# The
# PACIFIC
## IN THE WAKE OF CAPTAIN COOK

*The*

# PACIFIC

## IN THE WAKE OF CAPTAIN COOK

### *with Sam Neill*

MEAGHAN WILSON ANASTASIOS

HarperCollins*Publishers*

**HarperCollins***Publishers*

First published in Australia in 2018
by HarperCollins*Publishers* Australia Pty Limited
ABN 36 009 913 517
harpercollins.com.au

**HarperCollins***Publishers*
Level 13, 201 Elizabeth Street, Sydney NSW 2000, Australia
Unit D1, Apollo Drive, Rosedale, Auckland 0632, New Zealand
A 53, Sector 57, Noida, UP, India
1 London Bridge Street, London, SE1 9GF, United Kingdom
Bay Adelaide Centre, East Tower, 22 Adelaide Street West, 41st floor, Toronto,
Ontario M5H 4E3, Canada
195 Broadway, New York NY 10007, USA

A catalogue record for this book is available from
the National Library of Australia

ISBN: 978 1 4607 5639 3 (hardback)
ISBN: 978 1 4607 1036 4 (epub)

Cover design by Hazel Lam, HarperCollins Design Studio
Cover images: Photo by Johanna Gibson, © 2018, Essential Media & Entertainment;
background map *Nuova Guinea e Nuova Galles ed isole adjacente, Zatta, Antonio, active 1757-1797,*
courtesy National Library of Australia (Call No: MAP T 1432); Portrait of Captain James Cook
courtesy State Library of Victoria (H1842); back-cover painting *Captain Cook landing at Owyhee
(Hawaii)* courtesy Dixson Galleries, State Library of New South Wales (Call No: DGD 27)
Author photo by Lynton Crabb
Typeset in Bembo Std by Kirby Jones
Maps by Map Illustrations www.mapillustrations.com.au
Printed and bound in Australia by McPherson's Printing Group
The papers used by HarperCollins in the manufacture of this book are a natural,
recyclable product made from wood grown in sustainable plantation forests.
The fibre source and manufacturing processes meet recognised international
environmental standards, and carry certification.

*I can only speculate at what Cook's motives might have been when he embarked on his voyage because we don't get much from his logs. I can only guess at his inner thoughts. But the fact he kept going back to the Pacific — he couldn't stay away — shows he was completely taken by the place. In the end, it wasn't just that he changed the Pacific ... the Pacific also changed him. He became a man of the Pacific.*

*

*Most of the voices we hear on* Pacific *are indigenous, and for me that's important. The other side has been told so often — it's so familiar. The great Cook who comes along and plants a flag followed by all the benefits that come with European settlement. Law. Literacy. Technology. The wheel! We've heard it all before. But there's a whole other side to the story many of us have never heard — largely because we haven't been listening, and that's the indigenous story of the Pacific. Hopefully,* Pacific *might help change this.*

— Sam Neill

# CONTENTS

# FOREWORD
*by Sam Neill*

When I was a boy there was a huge map on the classroom wall. It was a map of the world, and most of that map was coloured pink, which meant that it was British, the old British Empire. This was supposedly a *very good thing*, because it brought order, enlightenment and above all cricket to the darkest places of the world.

Well. That was then. And of course now … I'm not sure of any of it.

That map was in large part pink as a result of the three voyages of the great explorer James Cook, at least in the third of the planet we call the Pacific. Cook's journeys, and the course of his reputation, particularly in Australia and New Zealand, fascinate me. Cook of course didn't actually 'discover' anything – everywhere he went had been discovered by other people hundreds, sometimes thousands, of years before him, though this certainly didn't deter the Europeans who followed in his wake. Which meant that most of the Pacific was eventually colonised, and thus our map, much of our corner of the world, was pink.

But for me, this *has* been a journey of discovery; the result being this book, as written by Meaghan Wilson Anastasios, and TV series. More than that, I think they became a love letter to my part of the world. I am more grateful than ever for growing up here, for being part of this place. I love this vast blue hemisphere.

Much of what we found on this voyage was new to me. For instance, I was not a little taken aback at the disparity of opinions on Cook: he is utterly loathed in some quarters, and yet adored in others. The project evolved, and became a story of an ocean as much as a story of people. It's as much about the present as it is about history. It's as much about me, I suppose, as it is about Cook – Cook being someone of enormous stature, and me … not particularly of any stature at all.

It is 250 years since Cook first sailed into this immense ocean, since those first fateful encounters. So perhaps it was no coincidence that even while we were shooting the series, the impending commemorations meant increasing controversy. How should we remember Cook? What are we to make of his claiming these lands for the Crown? How responsible was Cook himself for the devastating consequences of his 'discoveries' for the peoples who had populated the Pacific for so long – the people who had actually discovered and settled in this ocean?

And those original peoples – for all Cook's magnificent achievements and his consummate seamanship – how extraordinary were they? My own family now is in part Māori, so I have a particular and personal interest in the Polynesian diaspora – their incredible navigational skills, their great knowledge of the Pacific, their survival. Cook's arrival put that survival into immediate risk.

Of particular fascination to me are those initial awkward,

often funny, sometimes tragic first encounters. As in so many parts of the world, the arrival of Europeans was at best a puzzle. They looked like dead people. They must have had eyes in the backs of their heads since they paddled backwards. The reception by the Māori and Australian Aboriginal people could not have been more different – in New Zealand they were met with curiosity, hostility and often generosity. In many of the encounters in Australia, by contrast, the Indigenous people either retreated into the bush, or carried on with their lives completely ignoring these intruders. It was as if they were invisible. In Tahiti, Alaska and Hawai'i … that's another story again.

But here's the thing about Cook, the navigator – he always knew where he was. And for good or bad, he drew that map. And that map changed history.

It's been a privilege, as well as an education, to sail in his wake.

Here a disclaimer: I'm not a historian, I'm not a sailor, I'm not a navigator, I'm not an expert at anything much, I'm just a winemaking actor – but I *am* vitally interested, and I hope that you will be interested too. So follow me while I follow Cook. And just remember nothing is definitive, nothing is written in stone, make up your own mind, don't take my word for it!

There are many people to thank here. Essential Media's Chris Hilton, Frame Up Film's Owen Hughes, Foxtel History Channel's Jim Buchan, Duane Hatherly and Richard Stomps, and Prime TV's Annie Murray for their initial vision. The writers of the series – Owen Hughes, Sally Aitken and Meaghan Wilson Anastasios, who also wrote this book. Please feel free to criticise any inaccuracies as their fault! The excellent directors Kriv Stenders and Sally Aitken; our Executive Producer, David Alrich;

our doughty crew – Jules O'Loughlin, Mark Broadbent, Glenn Fitzpatrick, Ziggy Golden, Eamonn Dimmitt; the researchers who made it possible, Kirrilly Brentnall and Johanna Gibson; archive researchers Crystal Khoupraseuth and Penny Jope, the producers who kept us all in line, Aline Jacques and Joe Weatherstone; Indigenous consultants Larissa Behrendt in Australia and Annabelle Lee in New Zealand; the editors of the TV series, Karryn de Cinque and Adrian Rostirolla; and those close to me – Ann Churchill Brown, Sophy Jones and Lauren Major.

And above all, the many wonderful generous people we found from Alaska to Dusky Sound, from Cooktown to Hawai'i and all between.

# AUTHOR NOTE

'Captain Cook discovered Australia … New Zealand … Hawai'i.' To the original inhabitants of the Pacific, these are words that burn.

'We were not discovered' … it's a sentiment expressed from one end of the Pacific to the other. It's also the reason this book is structured as it is. Although half my surname may be Greek, it comes to me through marriage – my own family heritage can be traced to the moment the Angles met the Saxons. So when I embarked on this story, I knew that for me to speak for the indigenous Pacific experience would be plain wrong. While I feel qualified to relate the European side of the story, I wanted to leave the indigenous perspectives in *The Pacific: In the Wake of Captain Cook with Sam Neill* in the words of the people who own the history. In those accounts, you'll find contradictions and diverse opinions, as you'd expect of a gathering of intelligent individuals with strong opinions. One manifestation of this is that you'll notice not all the contributors are listed in the publication with cultural identifiers or tribal affiliations. This has been done at their request and for many and varied reasons. The point is, in this book I've attempted to honour the wishes of the people who were generous enough to share their time and wisdom with the production and to pass on their stories in their own words – as is right.

Another point that requires explanation is the use of the word 'indigenous'. In this book, 'Indigenous' is capitalised when it is specifically referring to Aboriginal Australians. For other First Nations of the Pacific, 'indigenous' is used. However, it's important to acknowledge that not all Aboriginal Australians choose to refer to themselves as 'Indigenous'; an adjective that could be seen as implying a homogeneity they find derogatory and offensive.

*Meaghan Wilson Anastasios*

# PART ONE

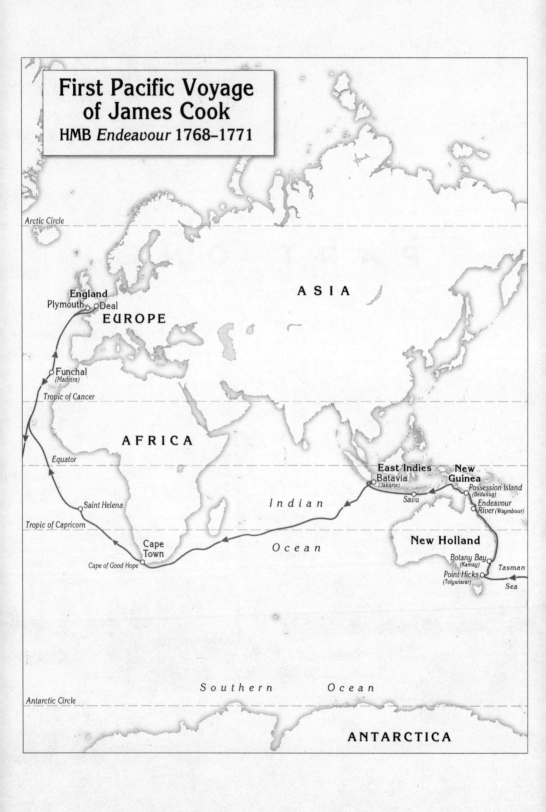

# First Pacific Voyage of James Cook
## HMB *Endeavour* 1768–1771

Arctic Circle

ASIA

England
Plymouth  Deal
EUROPE

Funchal
*(Madeira)*
Tropic of Cancer

AFRICA

Equator

East Indies
Batavia
*(Jakarta)*
Savu

New
Guinea
Possession Island
*(Bedanug)*
Endeavour
River *(Waymbuur)*

*Indian*

Saint Helena

New Holland

Tropic of Capricorn

*Ocean*

Cape
Town
Cape of Good Hope

Botany Bay
*(Kamay)*
Point Hicks
*(Tolywiarar)*

Tasman

Sea

*Southern    Ocean*

Antarctic Circle

ANTARCTICA

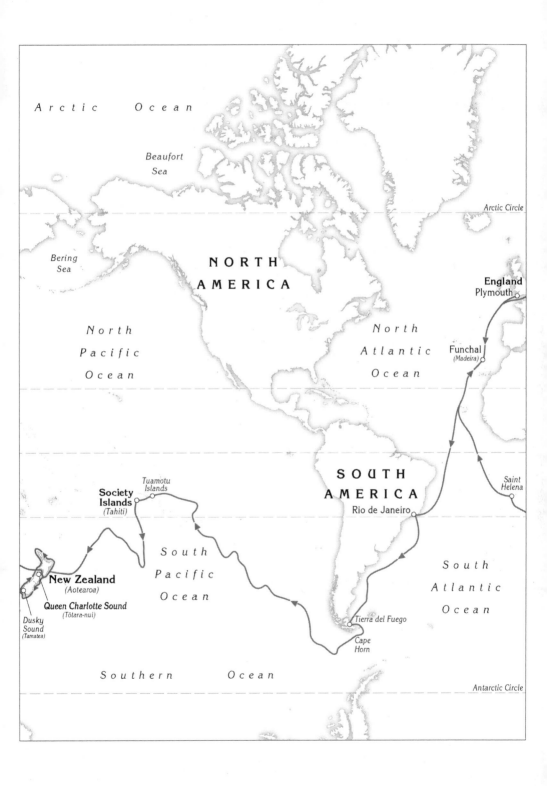

Arctic Ocean

Beaufort
Sea

Arctic Circle

NORTH
AMERICA

Bering
Sea

**England**
Plymouth

North
Pacific
Ocean

North
Atlantic
Ocean

Funchal
*(Madeira)*

Tuamotu
Islands

**Society
Islands**
*(Tahiti)*

**SOUTH
AMERICA**

Saint
Helena

Rio de Janeiro

South
Pacific
Ocean

New Zealand
*(Aotearoa)*

**Queen Charlotte Sound**
*(Tōtara-nui)*

Dusky
Sound
*(Tamatea)*

South
Atlantic
Ocean

Tierra del Fuego

Cape
Horn

Southern Ocean

Antarctic Circle

# ONE

# PARADISE ON EARTH

*As restrained as he was in his logbooks, Cook did describe*
*places like Tahiti as being particularly beautiful. How*
*could he not? The world is full of beautiful places but*
*there's nowhere quite like the Pacific.*
**SAM NEILL**

The Tahitians would have caught a whiff of them on the breeze before they saw them: ninety-four men jammed into a timber sailing vessel in the tropics. Although the captain of the *Endeavour* was as diligent as he could be about his crew's health and general sanitation, hot baths and bars of soap were few and far between on the high seas. Based solely upon the new arrivals' questionable personal hygiene, the Tahitians would have been justified in repelling the *Endeavour* and her crew from their shores.

**JOSIANE TEAMOTUAITAU PhD, Historian**
*When the* Endeavour *arrived here, and the men on the*
*ship saw those people on the beach who were not too dark*
*but just the right colour, and they were clean, and always*

*wearing scented flowers … the sailors were impressed because our people would bathe twice a day and they had all their teeth, which was not the case on board. So, of course, who wouldn't have been attracted?*

The locals standing on the soft sands of Matavai Bay and watching the approach of the British ship were fastidious about cleanliness. They washed themselves at least two times a day in a freshwater river near Point Venus, removed the hair from their armpits, dressed their silken tresses with snow-white blossoms, and anointed their skin with an intoxicating blend of coconut oil infused with *tiare* flowers known as *mono'i*.

**SAM NEILL**

*Everyone living on the island was like a god to the men on the* Endeavour *– they were muscular and beautiful. I don't know why they put up with these miserable little buggers from the East End … Why would you? But I suppose it was a matter of mutual curiosity. And so, the first thing that happened when the ship arrived was that sailors did what sailors do. It must have absolutely blown their minds.*

When the excited and malodorous crew of the *Endeavour* arrived on 13 April 1769, led by Captain James Cook, they received a warm welcome complete with a full array of sexual favours. One can only ask: why?

**MOETAI BROTHERSON, Mā'ohi Tribe, French MP**
*You have to put yourself in Polynesian shoes of the time. I can just imagine their curiosity. Those new weapons. The*

*language and the maps. All the written things that we*
*didn't have. It must have been very exciting for the*
*Polynesians, because we are curious people by nature. I'm*
*sure our ancestors were looking at everything these strange,*
*pale men had.*

The cause of the sailors' erotically charged reception can be laid firmly at the prow of the two European voyages that had found their way to Tahiti prior to Cook. In 1767, Samuel Wallis had arrived aboard the *Dolphin* and named Tahiti 'King George's Island'; and the two ships of French navigator Louis Antoine de Bougainville, the *Boudeuse* and the *Étoile*, had dropped anchor in 1768.

It hadn't taken long for the Tahitians to work out that the new arrivals could be useful.

### JOSIANE TEAMOTUAITAU PhD

*Tahitians are very pragmatic. We evolve and manage and*
*try to cope with what is given to us. When Cook and the*
*other Europeans arrived on the island they tried to make*
*the best of it. They knew they couldn't fight guns. So this*
*trade began: these exchanges, these friendships.*

There was one thing in particular the Tahitians knew they could get from the Europeans: metal. The Tahitians had been introduced to the wonders of metallurgy after salvaging parts from a European wreck that had foundered on a nearby island in 1722. To a people who worked architectural and nautical miracles with tools made of coral, stone, wood and (usually human) bone, the potential of metal was immediately apparent.

When the *Dolphin* turned up in 1767, it dawned on the Tahitians they had something the unwillingly abstinent sailors would happily exchange for iron: sex. And so a febrile and enthusiastic trade ensued. As one of the sailors on board put it, '*The women were far from being coy. For when a man found a girl to his mind, which he might easily do amongst so many, there was not much ceremony on either side.*' So eager were Wallis's men that they absconded with the iron nails used to hold their hammocks in place below deck. It must have made for an uncomfortable trip home for those sailors silly enough to dismantle their sleeping quarters.

Comfort was one thing, but seaworthiness was another altogether. When the *Dolphin*'s amorous crew began to pry the nails out of the ship's hull to continue their exploration of Tahiti's garden of earthly delights, things took a more serious turn. Shipwreck, piracy, mutiny and foundering at sea were all well-documented means of losing one's vessel – but sabotage by a randy crew didn't appear in the shipmaster's manual. Even the threat of a flogging wasn't enough to deter them, and as the Tahitian women began to up the ante, demanding longer nails – not in a metaphorical sense … they literally wanted longer nails – in exchange for a sexual encounter, the *Dolphin* was in serious danger of collapsing into a pile of floating planks.

Cook had been apprised of these perils before he set sail from Plymouth on 25 August 1768. So as the *Endeavour* dropped anchor in Matavai Bay and the Tahitians surrounded the boat calling out '*taio*' – 'friend', Cook knew that most of the men on board had more than friendship in mind. To discourage his crew – or 'The People', as he called them – from dismantling his ship, he had set in place a severe regime of punishment for any man caught trading necessities for sexual favours.

**CAPTAIN JAMES COOK**

*Endeavour by every fair means to cultivate a friendship with the natives and to treat them with all imaginable humanity ... No sort of iron, or anything that is made of iron, or any sort of cloth or other useful necessary articles are to be given in exchange for anything but provisions.*

He had the best of intentions. But it was a lost cause.

Cook was prone to wishful thinking. A fair to middling state of optimism must have featured fairly high on his list of personal attributes, considering the monumental challenges he would go on to confront and the milestones he achieved in a stellar naval career. Not that you'd guess it from his journal: more often than not, Cook's phlegmatic entries from his first voyage reveal more about his personality through what he doesn't tell us than what he does.

**SAM NEILL**

*Cook left a lot of stuff for historians – logs, journals, charts and sketches – but the man is still hard to read. He was the consummate professional. He didn't write about his hopes, his fears, his loves or ambitions. He just recorded his actions, those of the crew and the progress of his ship.*

Cook was disciplined, focused and temperate. At over six feet in height, he had a dark complexion and was strong featured and generally regarded as a bit of a looker. But a poet, he was not.

For a vivid description of the effect of the Tahitian welcome upon a ship full of sexually frustrated European sailors we must look, perhaps not surprisingly, to a Frenchman. The navigator

Bougainville, who had arrived on the island with his two ships in 1768, wrote in lyrical terms about the irresistible temptations laid at the French sailors' feet.

**LOUIS ANTOINE DE BOUGAINVILLE (1729–1811),**
**French Admiral and Explorer**

*I ask you, how was one to keep four hundred young French sailors, who hadn't seen women in six months, at their work in the midst of such a spectacle? Despite all the precautions which we took, a young girl got on board and came onto the forecastle and stood by one of the hatchways which are over the capstan. The girl negligently let fall her robe and stood for all to see, as Venus stood forth before the Phrygian shepherd; and she had the celestial shape of Venus ... We managed to restrain these bedevilled men, however, but it was no less difficult to control oneself.*

The men who arrived on Tahiti on board the *Endeavour* were no different, regardless of their commander's most fervent wishes. Part of the problem was that they already knew what to expect.

Of all the peddlers in tall tales, seamen would have to rank as the most creative. Embedded in Cook's crew were five men with firsthand experience of what the *Endeavour*'s sailors had to look forward to when they arrived on Tahiti's palm-fringed beaches. John Gore, Charles Clerke, Richard Pickersgill, Francis Wilkinson and Francis Haite had all visited the South Pacific on earlier voyages of exploration. The salty tales recounted on the excruciatingly long journey would have been fuelled by the prodigious amount of alcohol on tap – with 4500 litres of beer, 6000 litres of spirits and 11,500 litres of wine on board, the

*Endeavour*'s circumnavigation of the globe was as much booze cruise as it was voyage of exploration.

The ninety-four men on the *Endeavour* were a mixed bunch. Naval officers, gentlemen scientists, marine guards – to enforce order – and artists rubbed shoulders with the sailors, some of whom had barely entered their teens; the youngest amongst them was aged just twelve. But monotony, physical deprivation and discomfort know no class boundaries. The hardships experienced during the long voyage were common to all. Suffice to say as the emerald peaks of Tahiti appeared on the horizon, anticipation on board would have been high.

**SAM NEILL**

*Cook was quite a remote man. He was a working-class man from very humble origins. All his crew, apart from the officers, were from similar humble backgrounds. But Cook was remote from them and remote from his officers. He got on well with people but he didn't make any close connections with the other people on board. That's the thing about being commander – you can't be overly familiar with your shipmates.*

James Cook was cut of a different cloth. Debauchery and excess were anathema to him. Born on 27 October 1728 in North Riding, Yorkshire, to a Scottish labourer of modest means and his Yorkshire wife, Cook's outlook was shaped by the time he spent as an apprentice in Whitby with the Quaker coal-shipper, Captain John Walker. The constraints of this particular lifestyle are made clear in a line from the contract Cook signed with Walker; he agreed not to: '*play at dice, cards, bowls or any other unlawful games ... [nor] haunt taverns or play houses ... [or] commit fornication'.*

**JOHN ROBSON, Map Librarian, University of Waikato**

*He was a great leader of people, he was a great seaman, he was a great navigator, and a wonderful cartographer. As to whether he was somebody that you would invite to dinner and expect to be the life and soul of the party, I suspect not.*

Quakers cherish purity, plain speaking and a modest way of life, and they abhor drunkenness and hedonism – the latter being foremost in Cook's men's minds as the *Endeavour* dropped anchor. Cook would not have approved. But it soon became apparent there was little he could do to stop it. As the ship's master, Robert Molyneux, put it, *'The women begin to have a share in our friendship which is by no means platonic.'*

One man on board who took full advantage of all that Tahiti had to offer would, in years to come, become an intellectual and political heavyweight. To Australians today, Joseph Banks is best known as the renowned botanist whose venerable and hoary features once graced the five-dollar note and who gave his name to the fluffy-headed native Australian wildflower species, the banksia. But when he embarked with Cook in the *Endeavour*, he was, not to put too fine a point on it, a rake on the tear. He was a well-resourced, well-connected and dashing young man who contributed ten thousand pounds to the voyage – this at a time when the average sailor's wage was just fourteen pounds a year.

Banks was ambitious and determined to make a significant contribution to his chosen field of botany. As quite the man about town and a member of the notorious Hellfire Club, he was also keen to put paid to his peers' braggadocio about their adventurous wanderings across Europe on the well-worn Grand Tour. Not for Banks romancing his way around France and Italy – he intended to experience adventure on a much grander scale.

Judging by his journal entries from Tahiti, adventure he did.

> **SIR JOSEPH BANKS (1743–1820), 1st Baronet,**
> **Naturalist and Botanist on Cook's first voyage**
> *Love is the chief occupation, nay almost the sole luxury of the inhabitants; both the bodies and souls of the women are modelled into the utmost perfection for that soft science, idleness the father of love reigns here in almost unmolested ease.*

Banks' account is peppered with euphemistic tales of his amorous encounters on the islands, including a memorable evening spent with three beautiful girls, all of whom joined him in his tent and, the morning after, begged him to stay. He clearly had no difficulty overcoming his initial distaste for the smell of the coconut oil the Tahitian women used to anoint their skin, and it's little wonder that he declared it preferable *'to the odoriferous perfume of toes and armpits so frequent in Europe'*. Later in life he's said to have boasted that he had tasted *'woman's flesh in almost every part of the known habitable world'*.

It may well have been something more than Banks' well-cut pantaloons and air of entitlement that piqued the interest of the Tahitian women. Beyond the acquisition of metal, they had another very good reason for embracing the noisome seamen.

When Wallis had first arrived in the *Dolphin* two years earlier, his welcome had been far less congenial than the reception that greeted Cook and his men. In fact, it was outright hostile.

While the Tahitian warriors encircled the vessel and readied to attack, the women stood in canoes and exposed their genitals. In a classic – and understandable – example of cultural misunderstanding, the men on board the ship interpreted this to be a sexual invitation. The women were actually issuing them with a grave insult, showing them the passage to *Te Pō*, the place from which all men issue forth and to which they will all return after death. But there was no misreading the warriors' intent as they flung spears and hurled stones at the ship. The *Dolphin* fired its cannon and a battle ensued. When hostilities ceased, many Tahitians had been killed and their canoes shattered. It's difficult to fathom the shock and horror that must have overwhelmed the Tahitians after the massacre, their warriors torn apart by unfamiliar weaponry that caused such complete devastation. Wallis wielded his military might without mercy, and it was a lesson that wouldn't be forgotten.

For the Tahitians, the arrival of these men with their big guns was big news. In a region rife with intertribal rivalries, chieftains tussled to gain the favour of the new arrivals. These pale-skinned men bearing arms would be formidable allies. By drawing them into their world, the Tahitians would absorb their *mana* – their sacred power.

### JOSIANE TEAMOTUAITAU PhD

*When they saw those visitors with their uniforms, the white shirts, and those golden buttons, the Tahitians knew they had power. It was magic. They could take out things from their pockets. On Tahiti we didn't have pockets, you*

*see. When the visitors arrived, they realised that they were*
*men with* mana *and men with power because they had*
*guns, and so they wanted to befriend them. In those days*
*there was this thing called the bond friendship. They*
*exchanged names, but in doing so, they also exchanged*
*everything else. So the* taio *of Cook, for example, would*
*take his name, and Cook would take his* taio's *name. And*
*if Cook wanted, he could have had his wife and all his*
*property, too. But it was meant to work the other way too.*

In Tahiti, a formal alliance between two people was given a name: *taio*. Friend. These were friends with benefits. A chieftain's *taio* was permitted to lie with his wives and make use of his possessions. These men were also expected to defend each other in military conflicts.

Predictably, and very sensibly, the Tahitians rushed to form alliances with the British captain. Wallis had been a *taio* to Purea – the woman declared 'Queen' by the European visitors. When Cook arrived on the island, after an exchange of ceremonial gifts he was claimed by the chieftain, Tutaha, in order to forestall an alliance with Tutaha's adversary, Purea.

The usually libidinous Banks noted the response of the chieftain's wives after this ceremony, describing how they demonstrated themselves willing to partner with their husband's *taio*, despite being exposed to the curious gaze of a potential audience.

**SIR JOSEPH BANKS**

*[They] showed us all kind of civilities our situation could*
*admit of, but as there were no places of retirement ... we*

*had not an opportunity of putting their politeness to every test that maybe some of us would not have failed to have done had circumstances been more favourable ... by their frequently pointing to the mats on the ground and sometimes by force seating themselves and us upon them they plainly showed that they were much less jealous of observation than we were.*

But Banks declined the offer, his enthusiastic promiscuity stalled by a surprising coyness. Tahitian attitudes to public displays of sexuality were much more laissez-faire than the Englishman could entertain.

**PHILIBERT COMMERSON (1727–1773), Naturalist on Bougainville's voyage of circumnavigation**
*Here, modesty and prudery lose their tyranny. The act of procreation is an act of religion; its preludes are encouraged by the voices and songs of the assembled people, and its end is greeted by universal applause.*

In Cook's own journals, he described one of these ritual sex acts: '*A young fellow above 6 feet high lay with a little girl about 10 or 12 years of age publicly before several of our people and a number of the natives,*' as senior women coached her performance. Cook observed that it '*appeared to be done more from custom than from lewdness*'.

Often, the men and women participating in these public displays were 'arioi: a revered class of priests and priestesses devoted to the performance of erotic songs, dances and ritual sex. Travelling from island to island, they were members of a cult of beauty dedicated to the god 'Oro. But not just anyone could join; practitioners were expected to be gifted with great natural beauty and demonstrate physical strength, grace and endurance. As the *Endeavour*'s artist, Sydney Parkinson, observed, *'I never beheld statelier men.'*

The purpose of the *'ariois'* public displays on Tahiti was not to entertain audiences with the equivalent of a Pacific peepshow. The *'arioi* indulged in public sexual displays to stimulate the carnal appetites of the Tahitian gods during the seasonal festivals and ensure the fertility of the islands. It's possible that Purea arranged the ritual sex act described by Cook as a way of arousing the British gods. But of course the men on the *Endeavour* got the wrong end of the stick. Cook took it to mean that Tahitian society was generally lacking in sexual decorum.

### CAPTAIN JAMES COOK

*Both sexes express the most indecent ideas in conversation without the least emotion and they delight in such conversation beyond any other. Chastity indeed is but little valued.*

This attitude certainly carried with it a fair dose of hypocrisy. The *Endeavour* had just set sail from Georgian England, which was in the grip of what's been described as the first sexual revolution; prostitution was rife and public displays of sexuality not at all uncommon. Cook was aware of this and did caution his readers against tarring all Tahitian women with the same brush, noting that women who were married and of high social status did not participate in the trade for sexual favours.

> **WILLIAM WALES (1734–1798), Astronomer,**
> **Cook's second voyage**
> *The great part of these women admit of no such familiarities, or at least are very careful to whom they grant them. That there are prostitutes here as well as in London is true … and such no doubt were those who came on board the ship to our people. These seem not less skilful in their profession than ladies of the same stamp in England, nor does a person run less risk of injuring his health and constitution in their embraces.*

Cook feared less for his sailors' mortal souls than he did for their physical wellbeing. The thought that his men might be felled by a sexually transmitted disease would have bothered him terribly, if only because a ship crewed by men stricken down with the pox wouldn't go too far. He was also mindful of the grievous damage that would be visited upon the Tahitians if the pox were let loose amongst them.

Despite Cook's exhortations about the perils of the diseases dubbed 'the clap', 'this filthy distemper', 'the foul disease', 'that heavy curse', and 'that greatest plague that ever the human race was afflicted with', within five days of landing, symptoms began to spread amongst the men. Prior to disembarking, Cook had directed the *Endeavour*'s surgeon to examine the men for symptoms of venereal disease. He found that just one man was infected, and Cook forbade him from communicating with the Tahitians. It was decided, then, that the disease had already been on the island when Cook and his men arrived. That left two possible culprits: the crew of the *Dolphin*, or Bougainville's libertine sailors.

Cook tried his best but could do little to slow the disease's progress through his men. In his journal, he bemoaned the scourge while also finding some misguided comfort in the belief that the *Endeavour* was not responsible for bringing venereal disease to the island.

### CAPTAIN JAMES COOK

*All I could do was to little purpose for I may safely say that I was not assisted by one person in the ship ... and the women were so very liberal with their favours, or else nails, shirts &c were temptations that they could not withstand, that this distemper very soon spread itself over the greatest part of the ship's company but now I have the satisfaction to find that the natives all agree that we did not bring it here.*

Given there was no love lost between the French and the English, in years to come they predictably blamed each other for infecting the Tahitians. But the final word on the matter should be left to the locals, who called venereal disease *apa no Britannia*. English illness.

Cook knew the disease would spread like wildfire, predicting that it would '*in time spread itself over all the islands in the South Seas, to the eternal reproach of those who first brought it among them*'. He was right. Once tuberculosis, smallpox, measles and whooping cough were added into the mix, the indigenous Tahitian population was decimated. For their part, the Tahitians attributed the scourge to vengeful deities. In 1774, Cook estimated there to be 204,000 Tahitians living on the island. A French census in 1865 counted just 7169 indigenous Tahitians.

Once the romantic descriptions of these perfect tropical islands nestled in warm, aquamarine waters and populated by sexually uninhibited maidens were carried back to Europe and transmitted by lovesick sailors, Tahiti became a byword for paradise. Cook's description was typically restrained, but it was as close as he would ever come to being effusive.

### CAPTAIN JAMES COOK

*The whole exhibits a view which can only be described by the pencil of an able painter … No very agreeable discovery, to us whose ideas of plenty upon our arrival at this island was carried to the very highest pitch.*

As might be expected, Banks was more florid: '*The scene we saw was the truest picture of an arcadia of which we were going to be kings that the imagination can form.*' But it is to the Frenchman, Bougainville, that we must look for the most evocative description of Tahiti's appeal. He likened it to the Greek island of Cythera – the birthplace of Aphrodite, the goddess of love.

### LOUIS ANTOINE DE BOUGAINVILLE

*Nature had placed the island in the most perfect climate in the world, had embellished it with every pleasing prospect, had endowed it with all its riches, and filled it with large, strong, and beautiful people … Farewell, happy and wise people; remain always as you are now. I will always remember you with delight, and as long as I live I will celebrate the happy island of Cythera: it is the true Utopia.*

At the dawn of an era when monumental social, political and economic rupture would tear Western society asunder, prominent thinkers were grappling with the essence of human

*View of the inside of a house on the island of Ulietea, with representation of a dance*, Giovanni Battista Cipriani, 1773, drawn from Sydney Parkinson's 1769 sketches of dancing Raiateans. It appears that Cipriani took Banks' florid descriptions to heart, transforming Tahiti into a Grecian idyll far removed from Polynesia. National Library of Australia, 7411 #S1691

nature and trying to unravel humankind's place in a topsy-turvy world. Foremost amongst these philosophers were Denis Diderot and Jean-Jacques Rousseau. Diderot was inspired to compose a fictional account that celebrated the 'noble savagery' of the Tahitians after reading Bougainville's account. For his part, Rousseau confected the model of 'natural man' as an ideal creature unspoilt by cultured society and the corrupting forces of civilisation. Think Adam and Eve gambolling in the Garden of Eden while enjoying a state of divine innocence and ignorance before they each took a big bite of the forbidden fruit. As far as the first European arrivals in Tahiti were concerned, the locals were living this utopian ideal in what amounted to paradise on earth. Bougainville again: *'I thought I had been transported to the Garden of Eden. Restfulness, a quiet joy and all the semblances of happiness reign everywhere.'*

During the nineteenth century, as the wheels of progress drove the Industrial Revolution forward, and war and violent revolution turned society on its head, more and more people tried to find a way out. Tahiti had the misfortune of being cast as surrogate for frustrated Western fantasies. But the thing about fantasy is that it seldom has any basis in reality and fails to accommodate an extant society's history, culture and complexity.

**SAM NEILL**

*In a way, it's unfortunate the Europeans had such a good time in the Pacific because they brought back these stories of compliant women wearing next to nothing, and so the Pacific was seen as an exotic and desirable place ... That the Pacific became the South Pacific Paradise didn't do anyone any good at all – the cliché of the dusky South Seas maiden and so on.*

So it was for Tahitians. The countless foreigners who journeyed to their shores in Cook's wake were determined to find paradise, regardless of whether or not it wanted to be found. To the Western imagination, it was important that this idyllic island was populated by tribes of 'noble savages' offering the world-weary flotsam and jetsam who washed up on its beaches an easy way to relax and forget their troubles. But to the locals, it was simply home.

One of the worst culprits when it came to shaping the Western vision of Tahiti was the French post-impressionist painter, Paul Gauguin.

**JOSIANE TEAMOTUAITAU PhD**

*In those days the painters had a message to convey. We can see all the standards of the Enlightenment: fair-skinned people, untouched world, noble savage, and also the classical references. Because those women do not look Tahitian at all, of course. The message was that this is the untouched world. The message they wanted to bring back to Europe was that they were gods of this new Arcadia.*

Gauguin arrived in Papeete in 1891, having left France to live 'in a primitive and savage state'. But when he arrived there, he was shattered. What he found was not the pristine Arcadia he was seeking, but, as he put it, '*the Europe which I thought to shake off … It was the Tahiti of former times which I loved … That of the present filled me with horror.*' To voice a preference for the Tahiti of 'former times' was, in itself, something of an achievement, given he had never been there. It does show the power of the myth of the South Pacific being peddled about Europe at the time – the impressions Gauguin had formed were vivid enough to encourage him to abandon his life in France, yet they were based solely upon the written and spoken word.

Oh, the injustice. Gauguin mourned the loss of Tahiti's 'innocence' at the hands of corrupting Western influences, as he did the very same thing himself, sending fantastical visions of a tropical paradise back to Europe and inadvertently fuelling others' wanderlust. In his portraits of scantily clad Tahitian girls, their glossy black hair knotted into loose buns at the napes of their necks, he was perpetuating the very things he was railing against. How lacking in self-awareness must he have been as he bemoaned Tahiti's degradation, while bedding girls at the wrong end of their teens and contracting then spreading the syphilis that would eventually kill him in 1903?

There's no doubt that Tahiti is a place that has always encouraged people to jump ship. James Cook found that out to his detriment. When he announced on 8 July 1769 that their time in paradise had come to an end, two lovesick sailors, Samuel Gibson and Clement Webb, took to the hills with their newfound paramours. The two men were tempted by more than just a congenial climate and promise of amorous adventure; they were also promised land and status by the Tahitians – a great deal more than they could aspire to in the rigid social hierarchy of Georgian England.

To force them back on board, Cook initiated what was to become his go-to response when confronted by uncooperative locals. He held hostage a group of noblemen and women, including Cook's own *taio*, Tutaha, until the two absconders returned. This was a high-handed and myopic reaction that showed complete disregard for Tahitian social conventions. It also gives us some insight into the lapses of judgement that would ultimately lead to Cook's demise.

Cook wasn't unaware of the adverse effect his ill-chosen response had upon the relationship he had been nurturing with the locals. But he placed the blame squarely in the laps of the two lovesick deserters. He wrote, '*We are likely to leave these people in disgust with our behaviour towards them, owing wholly to the folly of two of our own people.*' After their release, the Tahitian captives didn't attempt to hide their displeasure. As Banks described it: '*I met them from the boat but no sign of forgiveness could I see in their faces, they looked sulky and affronted.*'

But the tactic accomplished what Cook had intended. Gibson

and Webb returned to the ship and were greeted by a hearty flogging: twenty-four lashes each. For his part, Samuel Gibson – who was described as a 'wild young man' by the *Endeavour*'s master – responded well to Cook's tough love. And he acquired proficiency in something more than the language of love. He turned his amorous adventure to good use by employing his knowledge of the Tahitian language to become a translator, and he went on to accompany Cook on all three of his voyages. Gibson was certainly keen to marry an islander in a hurry – when inclement weather forced the *Resolution* to seek shelter in Scotland's Orkney Islands on Cook's third and final voyage, Gibson met a local girl and wed her after just two weeks of courtship.

Gibson and Webb weren't alone in their desire to remain on Tahiti. It was later revealed by one of the midshipmen that many men aboard the *Endeavour* had planned to abscond as Cook prepared to weigh anchor. It was only fear of '*the Pox – the disease being there, their getting it certain & dying rotten most probable*' that kept them on the straight and narrow.

It certainly wasn't the last time European sailors deserted their posts. The most infamous of these cases was a mutiny that occurred in 1789. William Bligh, who had served on Cook's third voyage, was unceremoniously divested of his command of HMS *Bounty* and set adrift in an open launch by his crew, led by the notorious Fletcher Christian. Bligh believed that it was the '*allurements of dissipation*' on Tahiti that so addled his sailors' reason that they couldn't bear the thought of returning home.

It was only a matter of time before the missionaries arrived, intent on putting a dampener on all the so-called depravity and debauchery.

**MOANA'URA WALKER, Priest, Te Hivarereata Cult**

*Christianity only has one god. So they went all around the world colonising people, telling them their idols were pagan ... Because at the time there were a lot of diseases, the missionaries said, 'Well, you're dying because you're worshipping false gods' ... The French missionaries put into people's minds if they go to their traditional places of worship they'll be visited and haunted by ghosts ... Once we started worshipping just one god, everybody forgot the rest of them ... And every god had a purpose that was linked to a specific cultural practice.*

Emissaries from the London Missionary Society landed at Tahiti in the *Duff* on 5 March 1797, still celebrated in Tahiti as Missionary Day. When they arrived on the island and began to attempt to promote Christian values, one of the first missionaries observed that the locals *'in general treated our message with a great deal of levity and disregard'* – not altogether surprising given they were trying to enforce a ban on all songs, games and entertainment deemed 'lascivious'. But succeed the missionaries did.

**MOETAI BROTHERSON**

*The missionaries realised very quickly that if they wanted their god to be the one and only god, they had to show the Polynesians that he was the most powerful one of all. All the bullets and the guns were to support that theory. For the Polynesians, the god to be followed was the one who was the most powerful. The Polynesians realised that their ancient gods were powerless. They couldn't prevent their troops from losing battles or succumbing to disease. So they turned to Christianity within one generation.*

To commemorate this moment, the Tahitians erected a monument at the appropriately named Point Venus. An inscription on this monument reads: '*After years of resistance and indifference the people of Tahiti embraced the gospel and, following the path of the setting sun, bore its words to the uttermost islands of the Pacific Ocean.*' Tahitian women succumbed to the Christian exhortation to cover their shame and submitted to the restrictive yoke of the high-necked, full-length, loose-fitting gowns known as 'Mother Hubbards'.

Regardless of how good their intentions were, the destructive impact the missionaries had upon indigenous societies across the Pacific is beyond measure. What's important to remember is that this happened in communities where ancient spiritual beliefs and rituals, culture, history and ancestral knowledge were generally transmitted through oral means, and although culture was codified everywhere in symbolic representations, once the means of translating the message was lost, so too was the information recorded there. Once the chain was broken at the urging of the missionaries, the knowledge that had been passed from generation to generation was lost. There was no great book of knowledge from which it could be revived. It simply disappeared.

Now, an exercise. Shut your eyes. Conjure up a vision of paradise. Odds are your imagination has carried you to a place that looks remarkably like Tahiti, whether you've been there or not. Because that's the funny thing – its allure remains unchallenged even today. It has weathered some fierce criticism;

Robert Louis Stevenson of *Treasure Island* fame was scathing when he wrote, *'I don't much like Tahiti. It seems to me a sort of halfway house between savage life and civilisation, with the drawbacks of both and the advantages of neither.'* That's the problem with fantasies – they're ephemeral and need to be kept locked up in the imagination. If permitted to enter the real world, they can never live up to expectations. To impose an imported vision of paradise upon a people and a place is unfair and reckless.

So while Westerners mourned the demise of a world that never really existed, the Tahitians were forced to navigate rapidly changing circumstances they'd neither asked for nor desired.

*T W O*

# WE WEREN'T DISCOVERED

*This is my own personal view, but the missionaries – these men with the best of intentions – did the most to destroy Tahitian culture. Everything that was sacred became profane. They built their churches on the top of old sacred Marae sites, they banned tattoo, they banned dancing, they banned any kind of nudity of course. It was cultural vandalism.*

**SAM NEILL**

Sometime early in the first millennium AD, a convoy of intrepid souls set sail across the deep, blue waters of the Pacific and arrived in Tahiti. They knew the minute they arrived they'd found the perfect place to call home. No immediate neighbours to bother them, a perfect climate, and an environment blessed with an embarrassment of natural riches. Little wonder they decided to stay put.

They hadn't just stumbled on these islands by chance. They knew exactly what they were doing and where they were going. We know this because they brought with them all the comforts of home: pigs, taro, bananas, yams and dogs. Most notably, in the context of our story, their arrival predated the European 'discovery' of the archipelago by many, many hundreds of years.

During the intervening years, a complex and sophisticated culture evolved in Tahiti, and with it all the things you'd expect to see in a high-functioning society. Politics. Commerce. Religion. Art. Law. The only catch for the Tahitians? When the first European visitors arrived, they barely recognised anything they saw for what it was. This was less of an issue for the locals when the interlopers were just coming and going and making vaguely anthropological observations about the islanders' way of life. But things were bound to get more complicated once the British, French and Spanish began to cast more covetous eyes across the Tahitians' tropical home.

As far as Western traditions are concerned, there's no better way to lay claim to a person or a place than to name it. Why else do you think in Anglo-Saxon society women have traditionally taken their husbands' surnames? The word 'Polynesia' is itself a European construct. Derived from Ancient Greek, it means 'many islands' and was confected by the nineteenth-century French navigator Jules Dumont d'Urville. He also gave us 'Micronesia' ('small islands') and 'Melanesia' ('dark islands') named for the darkness of the inhabitants' skins and based on the same Greek root that gives us 'melanoma', the cancerous blight that has bedevilled the fair-skinned Europeans who unwisely chose to settle in this, one of the sunniest regions on the planet.

A Tahitian priest in a religious trance foresaw the arrival of the pallid and cancer-prone invaders. When Wallis appeared over the horizon in the *Dolphin*, many islanders recalled the priest's vision, which predicted the arrival of visitors in a *'canoe without an outrigger'*.

When the European 'outrigger-less canoes' arrived in Tahiti in the eighteenth century, the men on board didn't know what to make of the community they found on the Society Islands, as Cook was to call them – not in honour of the Royal Society that sponsored his voyage, but by virtue of the close proximity of the islands to one another.

The world James Cook found in the Pacific was extraordinary. He would confront many things on his voyages that would have made a less composed man break a sweat, but there was one thing that pushed him to breaking point. Theft. On Tahiti, its ubiquity would drive him to distraction.

Working against Cook was the Tahitian god, Hiro. Precociously clever, Hiro wasn't interested in petty thievery. He set his eyes on bigger prizes. Planets. Stars. That kind of thing. He was also renowned as a navigator. Hiro would arrive on islands by stealth and attack at night.

It was one of the many distinctions between Tahitian and British society. The Tahitians admired the attributes of cunning and guile so much that their pantheon included a god who would have been deemed a scoundrel by British standards. Of course, one of the cornerstones of British jurisprudence is the inviolability of property, a principle that would see men, women and children marooned on the far side of the world for thievery. But before a regime of crime and punishment can be enforced, all parties must share the same ideas about what constitutes 'property' and 'possession'.

The Tahitian word, hōro'a, means both 'to give' and 'to loan'. If you loan something you might not expect to see it again, and the borrower does not necessarily intend to return it to you. The nature of taio relationships complicated this further for Cook and his men. By exchanging gifts with Tahitians and formally accepting their ceremonial friendships, the crew were giving their tacit approval to share their possessions and wives with their *taio*. The *Endeavour* didn't have any women on board to share, but it had no dearth of material goods. It set sail from Plymouth with the equivalent of 34,000 chunks of ship's biscuit, 9000 pounds of flour, 4600 litres of beer, and 4000 pieces of beef and 6000 slabs of pork in casks, in addition to trinkets described as 'trifles' to gift indigenous people encountered on the voyage. The ship was also well stocked with weapons, ammunition, clothing, rope, sailcloth in addition to countless objects wrought in the material the Tahitians wanted more than anything. Iron. If Cook decided to give any of this away, he would do so only in what he deemed fair exchange for something offered up by the locals.

How must this have appeared to the Tahitians?

### JOSIANE TEAMOTUAITAU PhD, Historian

*It was quite easy to understand what the visitors wanted. The English learnt two Tahitian words:* pua'a *and* vahine. Pua'a *means 'pigs'. And* vahine *means 'women'. That was all they wanted.* Pua'a, *and* vahine. *Pigs and women.*

Yet the crew on the *Endeavour* were unwilling to share the bounty on board, even as they helped themselves to whatever they pleased from the air, land and sea. The natural resources on the island belonged to its chieftains. Gathering breadfruit, shooting birds and scooping fish from the sea was the equivalent of poaching deer from the royal forests in Britain.

In the Tahitian worldview, if you had surplus, you shared it. Only the most contemptible person would attempt to short-change his or her fellows by accumulating a stockpile. One of the *Bounty* mutineers would describe it this way: *'It is no disgrace for a man to be poor, and he is no less regarded on that account, but to be rich and covetous is a disgrace to human nature ... a man of such a description would be accounted a hateful person.'*

When visitors arrived in the Society Islands, they would be honoured with a feast of monumental proportions. But it was understood that they would bring with them provisions to support themselves after the initial welcome. With their existence reliant upon a predictable and unyielding annual cycle of feast and famine, the Polynesians knew exactly when and what to harvest and how to build up stores to make it through the lean times. It was all very straightforward to the locals. Messages from the gods were found in the flight of birds, and certain coconut groves were reserved for the use of chieftains. When times were lean, fishing and agriculture were restricted, and a summer ceremony heralded the return of the season of abundance.

Tahiti provided for its people. But provisioning a shipload of almost one hundred hungry men for months on end would not have figured in the islanders' calculations. By stripping their resources, the British were threatening their very existence.

As for the behaviour of the islanders that Cook classified as outright thievery, the *Endeavour's* botanist and resident bon vivant, Joseph Banks, observed that the local attitude to theft was anathema to British standards.

**SIR JOSEPH BANKS (1743–1820) 1st Baronet, English Naturalist and Botanist on Cook's first voyage**
*Great and small chiefs and common men are firmly of opinion that if they can once get possession of a thing it*

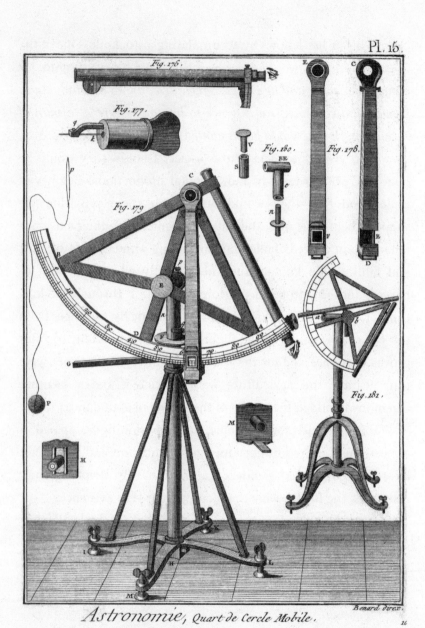

Pl. 15.

*Astronomie, Quart de Cercle Mobile.*

Benard direx.

*An astronomical quadrant*, 1760. A fantastic instrument, essential to Cook's measuring of the Transit of Venus and an object of desire for Tahitians.

Chronicle / Alamy Stock Photo, G38AWY

*immediately becomes their own ... the chiefs employed in
stealing what they could in the cabin while their dependents
too everything that was loose about the ship.*

It seems a pretty straightforward rule: take it, and it's yours. But
lacking the scaffolding required to acquire an understanding of
these cultural niceties, the endemic pilfering Cook experienced
in Polynesia and his increasingly despotic and brutal response to
it would eventually contribute to his demise.

Cook was fighting an uphill battle. From the Tahitian point
of view, stealing something without detection was quite an
achievement. But being caught red-handed was deeply
shameful – not because you were taking something that wasn't
yours; because you were caught.

Stealing another's treasured possession allowed the thief to
capture that person's *mana*. In the traditional Polynesian belief
system, it is *mana* that gave a person authority to lead and hold
sway over a community. The more prestigious the person, the
greater their *mana*. And that *mana* is transferred to those objects
a powerful person holds close.

What would the Tahitians have made, then, of an object so
venerated by Cook and his men that they stored it in a custom-
made box, hidden from sight? This prize was so cherished, the
British constructed a specially built fortress to house it,
surrounded by a ditch, a palisade and a steep bank. The Tahitians
rightly assumed that such a treasured article was most likely
sacred and a powerful reservoir of *mana*.

The object under guard in the fortress – Fort Venus – was
supremely important to Cook, though not in the way the
Tahitians imagined. Its value was not spiritual; it was scientific,

although one could argue that in the eighteenth century, the two concepts were one and the same. The quadrant represented the pinnacle of eighteenth-century maritime technology. By using it to measure the sun's angle over the horizon at noon, a navigator could calculate the line of latitude upon which their ship lay. But on Cook's first voyage, the quadrant played an even more crucial role. Without it, he'd have been unable to fulfil the primary purpose of his voyage: to track the planet Venus's passage across the face of the sun.

When the Tahitians distracted the guards and made off with the quadrant, Cook was apoplectic – to fail in his duties thanks to common thievery? Preposterous!

Joseph Banks set off in pursuit of the bandits with the astronomer Charles Green, a midshipman and Banks' Tahitian friend, Te Pau. Te Pau was able to mediate the return of the quadrant, now dismembered and its parts shared amongst many so all could partake in the purloined *mana*.

In the meantime, Cook had detained his *taio*, the chieftain Tutaha, and seized all the canoes in Matavai Bay until the quadrant was returned. Cook was dismayed to learn that Tutaha had attempted to escape, and that Cook's men had pulled him from the water by his hair. There was no greater insult to a chieftain, whose head and hair, where his ancestors' *mana* resided, were *tapu*: sacred and forbidden. That Tutaha was also Cook's ceremonial friend made the transgression all the more ghastly. Cook apologised as best he could, but although Tutaha appeared to accept this in good grace, it was an exercise in saving face. When Tutaha told his people to stop supplying food to the *Endeavour*, Cook knew his men had made a big mistake.

**TINA NGATA, Ngāti Porou Tribe**

*The Christian idea of God giving man dominion over the earth is the polar opposite of our ideas about our relationship to the environment. What stemmed from those two very different philosophies are two very different ways of interacting with our resources. The Western philosophy about dominion and hierarchy also impacted in a social sense of course, but it also manifested in an environmental sense and has had very harmful outcomes in terms of our relationship with the world around us.*

Cook and his men came from a society that believed humans were made in God's image and that everything existed on earth to serve or benefit humankind. As Joseph Banks saw it, '*the admirable chain of nature in which Man, alone endowed with reason, justly claims the highest rank*'. In contrast, Polynesian society embraced a communalist approach that exercised collective ownership of resources regulated by redistribution and reciprocity. Western culture celebrated the individual, but to the Polynesians, human beings were just one spoke of a very big wheel. The traditional, or *Mā'ohi*, ways were holistic, acknowledging the interconnectivity of all life on earth, while Cook and the Europeans who followed him brought a new way of thinking that venerated science and rationalism. The Tahitians must have marvelled at men who came to their island with not much in the way of fresh food, no women, and lacking the most basic knowledge of the natural world. Somehow, the power of the priests did not affect the European sailors, who had no concept of the central tenets of Tahitian society, including the rites and customs of *tapu*. For their part, the British did not understand that here, wealth was equated with prestige, and status acquired by accumulating social debts and sharing surplus with the needy.

For James Cook and his Enlightenment-era warriors, knowledge was the ultimate goal. There was a rational explanation for everything. They embarked on their voyages of exploration to map and measure, to classify and chart. Through the accumulation of knowledge, they would rule the world. So Cook was not one to miss an opportunity to learn more.

After Cook instructed the men to prepare the *Endeavour* to depart Tahiti on the next leg of his first voyage, he and Banks decided to set out to circumnavigate the island's coastline and trace its contours. It wasn't a journey without peril. They had only one musket and a few pistols, no food and only a pocketful of tradeable goods. But aided by local guides, they were honoured wherever they went. The Tahitians didn't realise that by drafting the outlines of their island, Cook was – in European terms, anyway – laying claim to their territory.

Without adding British ambitions into the mix, Tahiti and its neighbouring islands were already knotted up in a very complex intertribal skirmish. Cook arrived on Tahiti at a time of grave political conflict. Purea, who had formed a *taio* alliance with Wallis after he'd arrived on the *Dolphin*, was lobbying fiercely to promote her son to the position of great chief. As an *'arioi*, she had chosen to ignore her sacred obligation to kill her child when he was born – paradoxically for a fertility sect, *'arioi* were not permitted to procreate. Purea and her husband, Amo, constructed a monumental *marae* – a pyramidal-form temple – to advance their son's claims. Cook didn't realise it at the time, but when his sails appeared on the horizon, Purea's enemies assumed her *taio* had returned to avenge her, and all opposition to her rule disintegrated. Cook's arrival saved the two Tahitians and their allies.

Cook and his shipmates had no doubt about how they would be perceived when they put to shore. They knew Wallis's brutal response to the confrontation he'd faced in Matavai Bay had made quite an impression on the locals.

### SIR JOSEPH BANKS

*We shall soon by our connections with the inhabitants of Georges Island (who already know our strength and if they do not love at least fear us) gain some knowledge of the customs of these savages.*

Cook's presence in the Society Islands had a ripple effect that still resonates through the archipelago today. Cook, and the other Europeans who came after him, never really understood the complexity of the islands' politics. There was no single ruling clan. And by a quirk of fate and the fact that it happened to be the anchorage that was most appealing to European ships, Matavai Bay assumed a new importance. At the time, it was ruled by a fairly insignificant clan, but by associating themselves with the British and then the French, they would become the dominant family on the island. By 1788, the founder of the Tahitian royal family, Chief Tu, had unified the island of Tahiti. After adopting the name, Pomare, Tu and his descendants would eventually bring all the Society Islands under its rule.

In 1827, Queen Pomare assumed the throne of the Kingdom of Tahiti and became the fourth Pomare regent. She had, thanks to the efforts of the relentless Protestant missionaries, become a devout Christian who staunchly allied herself with the British. With their encouragement, she sent the Catholic missionaries packing. Needless to say, the French were less than enthused to see their keenest advocates drummed off the islands, so they arrived *en force* to compel Queen Pomare to reinstate the Papists. Pomare beseeched her fellow regent, Queen Victoria, to *'lend us your powerful hand, take us under your protection; let your flag cover us, and your lion defend us'*, but her pleas fell on deaf ears. Victoria had enough jewels in her Pacific crown already: Australia, New Zealand and Hong Kong amongst them.

The French, however, were keen to notch up a symbolic victory over their Anglo bêtes noires. They were trying desperately to forget the humiliation of the Napoleonic Wars, and the loss of Canada in 1754 still smarted. The opportunity to gain a foothold in the Pacific was far too tempting a proposition to ignore. And so, in 1842, a convoy of French ships and soldiers arrived and declared Tahiti a French possession, lumbering it with an unbelievably unwieldy and bureaucratic name: *Etablissements des Français en Océanie*, or 'French Settlements in Oceania'. After seizing the Royal Palace, they sent Queen Pomare into exile on Ra'iatea Island. Not that the Tahitians gave up without a fight. In the War of Independence of 1844 to 1846 they defended Bora Bora and Huahine, and drove the French off the islands. But lacking guns and ammunition, local resistance was doomed. The Queen returned from exile and agreed to rule under the French 'protectorate'. After her death in 1877, the monarchy was dissolved and, in 1880, Tahiti and its proximate islands were officially annexed as French Polynesia.

It seems that 'out of sight, out of mind' was the rule of thumb to the French colonisers. Tahiti was far enough removed from the

Gallic motherland in a physical sense that it would prove to be quite the boon in the twentieth century.

### RICHARD ARIIHAU TUHEIAVA,
#### Nohovao Tribe, Lawyer

*I am respectful of the past and of the relationship between our two countries. But we've been educated and conditioned to this lifestyle, and it's like being trapped in a box. We don't have any past and we don't have any future. I'm forty-three years old, and I've been brought up in a very French lifestyle. So there was a lot of pressure to never say anything against France. But as a Senator I now know the ambition of France throughout the region.*

In the late 1950s when the French started to build up their nuclear arsenal, they needed somewhere to test their new toys. Ideally, that would be somewhere as far removed from their own shores as possible. Geographically isolated and located on the opposite side of the planet, Tahiti was made to order.

#### MOETAI BROTHERSON, Mā'ohi Tribe, French MP

*Thirty years and 193 testings ... more than 5000 times the load of Hiroshima ... we have a rate of specific cancers, that are sometimes fourteen times the national average. If you talk about cancers that are scientifically tied to radiation, we have rates that are staggering. It's France's legacy to us.*

The French nuclear tests in the South Pacific between 1960 and 1996 exposed Tahitians to five hundred times the acceptable amount of radiation. That was the point, really – it kept all that nasty stuff away from *La Belle France*.

For Tahiti, the fallout has been both literal and figurative. Beyond the health repercussions, the high-handed manner in which Tahitians were treated by their French rulers and the lies they were told about the repercussions of nuclear testing on their wellbeing and environment were the straw that broke the camel's back.

### MOETAI BROTHERSON

*Deep down, I believe most Tahitians want independence. But there's this fear that has been instilled in our souls. But some of us haven't forgotten who we are and what we want to be for the future, which is Polynesians. Yes, we have a local government. But it's all farce. It's what we call here a political sandbox. They define the borders of that sandbox, and tell us we can play in that sandbox. But we're not allowed to forget this sandbox is painted with bleu, blanc and rouge – the colours of France.*

Today, the same determination and vision that inspired their ancestors to embark on one of the world's greatest migrations is stirring in contemporary Tahitian hearts. Driven, in part, by a desire to address the whitewashing of their pagan past, a cultural revival has been ignited.

### JOSIANE TEAMOTUAITAU PhD

*Tahitian culture in 2017 is just a result of 250 years of influences. Thanks to the revival movement that occurred in the 1970s we know more today than our parents –*

*maybe even more than our grandparents – because they*
*were under the influence of a religion that really forbids*
*this quest for the old times. Today we are more open-*
*minded to our own culture, and we tend to accept what*
*was, for our grandparents and parents, unacceptable – our*
*pagan past. Most of us are no longer ashamed of that part*
*of our history.*

Until very recently, speaking Tahitian was illegal on the French Polynesian islands – it has only been taught in schools since 2004.

Over the past few decades, the independence movement has been gaining ground, and with it a return to the *Māʻohi* ways of life that existed on Tahiti before the arrival of the British and French.

### MOETAI BROTHERSON
*We don't even know about part of what was lost, because it*
*was lost forever. Even our grandfathers, our elders – the*
*ones who are living – don't remember it. What we know*
*was lost were the traditions, the religion, the cults, and also*
*the way of living. All the knowledge about navigation was*
*also erased. This all had to be rediscovered.*

### MARGUERITE LAI, Dance Revivalist
*Our own memories were erased, replaced by European*
*fantasy images of ourselves.*

In a most remarkable circular development, the journals and accounts that Cook and his fellow travellers carted back to Europe are today important sources of information for the Tahitian cultural renaissance. These records are being used by Tahitians to revive dormant forms of cultural expression. Cook was an anthropologist before the term even existed. He was motivated to observe and record what he saw in the expectation that it would be of use to his masters back in Old Blighty. But he could never have imagined how important his work would become for the people whose world would be dismantled in his wake.

### SAM NEILL

*Pacific culture is only just beginning to recover. The whole fiction of the Pacific that everyone was libertine and sex was freely available and so on drove the missionary zeal. The old customs were thrown out the window – old gods were literally thrown into the sea. People had to cover up and dancing, music ... all the good stuff ... was destroyed. All the stories, all the old knowledge was thrown away and language was lost in many cases. That's one of the things that I saw on my own voyage – how Pacific people are recovering and reclaiming their languages, their old stories and their old religions.*

If only James Cook could see them now.

*THREE*

# PEACEFUL SEA

*These days travel is mostly sitting in airports waiting for*
*something to happen. I do wish I'd had more time at sea*
*on my journey because this program has become as much*
*as anything about the sea – about the Pacific – about this*
*immense ocean. And I'd have liked to have been on the*
*ocean more often rather than flying across it.*
**SAM NEILL**

Testicles lashed to the ship's rigging … Lugged along in the ship's wake by a rope tied beneath the armpits … Forced to sit for hours in a tidal pool as the waves wash around – and over – you … Deprived of sleep for days on end.

No, that's not an account of a fishing trip gone bad. It's not even a running list of medieval punishments meted out by brutal naval captains. Believe it or not, all of the above are reputed to be tried and true techniques for acquiring the skills required to become an exemplary navigator, Polynesian-style.

What better way to observe the ebb and flow of the tides than to sit as a youngster in the rockpools as the tide advances and retreats around you? And if you suffer from chronic seasickness, grabbing on to a rope and floundering along behind the ship for a while is a sure-fire way to take your mind off throwing up. As for the testicles, well, if the family jewels are quite literally on the line, a trainee navigator will very quickly learn to anticipate a vessel's movement through the waves and currents.

No matter what you think of their training regime, the first Polynesians were the consummate masters of open ocean seafaring. European history makes much of the accomplishments of the Viking adventurer Leif Eriksson, who crossed the Atlantic Ocean in 1000AD and was most likely the first European to set foot on the North American continent. Eriksson may have earned his navigating stripes, but a poet he was not, naming the first place he saw 'Stone Slab Land'. Compared to the Polynesians, though, the Viking adventurer was a Johnny-come-lately.

### SAM NEILL

*The Pacific is the centre of the world if you're Polynesian. This is home base and everything beyond its shores is as exotic to its inhabitants as Polynesia was for eighteenth-century Europeans.*

When Cook sailed into the Pacific, to all intents and purposes he was exploring a well-populated continent, albeit one that was water-based. And the people who inhabited these islands were not recent arrivals.

### MATAHI TUTAVAI, Tahitian Voyaging Society

*Still today in our history books and in documentaries I always hear that Europeans 'discovered' Tahiti ... that they discovered such and such. It really hurts me when I hear that, as if our ancestors didn't exist or were just part of the flora and fauna. That's why today we need to rewrite history. We will write it from our own perspective. But we've still got a lot of work to do to decolonise ourselves.*

Evidence drawn from linguistic, genetic and archaeological studies indicates that the Polynesians, who are classified as a subset of the Austronesian race, found their way to the Pacific via Taiwan from a point of origin on the island of Madagascar in the Indian Ocean. About seven thousand years ago – the same time that some bright spark in Western Asia worked out that it's much easier to move things around on vehicles that have wheels attached to them – the forebears of today's Polynesian people left Taiwan and headed for Melanesia. In 1500BC they took to the sea and sailed further east, populating Fiji, Samoa and Tonga. Sometime in the first millennium AD, Tahiti, the Cook Islands and the Marquesas were occupied, and after that, the outermost reaches of the Polynesian 'Triangle' – Rapa Nui, or Easter Island, in the east; Hawai'i in the north – had resident populations. The final great migration was to the south-west; somewhere between 1200 and 1300AD Polynesian culture arrived on the unpopulated islands of Aotearoa, or New Zealand, which was round about the time Leif Eriksson embarked upon his open ocean voyage to 'Stone Slab Land'.

### RICHARD ARIIHAU TUHEIAVA,
#### Nohovao Tribe, Lawyer
*We're all one people. We are ocean people. We are the ocean.*

To set sail across daunting stretches of open water was not an easy or particularly safe undertaking. And yet, the Polynesians did it repeatedly. Why? 'Fame and glory' certainly came into it. Whenever a brave navigator embarked on a long voyage by sea, this brought great prestige to his clan. According to traditional beliefs, every Polynesian is descended from the first human – Tiki – who initiated a diaspora that emerged from the setting sun in the west. But the eastern ocean led to the underworld where human spirits departed their bodies and plunged into the sea. To sail east into the rising sun ranked high on the bravery charts.

There was also a more pragmatic motivation. Polynesian society was rigidly hierarchical and inheritance tied to the 'winner takes all' principle of primogeniture, where to be the eldest child was to be the winner. So for those who were not firstborn and harboured a desire to accumulate wealth and gain status, their only option was to discover and settle a new world.

Not that these extraordinary voyages were all smooth sailing. Oral traditions suggest that at least half of those who set out across the ocean neither returned nor found safe passage to a new home.

The early navigators weren't exactly travelling blind, however. With all the wisdom accumulated by generations of sailors and transmitted through staunch oral traditions, the pioneers who set off from Melanesia and headed east knew what they were looking for and how to find it. It's thought many of the earliest relocations may have followed the seasonal migration paths of the birds that periodically crisscross the Pacific. The long-tailed cuckoo, for example, breeds and nests in New Zealand over summer before very wisely retreating to Tahiti at the approach of the icy fingers of the Kiwi winter. As the first Tahitians observed the life cycle of these birds, which took to the air en masse and headed south-west for a few months before returning to the tropics, they would have been fairly certain that a habitable land was within reach of the Polynesian ocean-going vessels.

However they did it, it worked. Within eighty generations, the Polynesians called almost all the Pacific's archipelagos home. They had dispersed their culture over twenty-five million square kilometres of the planet's surface.

### SAM NEILL

*When you look at the Pacific, there are just tiny little dots on this vast blue ocean. To be able to find those places just blows my mind. Easter Island – or Rapa Nui – it's so remote from anything at all. Yet the Polynesians settled it hundreds of years ago. How did they find it? The pinpoint accuracy of getting around the Pacific in a canoe – finding a tiny atoll, the highest point of which is a palm tree – now that is a miracle of technology and knowledge.*

In contrast, Europe was very late to the Pacific party. It wasn't until a Spaniard, Vasco Núñes de Balboa, crossed the Isthmus of Panama in 1513 and became the first European to glimpse the western Pacific that Europeans even realised the ocean existed. When Balboa waded into the waters of San Miguel Gulf and raised a standard sacred to the Holy Virgin in one hand and a sword in the other, he was staking a claim to the Pacific in the name of the Spanish Crown without having the slightest idea of the scale of this new watery territory.

At the time, the general consensus amongst European geographers was that there was just one great ocean encircling the globe. That's how Christopher Columbus got it wrong when he took off from Spain in search of a route to the Indies other than the protracted and perilous easterly approach via the Cape of Good Hope. When he landed in the Bahamas in 1492, he thought he was in Asia and was dead sure he had managed to find a westerly passage to the Indies. Hence: the 'West Indies'. He was blissfully unaware that he was sixteen thousand odd kilometres off the mark. There were other opportunities for Europe to make the Pacific's acquaintance – it's likely that Marco Polo had glimpsed its waters during his time in China in the thirteenth century, but he would not have recognised it for what it was. Ditto the Portuguese expeditions of 1512 and 1513 that approached the Pacific from the west in search of the Spice Islands.

It wasn't until 1520, when Ferdinand Magellan passed through the strait that still bears his name and entered the Pacific, that Europe began to have an inkling of what lay beyond the American continent. The Portuguese navigator, who was confusingly working for the Spanish Crown, named the vast expanse of water *Mar Pacifico* ('Peaceful Sea') if only because its relative calm was a pleasant change of pace after the washing machine–scale turbulence he had experienced in the passage through Tierra del Fuego. Thanks to some unwittingly clever political manoeuvring, the vast majority of Magellan's placid waters were already under Spanish control. They just didn't know what that meant yet. As for the ancient and well-established societies that lived there already, they had no idea about the storm clouds that were gathering beyond the horizon.

The shift in the Pacific's destiny came about, as such things so often did back then, as the result of a papal edict. On 7 June 1494, whether the world wanted it or not, it found itself chopped in two. The Spanish-born Pope Alexander VI bisected the globe along a demarcation line running from pole to pole, assigning one hemisphere to the Spanish and the other to the Portuguese. The Portuguese cried foul and accused the Pope of unfair bias; after some minor squabbling, the line was shifted slightly and ratified in 1506 by a pontiff deemed more impartial, the Italian-born Pope Julius II who also, incidentally, commissioned Michelangelo to paint the Sistine Chapel. Ultimately, the Treaty of Tordesillas resulted in a line that ran around the globe from a point roughly 370 leagues – 1900 kilometres or so – west of the Cape Verde Islands. At the time no thought was given to what this meant for the Pacific, because no European knew it existed. All the Spanish and Portuguese cared about was control of the New World. The line placed Brazil in the Portuguese realm and the rest of the Americas went to Spain. Which is why, in case you've ever wondered, Brazilians speak Portuguese while the rest of South America uses Spanish.

It's also why the westernmost borders of the Australian states of New South Wales and Victoria run along the same line of longitude as the border between Papua New Guinea and West Papua. The Dutch named the western, or nominally Portuguese, portion of the Australian continent 'New Holland'. When Cook took possession of the eastern coastline and it was subsequently named 'New South Wales', the lands corresponded to what would have been the Spanish Australian territories – which the Spaniards had never tried to claim.

And when Indonesia seized Netherlands New Guinea in 1962, they justified it by invoking the Treaty of Tordesillas that ran through the island – the same line that formed the border of New South Wales, which for the first half of the nineteenth century included the future state of Victoria.

But that was yet to come. In the eighteenth century when Cook embarked on his first voyage, the enormous body of water that lapped the shores of three continents was largely unknown to Europeans. The Portuguese, Spanish, Dutch and English explorers who had dipped toes into its briny depths prior to Cook had done so in a tentative manner, using its waters as little more than a passageway to get from A to B. Even the Spanish, whose galleon trade route operated in the Pacific between 1565 and 1815, just used its prevailing winds as the maritime equivalent of a super highway, rarely if ever wandering off the well-travelled track they established on the fortieth latitude. At least one Spanish vessel a year passed across the Pacific between Manila and Acapulco, carrying ivory, silk, spices and porcelain from Asia to the Spanish territories in America. From there they were transported overland and then across the Atlantic to a European populace hungry for 'exotic' knick-knacks. Heading back in the other direction was silver, sourced from American mines and highly sought after in Asia.

There was a fundamental difference between the original inhabitants of the Pacific and the early European explorers. For the Polynesians, the ocean was home.

**MATAHI TUTAVAI**

*We are ocean people. That's what defines us and our culture. That's what our ancestors were made of ... salt water.*

It was here that they had established a complex network of trade routes and a shared culture. But for Europeans, the Pacific was a daunting, expansive and barren space that was the antithesis of their definition of 'civilisation'. To them, 'civilisation' meant a kingdom of sovereign nations that shared, and frequently tussled over, terrestrial borders. In the Western psyche, to be lost at sea was an existential nightmare.

And get lost they did. In the eighteenth century more Europeans died at sea than in naval warfare because, more often than not, ship captains had no idea where they were, which made avoiding sandbanks and reefs rather challenging. Regardless of a chart's accuracy, it's next to useless if you can't pinpoint your location. The missing factor in this equation was an accurate way to measure longitude. Latitude was easy – all a ship's captain had to do was calculate the angle of the sun above the horizon relative to the ship's position and work out its relative proximity to the equator. But longitude was a great deal trickier. This meant European navigators were forced to hug coastlines – in itself a rather dangerous pastime – in order to identify a point at which they could break out into open water travelling east or west along what they hoped would be the correct line of latitude to reach their intended destination. It sounds a great deal easier than it was.

Intent on solving the problem, in 1714 the British government offered an eye-wateringly generous prize to crack the longitude code: £20,000, or 3.5 million of today's pound sterling. Astronomer Edmond Halley, he of the comet fame, had proposed that by measuring the passage of the planet Venus as it passed between earth and the face of the sun from various viewpoints on the earth's surface, it would be possible to calculate the earth's distance from the sun. This was key to calculating longitude. Not that he'd have the chance to test his theory in person. Unfortunately for Halley, who died in 1742, the Passage of Venus is such an infrequent event that he was long gone before it recurred; it occurs in pairs eight years apart with a century between events. The next passage was scheduled for 1761 and 1769.

But Halley's peers in the Royal Society weren't going to let all his good work go to waste. After lobbying King George III, the president of the Society, the Earl of Morton, secured royal assent and financial backing to send a voyage to the South Seas in order to observe and record the Passage of Venus. The earl's case was based on the argument that a great deal more than scientific curiosity was at stake – it was a matter of national pride.

### JAMES DOUGLAS, THE EARL OF MORTON
### (1702–1768), Scottish Scientist and President
### of the Royal Society 1764–1768

*The British Nation have been justly celebrated in the learned world, for their knowledge of astronomy, in which they are inferior to no nation upon Earth, ancient or modern; and it would cast dishonour upon them should they neglect to have correct observations made of this important phenomenon.*

This was why James Cook headed off into the big blue. He did so with the most cutting-edge navigational technology of the time. But judged by today's standards, once he left Old Blighty, Cook was on his own with the maritime equivalent of a couple of sticks to spark up a fire. Astronaut Neil Armstrong put it this way when he compared his own journey to the moon with Cook's circuit of the Pacific: *'at least we were in touch with mission control'*.

## SAM NEILL

*The sheer guts of the man – to go, blind, into a place that was virtually unknown in Europe. That takes remarkable bravery. That's why I admire Cook so much.*

Yes, Cook's navigational achievements were remarkable. But when he arrived on Tahiti, he encountered a race of people who had mastered open ocean navigation many centuries before he did. If it was so difficult for Cook and his peers, he must have wondered how on earth the Polynesians had done it.

And so we meet the theory of 'accidental drift'. Championed by the nineteenth-century Australian clergyman John Dunmore Lang as a way to explain Polynesian settlement of the Pacific, it requires us to accept that entire families – who happened to be accompanied by their dogs, pigs and conveniently transplanted paper mulberry trees and banana palms – were set adrift and off course on the high seas, then carried by benevolent winds to welcoming, uninhabited islands. In short, the theory removed Polynesians' agency from the equation and cast them in the role of passive subjects tossed about the Pacific at nature's whim. There are two reasons this theory may have gained such traction and survived well into the 1970s. Possibly it was fuelled by a Western inability to accept that something the European navigators found so challenging had been mastered by another race thousands of years beforehand. But a less generous interpretation is that it's easier to justify dispossessing a group of people who just happened to stumble on a place through dumb luck than it is to take a land that was chosen by another society as its home.

Cook wasn't so quick to dismiss the skills of the Polynesian navigators. He knew the Polynesian settlement of the Pacific was far too complicated to attribute to a series of lucky breaks. He may have been disparaging of his own lack of formal education, but he had an intuitive intelligence and remarkable powers of observation and deduction. Cook came from a humble background and in the absence of good family connections forged a naval career through hard work, exemplary skills and the patronage of powerful men who recognised his abilities. He didn't receive his commission as lieutenant until relatively late in life – he was just shy of forty, which in the eighteenth century was high time to hang up your tricorne hat. The Royal Navy was every bit as hierarchical as you would imagine; most commissioned officers had more than one high-society feather in their cap and came from a bloodline peopled by the landed gentry or, at the very least, (shudder) educated professionals. Cook had none of that and was, most likely, all the better for it.

When he encountered people in the Marquesas Islands who could understand the Polynesian dialect despite the 1600 kilometres that separated them, he reached the rather sensible conclusion that the two groups were related and in regular contact with each other. And this wasn't the first time it occurred to Cook that these people were related; journal entries from his first voyage show he was thinking about this even then.

### CAPTAIN JAMES COOK

*These people sail in those seas from island to island for several hundred leagues, the sun serving them for a compass by day and the moon and stars by night. When this comes to be proved we shall be no longer at a loss to know how the islands lying in those seas came to be peopled, for if the inhabitants of Uleitea have been at islands laying 2 or 300 leagues to the westward of them it cannot be doubted but that the inhabitants of those western islands may have been at others as far westward of them and so we may trace them from island to island quite to the East Indies.*

Over 150 years earlier, the Dutch had witnessed the Polynesians embarking on open ocean voyages. Jacob Le Maire and Willem Schouten were sailing between Tonga and Samoa in 1616 when they crossed paths with a convoy of canoes laden with trade goods. These Polynesian traders were neither lost, nor drifting – accidentally or otherwise.

**MOETAI BROTHERSON, Mā'ohi Tribe, French MP**
*At a time when most European sailors were just following the coasts, our ancestors were crossing the oceans without any compasses. I wish I could go back to a time where it was normal to cross the ocean and Polynesian people were reaching Asia and America. We have evidence of that. It must have been an incredible time.*

In order to ensure the British could become masters of the high seas, Cook was tasked with journeying to King George's Island, as Tahiti was then known to the British, to observe the Passage of Venus across the face of the sun. As the big day approached – 3 June 1769 – Cook was nervous. Or as nervous as a man like Cook could be. This was, literally, a twice-in-a-lifetime event, and he had missed it the first time. It was also one that he had travelled halfway around the world to witness. The one thing that's rather crucial to the correct observation of the sun is that

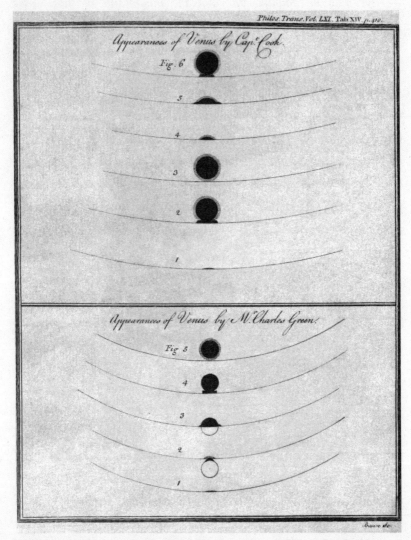

*Appearance of Venus.* The transit of Venus on 3 June 1769, as sketched by Cook and the astronomer Charles Green. A deceptively simple drawing that had profound consequences for navigation for nearly two centuries.

one can see it. Clouds rather spoil the fun. The day dawned, and he held his breath.

He had nothing to worry about. From the island of Tahiti, Cook and astronomer Charles Green observed the tiny black silhouette of Venus cross the blazing disc of the sun from nine in the morning until three in the afternoon. To cover all his bases, Cook sent Charles Clerke to the other side of the island to make the same observations, as did Banks on the nearby island of Mo'orea. Cook was concerned about some discrepancies in their reading. Due to what can best be described as a 'droplet' effect, which meant the outline of the planet distorted as it passed the outer rim of the sun, Cook and Green couldn't agree on the exact time the planet entered and exited the sun. But they needn't have worried. Once the results were combined with all the other results from the many observation points around the world, a figure was calculated that gave a distance between the earth and the sun that we now know was just 3 per cent off the mark.

As they watched what was going on, the Tahitians must have been perplexed. They, too, studied the planet Venus. They knew it as Ta'urua-nui, the beautiful eldest daughter of the mother of all stars, Ātea. Ta'urua-nui was also a Polynesian navigational star. But that's where the common ground with the British navigators ended.

For a start, while Cook and his men pored over charts and recorded everything in their journals and ledgers, the Tahitians did not write. Everything that was transmitted from generation to generation was communicated orally, most often in the form of a song. This was also true of the secrets of Polynesian navigation. Each island had a guild of navigators whose members enjoyed high social status and protected their trade secrets fiercely – and these were secrets worth protecting. They were the tricks of the trade that allowed the Polynesians to travel long distances across open water, not by measuring, calculating and consulting almanacs, but by observing the world around them.

### MATAHI TUTAVAI

*Navigators use everything around them. Signs they see in the sky, birds and clouds. They read the weather, but also the stars, and the moon as well as the sun. The navigators grew up doing just that out on the water. You learn your own limits, both physically and mentally. On the canoe, it's such a small place. Working together on the water can be really powerful. The canoe is an island, and the island is a canoe. Whatever experience you get on the va'a ('canoe'), it's your responsibility to bring it back to the land to the community, so all the community can share that experience with you.*

A Polynesian navigator would look to the sky's 'tone'. It would be darker over an island than over open ocean. A red sky at sunrise or sunset meant there was humidity in the air. Rain could be expected if the moon wore a halo. If there was a double halo, a gale was coming as well. When dolphins and porpoises turned tail and swam for sheltered waters, a storm was on the way. If a frigate bird, which has a chronic aversion to getting its feathers wet, was seen flying out to sea, then the navigator could expect calm seas. Certain birds will only roost on land. If a white tern was sighted over the water, this meant there was land within two hundred kilometres; if it was a brown tern, land was only sixty-five kilometres away.

The water itself spoke to the navigator. If there was poor visibility, the ocean showed the way. The navigators could distinguish between waves that were caused by a local weather system and those that were formed by pressure systems beyond the horizon line. They also looked to the deep ocean currents that flow through the Pacific, just as terrestrial explorers follow the great river systems to find their way through a landscape. It's even said that the greatest navigators could distinguish as many as five different swells at the same time and could sense an unseen island by reading the vibrations of the waves across a canoe's hull – islands create unique wave patterns, a signpost to those who are looking for them.

Polynesian navigators charted their voyages in their minds from their point of departure by visualising the destination. The Polynesians couldn't risk missing any of the signs encountered on the voyage and had to plot their route cerebrally as they progressed. Meaning that while they were on duty, they couldn't sleep. Ever. They would sit on a special platform on the ship's deck and were left to their business. These days, it's said you'll know a star navigator by their bloodshot eyes.

### RICHARD ARIIHAU TUHEIAVA

*The essence of celestial navigation is to master the art of visualisation. The navigator must keep the destination in mind. Even though you don't see the island or the country where you're going, you have to keep that destination and that island in your mind. If you lose that image – that picture – then you're lost on the ocean.*

Contemporary Polynesian navigators explain that other than the outer reaches of Rapa Nui, Hawai'i and New Zealand, the longest open water voyage in Polynesia is five hundred kilometres, and that at sea you can see fifty kilometres in all directions. That means the span of the area visible to the naked eye is one hundred kilometres. So, theoretically at least, that means land is always somewhere just over the horizon. Still. It sounds horribly daunting, not least because to contemporary Western eyes the vessels they took to sea look terrifyingly flimsy.

**MARGUERITE LAI, Dance Revivalist**

*The va'a were the backbone of our culture. Our canoes were the centre of daily life. Our villages were named for the va'a. It means everyone pulling together and working together. It's a broader metaphor for Polynesian society.*

These vessels were central to Tahitian society. The open catamarans were carved using tools made of coral, stone and human bone, and cracks sealed with sap and resin from breadfruit trees. Planking was bound together with rope made of coconut fibre, and sails were woven from pandanus leaves.

Cook had no concerns about the seaworthiness of Polynesian vessels. When he visited Tonga, he was particularly impressed by the double-hulled canoes he saw there. And they were speedy. He noted that they could reach seven miles an hour in a light breeze, which far outpaced Cook's own vessels. In a fine example of nautical one-upmanship, in New Zealand waters a Māori canoe approached the *Endeavour* and a warrior on board called out to the men on board, 'Are you alright? Are you sick? Why are you going so slowly?' When told the ship was under full sail and travelling at top speed, the Māori sailors fell about themselves laughing before taking off again across the waves.

As the means by which Polynesians interacted with their world, the canoe was a pillar of traditional Tahitian society. Watching the Tahitians and their brethren negotiate their way across the waves, Cook recognised kindred spirits. Like him, these people were sailors.

**MATAHI TUTAVAI**

*The big canoes would go out to other islands. They not only found those islands, they also went back and forth between them. We have family ties with Hawai'i, with Aotearoa, with Samoa, Tonga. To us, the ocean wasn't a barrier, it was a highway. We knew how to use it.*

They handled their canoes *'very dextrously'*, said Cook: *'I believe* [they] *perform long and distant voyages in them, otherwise they could not have the knowledge of the islands in these seas they seem to have.'* But the Polynesian ships were, in virtually every way, completely unlike the converted collier James Cook sailed into the Pacific. The newly minted lieutenant would have felt right at home in the coal-carting vessel formerly known as the *Earl of Pembroke*. Cook learnt to sail on Whitby 'cats', as they were called.

**DAVID PRYCE, Sailor and Adventurer**

*You look at the shape of the* Endeavour – *well, it is pretty much as close to your bathtub as you can get. It wasn't a very manoeuvrable ship.*

With their flat bottoms, massive space below deck and square bows, the British ships weren't much chop when it came to speed. But the ship renamed HM Bark *Endeavour* – 'bark' being the term used for those vessels that didn't easily fit the British Navy's classification system – was just the ticket for long-distance voyaging. Its 'bluff' bow was much stronger than a pointy hull, and its flat bottom and shallow draught meant it could be floated off troublesome reefs or shoals a great deal more easily than if it had a pointy bow. It may not have set any speed records, but as events later in the voyage would prove, the *Endeavour* was well chosen for the conditions. In any other vessel, Cook's great Pacific adventure might have gone no further than his first voyage.

What the high priest of 'Oro and navigator, Tupaia, thought of Cook's cumbersome vessel as he climbed on board in 1769 off the shores of Tahiti, we'll never know. But thanks to the various journals kept by the crew of the *Endeavour*, we do know something about the man who left his ancestral home on Ra'iatea and set out to sea with a boatload of noisome British sailors. Born around 1725, Tupaia was an *'arioi* and was blessed with all the traits that membership of the exclusive class of priests and priestesses entailed. He was statuesque and physically imposing, highly intelligent and charismatic, and a savvy diplomat. The ship's master, Robert Molyneux, deemed Tupaia to be: '*infinitely superior in every respect to any other Indian we have met with, he has conceived so strong a friendship for Mr Banks that he is determined to visit Britannia*'.

It was true that Joseph Banks formed a particularly close relationship with Tupaia, so much so that he harboured ambitions to take him back to England and keep him. Much like an exotic pet.

**SIR JOSEPH BANKS**

*Thank heaven I have a sufficiency and I do not know why I may not keep him as a curiosity, as well as some of my neighbours do lions and tigers at a larger expense than he will probably ever put me to; the amusement I shall have in his future conversation and the benefit he will be of to this ship, as well as what he may be if another should be sent into these seas, will I think fully repay me.*

Banks also knew it would be a boon to have Tupaia on board as a translator and local mediator when they encountered other Pacific Islanders. Even before the *Endeavour* arrived in Tahiti, he had been contemplating the benefits that a local guide would offer.

**SIR JOSEPH BANKS**

*[We should] persuade one of them to come with us who may serve as an interpreter, and give us an opportunity hereafter of landing wherever we please without running the risk of being obliged to commit the cruelties which the Spaniards and most others who have been in these seas have often brought themselves under the dreadful necessity of being guilty of, for guilty I must call it.*

As for Tupaia, his motivations for embarking with Cook and his men were crystal clear.

**RICHARD ARIIHAU TUHEIAVA**

*Tupaia did follow Cook because he wanted to discover how things were outside of this country. He had a personal quest. He was not simply being used by James Cook.*

*Tupaia had his own ambitions too. He had a very high level of wisdom and spiritual training – more so than James Cook. But he had no ship. He needed Cook to travel across the ocean and see the islands beyond.*

In the intertribal wars, Tupaia had been driven from his homeland, Ra'iatea, by a rival group from Bora Bora. He relocated to Tahiti, where he aligned himself with Queen Purea and became her advisor and lover. Naturally, he was keen to take his home back. He must have known that an alliance with the British and their impressive weapons certainly wouldn't hurt his ambitions.

Before the *Endeavour* set sail on the next leg of its voyage, Tupaia directed the ship to Ra'iatea and what we now know to be one of the most significant historical sites in the Pacific: Taputapuatea Marae.

### RICHARD ARIIHAU TUHEIAVA

*It was where the most beautiful ocean-going journeys of all time began. Celestial navigation was an art, but also a lifestyle. Taputapuatea was the navigational hub of all these people – these heroes – who crossed the ocean without any instruments, and returned to this place they considered their homeland.*

It was here that *Te Pō* – the world of darkness occupied by the sacred ancestors – intersected with the world of the living: *Te Ao*. It was where the god of war, 'Oro, held court, and was also the mythical Havaiki from which the great Pacific migrations traditionally set sail.

**SAM NEILL**

*Taputapuatea is the spiritual heart really of Polynesia. It's a very sacred place. It gives me the same sort of feeling I've had at the pyramids in Mexico or at Stonehenge. I don't really understand it, if I'm honest. It does feel quite dark to me, but perhaps that's just my feeling about religion as a whole. The only thought I have on religion is that I believe you should be able to practise whatever it is that you believe in ... as long as it doesn't hurt any other people. Human sacrifice was a feature of religious worship at Taputapuatea ... but we might just let that one go through to the keeper.*

As a star navigator, Tupaia knew that all those who departed and returned to the islands must pay their respects at Taputapuatea. So it was that Cook and Banks were witness to a ceremony complete with complex chants and offerings to 'Oro intended to elicit divine protection for the rest of the voyage. But the visitors weren't treated to the full show. When *arioi* usually arrived by canoe at Taputapuatea for a religious ceremony, sacrificial pairs of dead men and fish were strapped onto the prows of the boats, and other victims were hung in the trees ringing the stone platform by ropes strung through their heads or used as rollers beneath the keels of canoes as they were hefted up the shore from the sea.

Although Cook's diary entries betray an anthropological interest in describing what he saw of Tahitian religious traditions, in general he shied away from theology.

## CAPTAIN JAMES COOK

*The mysteries of most religions are very dark and not easily understood even by those who profess them ... it will be expected that I should give some account of their religion, which is a thing I have learned so little of that I hardly dare to touch upon it ... The Mories [marae], which we at first thought were burying places, are wholly built for places of worship, and for the performing of religious ceremonies in. The viands are laid upon altars erected 8, 10, or 12 feet high, by stout posts, and the table of the altar on which the viands lay, is generally made of palm leaves; they are not always in the Mories, but very often at some distance from them ... The viands laid near the tombs of the dead are, from what I can learn, not for the deceased, but as an offering ... for they believe of a future state of rewards and punishments; but what their ideas are of it I know not.*

Banks, however, got very hands on. Curious to understand the inner workings of Tahitian religious practices, he stuck his arm into a shrine in Taputapuatea and removed a sacred relic. This act was sacrilege on a grand scale, akin to reaching into a reliquary at the Vatican and pulling out St Peter's fibula. The locals were apoplectic. Without Tupaia's intercession on his behalf, Banks might well have found himself adorning the prow of a sacred canoe.

That disaster averted, the *Endeavour* readied to put out to sea, and the extent of Tupaia's navigational knowledge soon became apparent. It was a meeting of minds as Cook transcribed the chart onto paper that Tupaia carried about in his memory.

### RICHARD ARIIHAU TUHEIAVA

*Tupaia shared his map of Polynesia with James Cook. But the way of using this map is very difficult for a Western mind because it goes hand in hand with the technique of visualisation. When you see an island, you know there's another right after it. You draft the map in your mind and it's a way of thinking and of visualising things. It's easy for us. For Tupaia, it meant he had a way to come home. It's like a sea turtle. They don't get lost. Tupaia wouldn't either.*

What resulted was the perfect meeting of Enlightenment rationalism and Polynesian traditional wisdom. The chart records a total of 130 islands covering a rough circle with a diameter of 4700 kilometres, from the Marquesas in the east to Fiji in the west. Of those 130 islands, Tupaia had names for seventy-four, and although he had only visited thirteen of them, his father and grandfather had told him of the others. He explained to Cook the workings of the prevailing winds and currents that allowed the Polynesian people to travel and trade across the Pacific.

### CAPTAIN JAMES COOK

*Tupaia tells us that during the months of November, December & January westerly winds with rain prevail & as the inhabitants of the islands know very well how to make proper use of the winds there will no difficulty arise in trading or sailing from island to islands even though they lay in an east & west direction.*

This couldn't have failed to impress Cook, who was himself a cartographic prodigy, having taught himself mathematics, trigonometry, astronomy, surveying and charting. Cook left us a legacy that includes hydrographic surveys of Newfoundland and New Zealand that were still in use in the twentieth century – the last section of his chart of New Zealand was only retired in the 1990s.

They may have come from opposite sides of the planet, but when it came to their relationship with the sea, Cook and Tupaia had much in common. On the subsequent voyage between Tahiti and New Zealand, Cook marvelled at how Tupaia was able to identify the precise direction back to Tahiti without reference to any instruments.

> **ALEXANDER DALRYMPLE (1737–1808), Scottish Geographer and Hydrographer**
>
> *I have heard Captain Cook as well as others assert, Toobia [sic] could show them at all times during the course of their voyage, to half a point of the compass, the direction in which Otaheite [Tahiti] lay.*

And like Cook, Tupaia could sense the ship's movement through the water, intuitively knowing when they had shifted course.

Cook could read the signs on land as well. And as the season turned in the Tahitian archipelago, he knew it was time to go: *'the season for bread fruit was wholly over and what other fruits they had were hardly sufficient for themselves'*. As the *Endeavour* sailed out to sea with Tupaia on board, the Tahitians wept, crying out *'Auē! Auē!'* – 'Alas! Alas!'

But Cook ignored Tupaia's advice to bear west towards where the Tahitian navigator knew there were more islands to explore. Instead, the Englishman set a course to the south.

**RAYMOND SMITH, Ngāti Kuia,**

**Rongomaiwahine Tribes, Descendant of Kahura**

*Our opinion of Cook is that he was a reasonably fair person, a reasonably good navigator; however, he didn't take direction well. He had the most skilled navigator in Tupaia, and Cook suggests Tupaia was only a mere interpreter, but in Pacific nations he was highly respected. It was to the detriment of the crew that Lieutenant Cook disregarded Tupaia's knowledge.*

What few on the *Endeavour* realised was that the Admiralty had set Cook a far more dangerous mission than the relatively benign task of recording the Passage of Venus. From Tahiti, Cook and his men were heading out into the great unknown. They had no way of preparing themselves for what lay ahead and no idea of just how important Tupaia would prove to be.

As Banks wrote, '*We again launched out into the ocean in search of what chance and Tupaia might direct us to.*'

# PART TWO

*FOUR*

# LOST WORLDS

*If you look at the world from different angles, there are a
lot of interesting things going on – a lot of continents.
And then you turn 'round to the Pacific and from a
certain point in space all you see is blue. It's enormous; it's
a third of the planet. The scale of it just beggars belief –
particularly if, like Cook, you're in a little tub from
Whitby, or – like Tupaia and the Polynesian navigators –
you're in a double-hulled canoe. The scale of this thing
exceeds the limits of one's imagination.*

**SAM NEILL**

During an era when, thanks to Google Street View, we can
take a virtual stroll around exotic cities during our
lunchbreaks, and armchair amateurs use Google Earth to
discover ancient cities buried beneath the sands in the Saudi
Arabian desert, it's almost impossible to imagine a time when
the world beyond our shores was unknown in the most
profound sense. There were no satellites beaming live footage
from remote regions; no frontline reporters and cameramen
transmitting images and events for us to digest with our

evening meal; no National Geographic Channel; no Instagram; no Facebook; no YouTube; no smart camera recordings or live blogging. Any sense that there were unfamiliar lands and societies beyond the horizon existed only in the imagination, if at all.

Whether they lived in Moscow, Manchester or Matavai Bay, in the eighteenth century most people knew little if anything about the world beyond the proverbial back fence. In the absence of the fast, safe and comfortable means of modern mass transport we know today, long distance travel was an extreme sport. To say it was hard work is an understatement verging on the ridiculous. That's why so many European philosophers and thinkers could believe there was a massive unknown continent hidden somewhere in the southern hemisphere without ever having seen it. Just as theoretical physicists today posit ideas about the universe without ever thinking they'll jump in a spacecraft and head into outer space to test their theories in person, the European geographers had no intention of boarding a ship to sail into the great unknown. They left that up to men like James Cook.

The European fixation with the Great Southern Continent was spawned by the ancient Greeks. The obscenely gifted polymath Aristotle, who dabbled in everything from physics to poetry and ethics to biology, proposed in his *Meteorologica* that without a large landmass on the opposite side of the globe to counterbalance the lands in the northern hemisphere, the world would fly off kilter as it spun on its axis. After the geographer and mathematician Ptolemy picked up Aristotle's theory in the second century AD and his work was rediscovered during the Renaissance, the concept of *Terra Australis Incognita*, or the

'Unknown Southern Land', became a cornerstone of Western thinking. And because human beings are naturally inclined to believe that every lost continent hides unimaginable riches, as Europe stretched its colonial tentacles across the globe, the race was on to find it.

In its earliest imaginary form, the southern continent occupied about a quarter of the planet. Because Europeans had yet to find their way around the tip of Africa, and the Americas were still unknown to them, the proposed continent was depicted as joined to Asia by a land bridge. According to this model, the oceans were actually giant lakes encircled by land. At the time, the sea best known to the Europeans was the Mediterranean, a largely enclosed body of water. To them, it would have been inconceivable that the surface of the planet was covered by far more water than land.

All it took to make this conceivable was Columbus's landing in the Americas in 1498 and Magellan's passage into the Pacific in 1520. But the terraqueous world the new voyages of exploration gave Europe didn't put paid to the concept of the Great Southern Continent. In his 1569 map of the world, Gerard Mercator included a vast continent spreading from the fiftieth line of latitude south of the equator with two peninsulas, each the size of southern Africa, reaching north beyond the Tropic of Capricorn towards Java and New Guinea. When the Dutch cartographer Abraham Ortelius put his mind to creating the *Theatrum Orbis Terrarum* in 1570, which was the first complete atlas of the world – well, as 'complete' as it could be at the time – he depicted the Great Southern Continent as extending around the world and covering a greater area than North and South America combined.

Mercator and Ortelius were the leading lights of the great school of Dutch cartography that emerged during the sixteenth and seventeenth centuries. It's no accident that this coincided with the expansion of Dutch commercial and colonial ambitions. Without maps to show the way, the ambitious Dutch plans to spread their interests across the globe would have been very short-lived. The information on these maps was valuable beyond measure even where, as was the case of the posited Great Southern Continent, it was somewhat less than accurate. Better a fair guess than nothing at all. Dutch cartography would shape the future of the planet – on paper and on the ground. Even before they launched their expansion into South-East Asia and the Pacific, they positioned themselves firmly in the pro–Great Southern Continent camp. Whether or not it was just wishful thinking, if the missing continent appeared across the waves it would provide them with a raft of new territories to occupy and exploit.

The French had no intention of being left out of the race as they watched the Portuguese and Spanish, and then the Dutch, spread their sails and race across the water towards unimaginable wealth – because what else would a lost continent contain if not lashings of gold, silver and precious gemstones? In 1582, the French politician Lancelot Voisin de La Popelinière wrote *Les Trois Mondes*, an influential history recounting the exploration of the world. In it, he argued that French interests would best be served by their sailors setting out to find and settle the vast southern continent, as yet unknown to European interests. '*Terre Australe could only benefit France*,' he said. And of course, it '*is impossible that there would not be marvellous things and delights, riches and other benefits of life there*'.

By the turn of the seventeenth century, the Dutch had quite a head start on the French. They were already well established in Indonesia – or the Dutch East Indies, as they were then known – where the Dutch East India Company, or VOC, had the sole Dutch rights over the lucrative spice trade. One of the largest shareholders in the VOC was Isaac Le Maire who, after a falling out with the company, founded the *Austraalse Compagnie* with the express intent of discovering the Great Southern Continent and breaking the VOC's stranglehold on trade in the region. The company's founding principle was that it was inconceivable that God would be anything but even-handed in His distribution of natural resources and mineral wealth between the northern and southern hemispheres, and therefore unimaginable wealth awaited those who were fortunate enough to take control of the undiscovered lands in the south. Le Maire and his son, Jacob, set sail with two ships captained by Willem Schouten in 1615. As Cook was to discover on his second voyage, they played an important role in the early European exploration of the Pacific. But a Great Southern Continent they did not find.

After this, many reports found their way to the Dutch about a large, mysterious continent to the south-east of Java. They already knew about the western and northern Australian coastlines, thanks to the many VOC near misses along its dangerous shore. But they didn't know how far south the landmass extended and whether or not it was connected to the long sought-after southern continent, a place many in the VOC believed must be at least as large as the known world, and where – you guessed it – gold and silver would abound.

In 1642 the VOC appointed the seafarer and merchant Abel Tasman to test that theory. Tasman sailed west from Batavia to

Mauritius, then travelled south. Once he got to the fortieth latitude, he hitched a ride on the Roaring Forties – the prevailing winds that tear around the globe at that bearing and only pause their relentless circumnavigation when they meet the southern tip of South America, the island of Tasmania and New Zealand. Tasman carved a path across the Indian Ocean to the south of Australia until he met up with the tiny island that would later bear his name. But at the time, he named it Van Diemen's Land for Anthony van Diemen, the Governor of the Dutch East Indies. He then turned east and in 1642 became the first European to sight New Zealand, a place he confidently declared was the *'mainland coast of the unknown southern continent'*. He named it 'Staten Landt'. He used nothing other than fairly wild conjecture to reach the conclusion that it must be connected to the land south of Tierra del Fuego that was first described by Jacob Le Maire and Willem Schouten when they passed Cape Horn in 1615, and also named by them 'Staten Landt'. According to Tasman's reasoning, a massive coastline linked New Zealand to a land just south of the southernmost tip of South America. If it had existed, it certainly would have been a continent that would warrant the name 'Great'.

This is where Tasman's story intersects with Cook's. Tasman returned to Batavia in June 1643, having sailed around the Australian continent – though as we'll see, he didn't sight the eastern coastline. By doing so, he proved that the landmass had nothing to do with the much-vaunted Great Southern Continent, which theoretical geographers asserted must be a far larger body of land than the relatively small continent that was then known as New Holland. But there were those who held out hope that as Tasman had proposed, New Zealand was going to deliver the goods. That's why, after leaving the Society Islands on 9 August 1769, Cook turned the *Endeavour* south-west towards the fortieth parallel, the same latitude Tasman was travelling along when he bumped into New Zealand. He was carrying with him instructions from the Admiralty marked 'Secret' that left him in no doubt that he was expected to continue the search for the elusive land so many believed lay in southern latitudes:

> <u>Secret</u>. … *there is reason to imagine that a continent or land of great extent, may be found to the southward of the tract lately made by Captain Wallis in his Majesty's ship the* Dolphin … *you are therefore … required and directed to put to sea with the bark you command … to pursue to the southward in order to make discovery of the continent abovementioned … If you discover the continent abovementioned either in your run to the southward or to the westward as above directed, you are to employ yourself diligently in exploring as great an extent of the coast as you can.*

Tupaia, who had already demonstrated his encyclopaedic knowledge of Polynesian geography, knew Cook was barking up the wrong tree and told him so. He'd find no great continent in the south – only open water. But Cook was a man of science. He believed in things he could measure, and things that could be learnt in books. The accumulated knowledge and ancient oral traditions that informed Tupaia's worldview just didn't cut it for Cook. So he sailed on into some of the most appalling seas on the planet.

**SYDNEY PARKINSON (1745–1771), Scottish Botanical and Natural History Illustrator on Cook's first voyage**

*The sea ran mountain-high and tossed the ship upon the waves. She rolled so much, that we could get no rest, or scarcely lie in bed, and almost every moveable on board was thrown down, and rolled about from place to place.*

For many of the fifty-nine days that followed, the *Endeavour* was smashed by unrelenting storms driven by the same prevailing winds – the Roaring Forties – that had carried Tasman across the Southern Ocean. Even the usually loquacious Joseph Banks was lost for words. All he could bring himself to write in his journal was: *'Myself sick all day.'* As anyone who has ever experienced a brutal sea voyage can attest, that's all that needed to be said.

It was two o'clock in the afternoon of 6 October 1769. The men on board heard a cry from the starboard bow. *Land ho!*

And not a moment too soon. After a voyage covering more than six thousand kilometres, the communal sigh of relief on board must have been quite something. The men were so desperate for a break from the unrelentingly brutal weather that Cook had offered a generous reward to whoever was first to sight land – so it was that the surgeon's boy had a headland named for him. Young Nick's actual head would be feeling a little the worse for wear as the voyage progressed, given his other reward: an imperial gallon – four and a half litres – of 94 per cent proof rum. For a twelve year old.

Once land was sighted, much feverish speculation ensued.

Could this actually be the fabled Great Southern Continent? Cook was sceptical. Not that this would stop him from proving the land's identity beyond doubt, one way or another. He wasn't going to leave anything to chance, even if he had a sneaking suspicion that Tupaia was closer to the truth than many of those on board who thought they had, at last, found the lost lands. The strongest supporter of the continental cause was the eternally optimistic Joseph Banks.

**SIR JOSEPH BANKS (1743–1820), 1st Baronet,**
**Naturalist and Botanist on Cook's first voyage**
*We were now on board of two parties, one who wished that the land in sight might, the other that it might not be a continent: myself have always been most firm for the former.*

Whether or not they were part of a southern continent was of little import to the Māori who had arrived on these islands at least five hundred years before the *Endeavour* sailed into their waters. To them, New Zealand was, and is, Aotearoa. The Land of the Long White Cloud. To state the bleeding obvious, most of the places Cook rushed about assiduously naming from one side of the Pacific to the other already had well-established names given to them by their indigenous inhabitants.

*SAM NEILL: Let's talk about naming for a minute. It's occurred to me that every act of possession is also an act of dispossession, and that every time someone like Cook names something that already has a name, he's disempowering the name that was there before.*
**KIHI HOWE-RIRINUI, Ngāpuhi ki Tauranga Moana**
**Tribe, Tour Guide:** *You'll never see Māori names in his country. So why have we got his names in our country?*

To the Māori, the newly christened Young Nick's Head was Te Kuri-a-Paoa.

New Zealand would become Cook's favourite anchorage in the Pacific. Over the course of his three voyages, he would visit six times. In years to come, he would write in typically restrained prose of his pleasure at returning to the southern islands. But this was his first visit and he didn't know what to expect.

### NICK TUPARA, Ngāti Oneone Tribe, Descendant of Te Maro

*I don't feel that Cook felt any anxiety at all. The British have conquered half the planet already as an empire, and this is perhaps the last bit left. England had been doing this sort of stuff for a very, very long time. I think this land was a brand-new land with new resources, and they found some natives on it. They needed to just go and sort it out. And that was their mission.*

The sight of columns of smoke on the shore confirmed to Cook what he already knew – that this land was populated. And what he had learnt of the locals would not have filled him with optimism.

Popular legend held that the remote regions of the Antipodes were populated by fabulous hybrid beings. Dog-faced men. Men without noses. Men without tongues. Others whose heads had sunk so low beneath shoulder level they had been absorbed into their chests. And the *skiapodes*, who were creatures with a single foot so large they used it as a sunshade to protect themselves from the scorching heat of these desolate lands. Cook, of course, knew enough to disregard such wild tales. He was less concerned about having to fight off a tribe of men with unfeasibly large feet than he was about meeting the locals whom he knew, from Tasman's experience, were ferocious warriors.

What Cook couldn't know was that the smoke on shore came from signal fires summoning those warriors to repel the new arrivals. He could only guess at what might happen next. But one thing was certain: this would be nothing like the idyllic tropical islands they had just left behind. When the *Endeavour* arrived on Tahiti, Wallis and Bougainville had already laid the foundations for his arrival. But in New Zealand, things were totally different. For one thing, the locals had only had one European visitor, and that was over a century before. It was brief, and it didn't end well. One Māori warrior was felled and four Dutchmen were killed. Tasman's assessment of the place was summed up rather bluntly in the name he gave the inlet: 'Murderers Bay'.

The tragic outcome of Tasman's encounter with the Māori came despite the fact he had been issued with very clear instructions about how to negotiate relationships with indigenous people encountered on his voyage. These instructions were, given the otherwise brutal times in which they were written, surprisingly humane – notwithstanding the liberal use of the world 'barbarian':

> [E]xtreme caution will everywhere have to be used ... the
> southern regions are peopled with fierce savages ...
> barbarian men are no wise to be trusted because they
> commonly think that the foreigners who so unexpectedly
> appear before them, have come only to seize their land ...
> you will treat with amity and kindness such barbarian

> *men as you shall meet and come to parley with, and*
> *connive at small affronts, thefts and the like … lest*
> *punishments inflicted should give them a grudge against*
> *us … You will prudently prevent all manner of insolence*
> *and all arbitrary action on the part of our men against*
> *the nations discovered, and take good care that no injury*
> *be done to them in their houses, gardens, vessels, or their*
> *property, their wives etc.*

Most noteworthy is the observation that '*barbarian men …
commonly think that the foreigners who so unexpectedly appear
before them, have come only to seize their land*'. Goodness knows
how they might have got that impression.

Cook also carried with him a list of best possible intentions
issued by the Royal Society. In a document drafted in impeccable
eighteenth-century copperplate, James Douglas, the fourteenth
Earl of Morton and President of the Society, put forth '*hints
offered to the consideration of Captain Cook, Mr Banks, Doctor
Solander and the other gentlemen who go upon the expedition on
board the* Endeavour'. It was the consummate Enlightenment-era
document:

> *To exercise the utmost patience and forbearance with*
> *respect to the natives … To check the petulance of the*
> *sailors, and restrain the wanton use of firearms … [S]*
> *hedding the blood of those people is a crime of the highest*
> *nature. They are human creatures, the work of the same*
> *omnipotent Author, equally under his care with the most*
> *polished Europeans … Should they in a hostile manner*
> *oppose a landing, and kill some men in the attempt, even*

*this would hardly justify firing among them, till every
other gentle method has been tried ... They [the
indigenous inhabitants] are the natural, and in the
strictest sense of the word, the legal possessors of the several
regions they inhabit ... No European nation has a right
to occupy any part of their country, or settle among them
without their voluntary consent.*

There's no reason to doubt that the Earl was sincere when he penned the most heartfelt passages. With what was about to happen as the *Endeavour* approached shore, it was a statement that would come back to haunt Cook.

At the Tūranganui River on the eastern coast of New Zealand's North Island, the Māori watched the approach of the curious vessel.

### NICK TUPARA

*A visionary three years before Cook's arrival foretold that
Cook would come. He said that a white person would
arrive here, and that person would bring one god with him,
and that god would be the god of the dead son.*

When they first saw the *Endeavour*, the Māori were astonished. Some thought it was a floating island, its sails the clouds billowing above it. Others imagined it to be Ruakapanga, the mythical bird from Havaiki; the smaller boat they saw lowered into the water beside it a fledgling that bore multi-coloured beings in human form. And some saw the red and white strangers arriving from the spirit world as the fulfilment of a prophecy.

**KILEY NEPIA, Ngāti Apa ki te Rā Tō, Ngāti Kuia,
Rangitāne Tribes, Descendant of Kahura**

*Imagine – you've got the strange ship that's parked out over
there, everybody musters inside the village and then you
are sending scouts out to have a look at what this new
intrusion is … What is that spacecraft over yonder and
what is it bringing? So, you could imagine that it was a
time of anxiety for our people.*

Try this for a mental exercise. You've had a call from the
neighbours – something peculiar has appeared in the sky above
your street. You gather in a group outside in time to see a
spaceship descend from the heavens, the aliens on board waving
at you. It's not too long a bow to draw, because as far as the Māori
were concerned, Cook, his men and their ship were totally, utterly
and completely alien. Not foreign – because that implies the
Māori knew they were men from a distant and unfamiliar land –
but alien. Though to their great misfortune, it wouldn't take long
before the Māori realised the visitors were mortals and suffered
from all-too-human failings.

Cook stepped ashore from the cutter and became the first
Englishman to plant a foot on New Zealand soil. As was his way,
he led from the front.

**SAM NEILL**

*On a good day, Cook could be a great politician and a true
diplomat. On other days, he handled things very, very
badly. When he was clumsy, shit happened.*

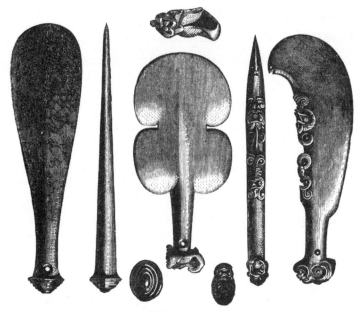

MAORI WEAPONS.

*Maori weapons* (engraving), English School (19th century). The basis of Māori warfare was clubs and spikes, used in hand-to-hand combat. Hence the appeal and destructive force of the musket – it brought death inflicted from afar. Bridgeman Images, LLM965340

He was not a man to hang back while others took the first – most dangerous – steps towards the unknown. True to form, he approached indigenous people with one hand outstretched in greeting and the other resting on a loaded musket. But on this day, it wasn't necessary. The Māori had seemingly disappeared. Cook left four men on the beach to keep an eye on the boat as he wandered further afield. Once he was out of sight he heard a shot. He had no way of knowing what had happened. But he suspected it wouldn't be good.

After Cook had left, a group of Māori brandishing their weapons had advanced towards the men on the beach. An attempt to warn them off had failed and the anxious sailors panicked Now, a Māori man was lying dead. When he fell, downed by a shot through the heart, his kin tried to pick him up. But when they realised he was dead, they were deeply shocked and dropped him to the ground. They could only think that Te Maro had been killed by *atua*: ancestral spirits. To touch him was *tapu*. This was the first time these Māori had ever seen a gun.

### NICK TUPARA

*Cook brought sailors ashore who were carrying arms. In the back of his mind there was a prospect there would be violence. I don't think it was anything of too much consequence to him that a few natives would be lost along the way. How do I know this story? The better question is – why don't others know about it? Everybody knows about Cook. When you grow up cast in the role as one of the 'natives' who approached the British and got shot, you don't get a chance to talk about it a lot. This is one of the rare times where we've actually been asked. Now, the written history takes a priority over the oral history. But we've retained the stories amongst ourselves, and they've been passed down from generation to generation. Cook gets a huge amount of attention, while our ancestors get nothing. It's annoying.*

Cook was shaken. It wasn't the auspicious start he was hoping for. As a gesture of apology, he placed an offering of beads and nails on Te Maro's body and retreated to the *Endeavour*.

After a restless night, Cook made another attempt to land. But this time, there was one crucial difference; Tupaia was with him. As Cook and Tupaia landed on the east bank, they were confronted by a group of fearsome warriors who greeted them with a *haka*, the terrifying war dance that's familiar to anyone who's ever seen the New Zealand rugby team, the All Blacks, greet their opponents on the field before the start of a game.

> **JOHN GORE (1730–1790) British American Officer, crew member, Samuel Wallis's circumnavigation on the *Dolphin* and Cook's first and third voyages**
>
> *About a hundred of the natives all armed came down on the opposite side of the Salt River, drew themselves up in lines. Then with a regular jump from left to right and the reverse, they brandished their weapons, distorted their mouths, lolling out their tongues, and turned up the whites of their eyes accompanied with a strong hoarse song. Calculated in my opinion to cheer each other and intimidate their enemies, and may be called perhaps with propriety a dancing war song.*

There was certainly no mistaking it for a welcome dance.

> **NICK TUPARA**
>
> *I think Cook assumes the performance of the* haka *is in fact for him, whereas every time I've ever done the* haka *it's generally about the place that you are. If you keep in mind they are facing Titirangi Mountain, and so their* haka *in the first instance would be back to the mountain. It will be also to the river that flows between Cook and them. The* haka *will be to all the ancestors – those that are there and those who have lived there over their time. It will also be to Te Maro who's lying there dead.*

The tension on the opposite side of the river must have been unbearable as the Māori warriors stamped and shrieked. Then, suddenly, a single man called out from amongst the group of strangers. Everybody froze. 'We have only come for food and water,' Tupaia called across the river, speaking in Tahitian. Tupaia and the Māori warriors were separated by hundreds of years of history and thousands of miles of open ocean. Yet they understood each other.

**WILLIAM MONKHOUSE (d. 1770),**
**Surgeon, Cook's first voyage**

*We found they understood his language. A long conversation ensued, which seemed to consist on their part of inquiries from whence we came, of complaints that we had killed one of their people, and of many expressions of doubt of our friendship.*

Tupaia managed to convince one of the Māori warriors to abandon his weapons and swim to a rock in the centre of the river. Cook reciprocated, handing his gun to one of his men and wading into the water, his hands held open at his sides to show he had nothing to hide. Somehow, in some way, Cook knew how to respond to the gesture of friendship offered by the warrior; they greeted each other in the Polynesian way, by touching noses.

Just as the Māori god Tane once blew the breath of life into the nostrils of the first Māori woman, Hineahuone, the *hongi* is an exchange of sacred breath between two people.

It was a profound moment.

**NICK TUPARA**

*Having statues of Cook on our sacred mountain ... having to live in streets named after him ... go to public places named after him but to have no places named after our ancestors in this city ... it is just abhorrent. Now, we're looking to bring a balance back. We're looking at the duality of history and it can't come quick enough really. Eventually we will all – as a community – begin to respect all the ancestors that came through here.*

Despite the détente, Tupaia remained cautious. *'Be on guard, for they are not our friends,'* he warned Cook and his men. Unfortunately in days to come, Tupaia's pessimism would prove to be justified. But at this moment, it seemed a peace of sorts might be possible.

Above all else, in an instant the truth of Polynesian migration was laid bare. Cook realised, perhaps for the first time, just how valuable Tupaia was going to be on this and subsequent voyages. As events would show, it's not too much of a stretch to say that without Tupaia there would be no Cook.

# FIVE

# KINDRED SPIRITS

*There is a totally different view of Māori culture than there was when I was a kid. Māori language is becoming much more part of the mainstream and people are much prouder in general of all things Māori. That's what distinguishes us in New Zealand so much from the rest of the world. People are really proud of that, but it is an enormous change.*

**SAM NEILL**

Whether they liked it or not, the people of Aotearoa had just acquired themselves a boatload of European sailors determined to get to know them. And the best way to do that is to find something you have in common. With the Ra'iatean priest Tupaia on board the *Endeavour*, that would turn out to be a whole lot easier than might have been expected.

It was something of a miracle that Tupaia had deigned to join Cook. Although it was still early days and things in New Zealand would get much worse before they reached equilibrium, the insights Tupaia gave Cook about Māori society, culture and faith would prove to be priceless.

**KILEY NEPIA, Ngāti Apa ki te Rā Tō, Ngāti Kuia,**
**Rangitāne Tribes, Descendant of Kahura**
*Tupaia played an important role. He was more than a*
*translator. When he came to these shores his interaction*
*would've been from a chief to a chief. There was a cultural*
*bridge that was crossed between Tupaia and our people.*

The Admiralty had given Cook instructions to make formal, amicable connections with any indigenous people he encountered, and Tupaia's knowledge and connections were worth their weight in gold:

> *You are likewise to observe the genius, temper, disposition*
> *and number of the natives, if there be any and endeavour*
> *by all proper means to cultivate a friendship and alliance*
> *with them, making them presents of such trifles as they*
> *may value inviting them to traffic, and showing them*
> *every kind of civility and regard.*

Tupaia essentially gifted Cook a passport he could use to gain access to the other Polynesian societies he encountered during his exploration of the Pacific.

The fact that Tupaia could communicate with his distant Māori kin was remarkable. It's not that Cook and his men would have been completely at a loss for words. As the voyage progressed, it became quite the thing to assemble a lexicon of indigenous languages, and a number of the learned gentlemen on the *Endeavour* showed a proficiency at mastering foreign languages at speed. But to have someone on board who could access Māori society at all levels was a benefit beyond measure.

They still had some way to go, though. There would be no alliances unless Cook managed to defuse the tinderbox he had ignited on the banks of the Tūranganui River. The spirit of friendship signified by the *hongi* between Cook and the Māori warrior had been short-lived. After that exchange, Cook and his men were surrounded as the other warriors snatched at the British weapons. One Māori man had a brief taste of victory after he lifted an officer's sword and took off with it – but it was a pyrrhic victory. Cook, who as we know just loved a bit of thievery, called for his men to retaliate. Shots were fired, and the man fell to the beach. His name was Te Rakau, and he was an important chieftain.

Two deaths in as many days. It was a terrible start.

Cook and his men beat a hasty retreat to the *Endeavour* without restocking any provisions and leaving two dead Māori men in their wake. Both Cook and Banks were shaken by how quickly they had lost control. The orders in Lord Morton's 'hints' and the missive penned by the powers that be in the Admiralty hadn't just been ignored, they'd been torn up and stomped over. And it weighed heavily on the two men's consciences. Regardless of their failings, Cook and Banks fancied themselves honourable men whose conduct under pressure erred on the side of restraint and reason. For Banks, this was '*the most disagreeable day my life has yet seen, black be the mark for it*'. Cook's own horror at how things turned out is captured in a journal entry heavily laden with self-recrimination.

**CAPTAIN JAMES COOK**

*I am conscious that the feeling of every reader of humanity will censure me for having fired upon these unhappy people, and it is impossible that, upon a calm review, I should approve it myself ... the nature of my service required me to obtain a knowledge of their country, which I could no otherwise effect than by forcing my way into it in a hostile manner.*

Despite his deep regret about what had occurred at the first landing, Cook was more determined than ever to establish meaningful contact with the Māori people. That he now knew Tupaia was able to communicate with the locals would have made it all the more enticing.

Departing the ill-fated landing place, Cook spied some fishing canoes returning from a jaunt out to sea, he decided to try again. Cook's plan was simple. He would grab some of the paddlers and bring them on board the *Endeavour*, where he and his men would put on a good show of British hospitality to convey their good intentions. Easy. What could go wrong?

As it happened, quite a lot. What Cook couldn't possibly have known was that virtually every place he went in New Zealand was on a war footing. It was a land torn apart by almost constant intertribal warfare. Under those conditions, what were the Māori in the canoe to think when Cook's ship loomed over them? With only men on board the strange vessel, they assumed it was an enormous war canoe. When Cook's men attempted to approach them, the Māori thought they were under attack. They had no idea Cook only wanted to invite them on board for tea and crumpets. So they fought back, hurling paddles, rocks – even fish – at the British ships.

Muskets were fired, and some of the Māori warriors who were shot fell into the sea and drowned. There's no consensus about how many men died that day. But one thing is irrefutable – even a single mortality was one too many.

Cook did manage to abduct three young men, who were hauled into a rowboat and dragged onto the *Endeavour*'s deck to enjoy the full splendour of British 'hospitality'. They were, at first, understandably terrified. But after being offered food and gifts, they reached the conclusion that their lives were not at risk and chatted amicably with Tupaia, later dancing and singing for Cook and the crew. After spending the night on board, the three boys were returned to shore.

What on earth was Cook thinking? More to the point, after they got over their shock, what might the Māori boys have been thinking?

Remarkably, we do have a firsthand account of the impressions the pale-skinned strangers made on one young Māori boy. In the mid-nineteenth century, a venerable chieftain by the name of Te Hōreta, whose adventures included a visit to Sydney in 1821, told British settlers in New Zealand an extraordinary story. He had been a young boy when Cook arrived in his homeland of Te Whitianga o Kupe, or Mercury Bay, on the eastern coast of the North Island's Coromandel Peninsula. He had extremely vivid recollections of that time, preserved in such clear detail thanks to the oral traditions that formed a cornerstone of Māori culture.

**TINA NGATA, Ngāti Porou Tribe**

*So much has been lost because our ancestors could retain an incredible amount of knowledge, but we didn't write things down. They could sit and speak for days and days – months, even – non-stop. Their ability to be able to retain knowledge and information far surpassed anything that we have today.*

Te Hōreta's mental faculties were honed to a razor-sharp edge because in a society that didn't commit things to paper, memory was everything. He recounted in great detail the impressions he and the other members of his *iwi* (tribe) formed of Cook and his men. At first they were struck with horror at the sudden appearance of what they decided could only be goblins, because these strange creatures had their eyes on the back of their heads as they rowed to shore; the British sailors sat in the cutter with their backs facing the direction they were headed, but the Māori warriors and the boys on the shore were only familiar with paddling while facing the front of their *waka*.

### TE HŌRETA TE TAHIWHA, Ngāti Whanaunga Tribe, Te Mateawa Hapū

*We lived at Whitianga, and a vessel came there, and when our old men saw the ship they said it was a* tupua, *a god, and the people on board were strange beings. The ship came to anchor, and the boats pulled on shore. As our old men looked at the manner in which they came on shore ... the old people said, 'Yes, it is so: these people are goblins; their eyes are at the back of their heads; they pull on shore with their backs to the land to which they are going.'*

\*

Over time, the Māori of Mercury Bay established a cautiously benign relationship with Cook and his men. The children joined the warriors on board, and whereas the exchange between the adults might have been guarded, Te Hōreta and his friends laughed at the way the sailors made 'much gabbling noise in talking'. The sailors laughed back and ruffled the children's hair affectionately.

### TE HŌRETA TE TAHIWHA

*As the goblins stayed some time, and did not do any evil to our braves, we came back one by one, and gazed at them, and we stroked their garments with our hands, and we were pleased with the whiteness of their skins and the blue eyes of some of them … When we got on board the ship we were welcomed by the goblins, whom our warriors answered in our language. We sat on the deck of the ship, where we were looked at by the goblins, who with their hands stroked our mats and the hair of the heads of us children; at the same time they made much gabbling noise in talking, which we thought were questions regarding our mats and the sharks' teeth we wore in our ears, and the* hei-tiki *we wore suspended on our chests; but as we could not understand them we laughed, and they laughed also … They held some garments up and showed them to us, touching ours at the same time; so we gave our mats for their mats, to which some of our warriors said 'Ka pai', which words were repeated by some of the goblins, at which we laughed, and were joined in the laugh by the goblins.*

As for Cook, Te Hōreta knew he was the most senior man on the *Endeavour*, from:

*his perfect gentlemanly and noble demeanour. He seldom*
*spoke, but some of the goblins spoke much. But this man*
*did not utter many words: all that he did was to handle*
*our mats and hold our* mere, *spears and* wahaika, *and*
*touch the hair of our heads. He was a very good man,*
*and came to us – the children – and patted our cheeks,*
*and gently touched our heads.*

The Māori boys agreed he was *tino tangata* (a great chief) and *tino rangatira* (a perfect gentleman). Te Hōreta's depiction of Cook is a tender and very human portrait of a man known to us only through the accounts of his peers and his own words, which were necessarily edited to convey the air of authority and detachment expected of an officer in the Royal Navy. The picture of the tall, raw-boned Englishman bending to pat young Te Hōreta's head is poignant and deeply moving. Through the eyes of a child we're given a rare glimpse of Cook, the man. This is not a side of him we see reflected anywhere else in the historical record.

As the *Endeavour* continued its journey along the shore, it was greeted with open hostility at every attempted landing spot. If Cook had known anything about the North Island of New Zealand, he might have anticipated such a reception. Conflict was a way of life there, and new arrivals just meant more people to fight.

It became something of a routine. The *Endeavour* would sail into an inviting anchorage, only to be confronted by a phalanx of *waka* with warriors on board brandishing weapons and pelting the ship with stones. Their war songs promised the British a bloody end.

Joseph Banks held to the principle that the only way to broker a peace under these terms was to terrify the Māori into submission, writing in his journal: *'till these warlike people have severely felt our superiority in the art of war they will never behave to us in a friendly manner'*.

The constant aggression soon began to grate on the men on board. Proving that the language of contempt is universal, a Māori warrior turned and bared his backside at the *Endeavour* in a move known to the Māori as *whakapohane*. The less technical term is 'mooning'. Later, when confronted by a long line of armed and threatening warriors on a clifftop, the surgeon William Monkhouse could no longer restrain himself. He decided to respond in kind. And he had the perfect retort – one he knew they would understand.

*New Zealand war canoe bidding defiance to the ship*, Sydney Parkinson, 1770. The majority of Māori saw Cook as an intruder and regularly welcomed the Endeavour with hails of stones, curses and bared buttocks.
Bridgeman Images, BL3284310

**WILLIAM MONKHOUSE (d. 1770), Surgeon,**
**Cook's first voyage**
*Seeing one man brandish his lance with great fury I was induced to retort the compliment we had received in the morning merely to try its effect upon this Quixotic hero – enraged at the insult he instantly threw his lance towards me with all his might, and took up another to try a second effort.*

The now furious Māori missed his mark.

Things were degenerating quickly. Just when it was looking terribly bleak, Cook did what he always managed to do – he sailed out of trouble into safe waters.

*

Until the tragic confrontation that would end his life, Cook's time in the Pacific was notable for the many near-death experiences he escaped by the skin of his teeth. On 23 October 1769, he sailed into an anchorage that he named 'Tolaga Bay'.

**ANNIE MCGUIRE, Te Aitanga-a-Hauiti**
**Tribe, Sociologist**
*The name of this place was Uawa. That's the name of our river now. It means the great river Uawa – the great river of our parents, the legendary or mythical earth mother and sky father being the two parents.*

Cook had found a safe haven. Here, the *Endeavour* would enjoy a cordial reception.

The crew were immediately struck by the natural beauty of the bay, calling it *'agreeable beyond belief – a second Paradise'*. As the sailors set to replenishing supplies, Joseph Banks and his assistant, Herman Spöring, spent countless hours exploring the area. There was one geographic feature that transfixed them – a pierced rock Banks described as an *'extraordinary natural curiosity ... far superior to any of the contrivances of art'*. It's a blessing that he didn't know the Māori name for it: *Te Kotore o te Whenua*. The Anus of the Land.

Tolaga Bay would offer up a great deal more than the Land's Anus to one man on board the *Endeavour*. Tupaia, a tall man, was accustomed to a tropical lifestyle and had just spent two months crammed into a small, foul-smelling ship ploughing through mountainous seas. He deserved some respite. So as soon as Cook dropped anchor, he went ashore. Finding an inviting rocky overhang, he took up residence on land. It didn't take long for the curious locals to strike up a conversation with him. He told them about the British and the great journey they had made from a far-distant island called 'Peretane' (Britain) via the Māori ancestral homes in Tahiti and Ra'iatea.

Cook would eventually encounter people in the Marquesas Islands who could understand the Tahitian language, even though 1600 kilometres separated the two archipelagos. This, for Cook, was proof of the great Polynesian migration.

> **GORDON TOI, Hokianga, Ngāti Wharara Tribe,**
> **Artist and Actor**
> *For a long time the Europeans thought if they went to the end of the horizon they're gonna slip off the edge of the earth. But our ancestors were strapping logs together and*

*sailing around the Pacific like madmen. They were*
*traversing the largest spans of water on the planet like they*
*were just going down the road to get some bananas ...*
*'Let's go to Tahiti ... or Hawai'i!'*

Tupaia and the Māori didn't need any evidence. They knew they were kin. And the Māori knew straight away that Tupaia was an eminent man. They welcomed him as a senior priest and eagerly absorbed the knowledge he shared with them about their history and culture.

### SIR JOSEPH BANKS (1743–1820), 1st Baronet, Naturalist and Botanist on Cook's first voyage

*Tupaia ... had much conversation with one of their priests;*
*they seemed to agree very well in their notions of religion*
*only Tupaia was much more learned than the other and all*
*his discourse was heard with much attention.*

When the *Endeavour* arrived in Tolaga Bay, it was a centre for a Māori school of learning known as *Te Rawheoro*. But the senior priests had large gaps in their knowledge that Tupaia was able to fill.

### ANNIE MCGUIRE

*The news had come up from Poverty Bay that there had*
*been deaths and that those deaths were caused by a firestick.*
*They also heard there was a man on board who spoke our*
*language or spoke a language we could understand. At the*
*time, Te Rawheoro – the learning centre – was going very*
*strongly, and they wanted to know what this firestick was*
*that could kill somebody at a distance.*

Tupaia told them that his homeland, Ra'iatea, was the mythical launching place for all the great Polynesian voyages that had populated the Pacific, including New Zealand. It was also the home of the Māori ancestors. Havaiki – Ra'iatea – was already embedded in the local belief system. After death, it was believed that Māori spirits would plunge into the sea from Cape Reinga at the northernmost tip of New Zealand's North Island and travel through the Pacific to Ra'iatea. It was little wonder that the Māori were so elated to meet Tupaia, a high priest who hailed from that very island.

Cook, who noted that *'Tupaia always accompanies us in every excursion we make and proves of infinite service'*, was fast learning how useful he would be for this and future voyages of Pacific exploration.

### CAPTAIN JAMES COOK

*Should it be thought proper to send a ship out upon this service while Tupaia lives and he to come out in her, in that case she would have a prodigious advantage over every ship that have been upon discoveries in those seas before ... you would always get people to direct you from island to island and would be sure of meeting with a friendly reception and refreshments at every island you came to.*

But to the Māori, Tupaia's presence here was something else altogether. His arrival was life-changing. He was filling in the blanks of Māori history and giving the locals an understanding of their place within an ancient, powerful and expansive seafaring civilisation.

One other aspect of Tolaga Bay's position as a centre of Māori learning was its focus on canoe construction and the ancillary skills of carving and weaving. The esoteric lore absorbed at Te Rawheoro was closely aligned with the carving skills that young Māori learnt there. In a non-literate society, art forms – from woodcarving to tattoos – communicated information and preserved knowledge that in Cook's Europe was recorded and circulated on paper.

> **GORDON TOI**
>
> *That's the journey. That's what's recorded in all these carvings. We're lucky and really fortunate in this country to be able to have a culture that still exists and lives and breathes. We get to tell all these stories about our ancestors and how we're connected to them and how they're connected to us.*

For example, the carving that goes into the construction of a *marae*, which in New Zealand is a roofed meeting house, creates something much more spiritually meaningful than just four walls and a roof. *Marae* were, and are, symbols of tribal prestige. Many represent a tribal ancestor. At the apex is a carved head from which extends a ridgepole representing the backbone. The bargeboards are the arms with the lower ends splayed to represent fingers. Inside, the roof's rafters are ribs, and the interior is the ancestor's chest and belly. A tribe's prestige was heavily invested in elaborate carving, including of *pataka*, the elevated food stores that reflected a tribe's prosperity, and – of course – the massive *waka* that confronted Cook and his men as they travelled around New Zealand's coastline.

The exquisite beauty of Māori carving impressed Cook and his men. Even in the absence of knowledge about the deeper meaning of the sculptural work, it was acknowledged that the Tolaga Bay artists were masters. They were beneficiaries of a long lineage of Polynesian artisans. The high priests of Polynesian society – Tupaia, as an *arioi*, was one – were expected to acquire artistic skills; art was yet another implement in their professional toolbox. On the Society Islands, the *arioi* were a class of artists in their own right; the priests would master woodcarving, dance, music and tattooing. Which is probably why, when given the chance, Tupaia seized upon the opportunity to try out a new medium. Watercolour painting.

The British Library has in its collection a delightful series of watercolour studies from Cook's first voyage. They are naïve in style, in the sense that they are clearly the work of an untrained artist, but until relatively recently nobody knew who painted them. Because watercolour paints were expensive and as there is a focus on plant life in a number of the studies, it was assumed that the mystery painter was Joseph Banks. But painstaking research has shown that the man who painted these exquisite works of art was Tupaia, whose preternatural skills as an artist were described by Banks.

**SIR JOSEPH BANKS**

*Tupaia the Indian who came with me from Otaheite learnt to draw in a way not quite unintelligible. The genius for caricature which all wild people possess led him to caricature me and he drew me with a nail in my hand delivering it to an Indian who sold me a lobster but with my other hand I had a firm fist on the lobster determined not to quit the nail till I had delivery and seizing of the article.*

The caricature is also noteworthy as it's the only portrait of Banks executed on the voyage itself.

Tupaia's arrival in New Zealand made an enormous impression on the Māori people.

### ANNIE MCGUIRE

*Tupaia, standing up in his cave with his audience below, really captured the audience by telling them about his homeland, which it turned out was also their homeland. Tupaia was the interpreter and the carrier of messages for both sides, and the Māori living here decided he was the captain of that* waka *with sails. He ordered Cook's crew around in his own language like he was in command and when he spoke to them in English he spoke to them in such a way that it seemed he was giving orders. That's typical Polynesian humour. Tupaia would've had a marvellous time telling them he was the boss here. Cook and the rest of the crew wouldn't have been aware of what he was saying back to the locals.*

News of his presence on board the *Endeavour* was telegraphed up and down the coast. Each time the British ships appeared in a bay or harbour, canoes would arrive alongside the ship and the men on board would hail Tupaia by name. After the ship departed New Zealand's shores, it was Tupaia, not Cook, who was remembered.

As for Cook, he developed an enormous respect for the Māori people. He understood why they were trying to keep him from their shores and admired the determination with which they fought him off. He also knew they were people he could do business with. On his second voyage, he described the Māori as having *a brave, noble, open and benevolent disposition, but they are a people that will never put up with an insult if they have an opportunity to resent it*.

Cook's admiration for the Māori remained steadfast, even as the journey progressed and the men on the *Endeavour* began to see hints of practices that had previously been unimaginable to a boatload of eighteenth-century Enlightened Englishmen. But many of his crewmates – including Tupaia – would be shaken to the core by what was to come.

*SIX*

# MORTAL REMAINS

*The Bay of Islands is such a peaceful and beautiful place.
But of course it wasn't always like this. It was a very
violent and disturbing place in the early 1800s. There's a
part of me that rather wishes that some of that excitement
was back. I don't know – perhaps we're all a little
attracted to the dangerous side of life. Anyway, I'm too
old for that now. So, forget about it.*
### SAM NEILL

Who'd be a sailor in the eighteenth century? To start with, there was an exhaustive list of superstitions to keep up with. No bananas on board. No singing or whistling into the wind. No people with flat feet, no women and no redheads, and certainly not anyone who was unfortunate enough to be all three. And don't learn to swim.

From a superstitious viewpoint, the no-swimming edict came from the idea that you'd goad the sea gods into whipping up a storm if you taught yourself to stay afloat. But there was also a practical consideration. Back in the day, the lumbering great sailing ships that plied the ocean weren't exactly nimble. If you fell overboard, there was no slamming the motor into reverse to come back and pick you up. Unless you were in a shallow bay or harbour where the anchor could be used, the crew had no way of halting the ship's progress. It was deemed better to sink quickly beneath the waves than to tread water and dog paddle for hours – or days – before finally succumbing to exhaustion ... or to circling sharks.

The fact of the matter is, few of the men on the *Endeavour*, including Cook, learnt to swim because the thing that terrified them more than anything was the thought of being lost at sea. That would change once they spent time in New Zealand. They then realised there might be a far more horrifying fate awaiting them.

That fate? Well, there's no more avoiding it. The pachyderm in the room demands attention. Cannibalism. There. It's been said.

On his return to England, Cook brought two legends of the South Pacific that captured the public imagination and would persist above all others. One was the seductive myth of pliant Tahitian maidens basking on sugar-soft beaches in the shade of emerald coconut palms. The other was a tale of fierce, tattooed warriors so enflamed by blood lust they tore each other limb from limb and devoured each other's flesh.

To Cook and the men on board the *Endeavour*, cannibalism was the ultimate taboo. According to the Western way of thinking, the only vaguely acceptable reason for indulging in cannibalism has been when people are pushed to extremes. In what would become known as the 'Custom of the Sea', shipwrecked sailors would draw straws to determine which of them should be sacrificed to save their crewmates. And in the frequent and protracted sieges of cities and towns during wartime, starvation would force people to throw the deceased in the pot. This was widely accepted as aberrant, if justifiable, behaviour – a last resort.

In short, in Western society cannibalism has never been something you generally discuss over biscuits and a cup of tea.

\*

When James Cook and his men returned to England, their accounts of Māori cannibalism fed the appetite of an eighteenth-century public ravenous for implausible tales from exotic lands. But they viewed these stories through a lens coloured by their own heritage and preconceived ideas. As far as the English public were concerned, 'cannibal' meant 'savage'. Uncivilised. To eat another human's flesh was, to most of these Englishmen and women, unimaginable. When Māori people were labelled 'cannibals', they were lumbered with all the baggage that came with it in Western culture, without allowing for the likelihood that the practice meant something altogether different in the Pacific islands of Aotearoa than it did in the backstreets of London town.

The practice of cannibalism in Māori society was underpinned by complex cultural and spiritual meaning.

**KILEY NEPIA, Ngāti Apa ki te Rā Tō, Ngāti Kuia, Rangitāne Tribes, Descendant of Kahura**
Kaitangata, *or the eating of people, wasn't for protein or the eating of nutrients. It wasn't an everyday occurrence. It was very rare. You're talking about strict* tapu *rules, so a specific type of person would have carried out that ritual. Not everybody was permitted to do those things.*

It was an important ritual associated with war. After a battle, warriors would consume flesh taken from the bodies of their fallen enemies. This was all tied up with the sacred Māori concept of *mana*. As Cook had encountered on Tahiti, for the Polynesians, *mana* is the force that determines an individual's prestige, status and authority – a spiritual gift that works through that person. A man or woman is not the source of *mana*; the human being is its agent. So for the Māori, when an enemy fell on a battlefield, a warrior could diminish his victim's *mana* by consuming his flesh, while also enhancing his own prestige.

At first, Cook and the other occupants of the *Endeavour* couldn't credit the idea that the Māori ate each other. The first hint they had of it came from the three boys they had abducted near Poverty Bay. When Cook indicated he was going to put the abductees ashore, the boys were less than thrilled when they realised the landing spot chosen was enemy turf. When Tupaia questioned them about their fears, they told him the members of the other tribe – or *iwi* – would kill and eat them.

### SIR JOSEPH BANKS (1743–1820), 1st Baronet, Naturalist and Botanist on Cook's first voyage

*[Tupaia] asked them ... whether or not they really eat men which he was very loath to believe; they answered in the affirmative saying that they eat the bodies only of those of their enemies who were killed in war.*

The boys' terror was existential in scale. They weren't simply horrified at the thought that they might be slaughtered and devoured. It was a great deal more than that. To be consumed by their enemies meant their honour – their prestige – would be extinguished.

Tupaia was aghast. Here was one key difference between the Polynesians of the Tahitian archipelago and the Māori of Aotearoa. As the Ra'iatean priest travelled around New Zealand on board the *Endeavour*, whenever he had the chance he spoke out against the practice of cannibalism, attempting to convince his Māori brethren to cease and desist.

### SIR JOSEPH BANKS

*I was loath a long time to believe that any human beings could have among them so brutal a custom … we have never failed wherever we went ashore and often when we conversed with canoes to ask the question; we have without one exception been answered in the affirmative … Tupaia who had never before heard of such a thing takes every occasion to speak ill of [it], exhorting them often to leave it off … [T]hey eat none but the bodies of their enemies who are killed in war, all others are buried.*

It has been suggested that Tupaia's reaction may have been motivated, in part at least, by the fact that human sacrifice in the Tahitian archipelago was a privilege of the gods. To partake of human flesh was, according to Tupaia's belief system, a grave sacrilege.

As for the Europeans on board the *Endeavour*, they couldn't credit it. Were these just tall tales, concocted to terrify the foreign arrivals?

\*

Their worst fears wouldn't be confirmed until January 1770, in the place that would become Cook's favourite spot to drop anchor in the whole Pacific: Tōtara-nui, which Cook named Queen Charlotte Sound.

The ship was careened on shore and the crew set to work doing what they did on such occasions – removing barnacles, scrubbing the hull, and recaulking the ship with a sticky mix of oil and tar.

Cook, Banks and Tupaia took off to explore in the ship's pinnace (a light sailing boat carried on the *Endeavour*), marvelling at the picturesque vista of heavily forested islands and inlets fringed with golden beaches. Spying a small family group on shore partaking of what seemed to be a beach cook-up, the men approached. Any thought they may have had of joining the feast was quickly put to rest when the three visitors saw a pile of bones sitting on the beach, picked clean but for a few tendons. Cook was in no doubt about what he saw. Amongst the bones was a human forearm. Not quite wanting to believe it, the men sought confirmation from the Māori. Yes, they insisted, a few days prior the arm had been attached to one of their enemies. When he fell, they dismembered him. And, yes, they had eaten the flesh off his bones.

When Cook, Banks and Tupaia returned to the *Endeavour* and reported what they had seen, it caused an uproar. Many of the sailors were deeply shocked.

The 'learned gentlemen' and officers were more philosophical, drawing on Enlightenment thinking in an attempt to rationalise something they had no way of understanding.

**JAMES MAGRA (1746?–1806), Corsican/American**
**Midshipman, Cook's first voyage**

*Perhaps they thought, like a celebrated philosopher, that it*
*was as well to feed on the bodies of their enemies ... as to*
*leave them to be devoured by crows. It is however certain that*
*they had no belief of any turpitude in this practice, because*
*they were not ashamed of it; but, on the contrary, when we*
*took up an arm for examination, they imagined us to be*
*desirous of the same kind of food, and with great good nature*
*promised that they would the next day spare a human head*
*ready roasted, if we would come or send to fetch it.*

While his men were universally horrified, Cook himself was remarkably sanguine, writing: '*They eat their enemies slain in battle – this seems to come from custom and not from a savage disposition – this they cannot be charged with.*' As commendable as this open-minded attitude might seem to us today, it would come back to haunt Cook on his third voyage.

As the *Endeavour* sailed away from Queen Charlotte Sound, an all-new terror had been added to the list of perils on the high seas. As Joseph Banks put it, '*the almost certainty of being eat [sic] as soon as you come ashore adds not a little to the terrors of shipwreck*'.

\*

The confirmation that the Māori did practise cannibalism shocked the men on board Cook's ship. But there was another exchange that occurred in Queen Charlotte Sound that would snowball and ultimately have an enormous impact on Māori – and New Zealand – society.

It all started with Tupaia, who asked an old Māori man whether or not they collected – and ate – the heads of their slain enemies. Not the heads, the man told him. But they did eat the brains. To demonstrate, he brought a selection of preserved heads out to the *Endeavour*. When they first arrived in New Zealand, Cook and his men were intrigued by the elaborate facial tattoos – *moko* – worn by the Māori. The preserved heads displayed these tattoos and Banks was determined to get his hands on one – all in the name of science, of course. He cajoled and attempted to barter, offering the old man a pair of his white linen undershorts in exchange for one of the heads.

**EMERITUS PROFESSOR NGAHUIA TE AWEKOTUKU,**
**Te Arawa, Tūhoe, Waikato Tribes, Academic**

*The notion of a pair of old white underpants being exchanged for a human head seems really heinous. But those underpants were white linen, and to the Māori they were an interesting shape. No Māori textile could equal white linen. You could put one leg in one side, and the other leg in the other, and they were warm. And you also had something that no one else in the village, or in the community, or even on the island, had ever seen or worn. I don't want to defend what Banks did, but I do think it's important to get a sense of the perspective of what was being offered, and what was being received.*

The old man was reluctant, but when Banks 'enforced my threats by showing him a musket', he handed the booty over. Because who can say no when a loaded gun is shoved in your face?

When Banks returned to England bearing his macabre, tattooed souvenir, he unwittingly kicked off a new fad.

**EMERITUS PROFESSOR NGAHUIA TE AWEKOTUKU**

*From a distance they wouldn't have actually seen the* moko *[facial tattoos]. But as they approached they would have realised those white flashing eyes and bright flashing teeth were actually ornamented and surrounded by a swirl of colour – of black lines. Moko can be menacing and fearsome and ugly. But it can also be erotic … desirable … appealing. There's a mixed aesthetic. Even today people meet* moko *Māori, and they don't know quite where to look. It's very funny.*

Before long, no fashionable home was complete without a preserved and tattooed Māori cranium above the fireplace. The booming trade in *toi moko*, as they were called in New Zealand, reached its peak in the early 1800s when it's believed hundreds of preserved Māori heads were exported to Europe. But these relics weren't stolen – they were traded by Māori who bartered with the heads of their enemies to supply this gruesome demand. This was the crowning insult and ultimate debasement to a defeated adversary, piling shame on their *iwi* and taking the gloss off their *mana*.

**EMERITUS PROFESSOR NGAHUIA TE AWEKOTUKU**

*Not all heads were preserved. Only those of the aristocratic, or the revered, or the admired. Certainly the particularly handsome. The* moko *– the ornamentation of the human face – were made using a technique no other people in the world actually achieved. That is the intense and ridged* *scarification of the facial skin with very fine and razor-sharp instruments that cause furrows and made the skin ridges. It's a creative and aesthetic response to what is beneath the skin, which is why each moko is so different and unique. Each individual's musculature, bone structure and sinews – what's underneath – brings out the design. Just as no two faces are the same, no two moko are the same.*

The most highly prized heads were those that were embellished with the ornate and masterful tattoos that made such an impression on Cook and the men on the *Endeavour* as they travelled around New Zealand.

**CAPTAIN JAMES COOK**

*The marks in general are spirals drawn with great nicety and even elegance …. [T]hey resemble the foliage in old … convolutions of filigree work, but in these they have such a luxury of forms that of a hundred which at first appeared exactly the same no two were formed alike.*

Both men and women were tattooed, although men were given designs that covered much of their face while women were tattooed only on their lips and chin. The traditional Māori method of tattooing is brutal and effective. The design is chiselled into the skin, with ink rubbed into the grooves, creating an effect that looks as if it were carved out of the bearer's flesh. An elaborate facial tattoo sent a very clear message to the beholder: its bearer had superhuman endurance and a very high pain threshold.

In Māori culture, where the head is the most revered part of the body, facial tattooing enhanced its sanctity. The design was formulated to complement and highlight the bearer's facial features, and it was also highly formalised.

**GORDON TOI, Hokianga, Ngāti Wharara Tribes, Artist and Actor**

*Tattoos are a map of somebody's life. That's why it is so personal. That separates it from the Western tattoo tradition. Māori tattoo is connected to the importance of knowing who you are and where you come from. For us it's really important. It makes you who you are and if you don't know that then you're just lost.*

Māori tattoos incorporated information about genealogy and hereditary rank in the most permanent and obvious manner imaginable. Because the ornate Māori tattoos were unique and acted as an anthology of an individual's family history, a deceased person's head had the potential to become a deeply significant and treasured object. For that reason, when important chiefs died, their heads were removed and preserved, often by smoking them and then drying them in the sun. The heads could then be displayed and revered, and the deceased chieftain would remain a part of the *iwi*. If that sounds ghoulish to you, pause for a minute to consider the Catholic Church's obsession with reliquaries containing body parts from Christian saints.

Head preservation wasn't reserved for those deemed worthy of veneration. Fallen enemies were also often decapitated and their skulls preserved, although in that instance those *toi moko* were treated as trophies of war and perched on posts where they became the focus of derision and mockery. This was where the heads that entered the global market came from.

In the early nineteenth century, demand outstripped supply. And so when fallen warriors were unavailable, slaves and even captured children were tattooed and killed, sometimes to order. Because *ta moko* were only given to Māori who had reached maturity, reports that children's heads were sold with facial tattoos suggest that at times tattooing occurred in a strictly commercial transaction. The same is true of heads that bore tattoos with iconographic blunders – these weren't venerable chieftains; they were slaves who had been marked up for sale. But don't think for a moment that this was customary practice; it only occurred after British colonisation and because the new arrivals had an apparently insatiable appetite for these morbid curios.

## EMERITUS PROFESSOR NGAHUIA TE AWEKOTUKU

*Today, we tend to romanticise and idealise how Māori were. So often we're portrayed as being either stolen from, or exploited, or somehow hard done by, or gifted with diseases and despair by Cook and the French. But the truth is, we had agency. We had control of our lives. In the harvesting of heads, we were in control. Māori were conscious of what they were doing, even though now we have taken the more righteous view of the preyed upon.*

*But we were predators too. And that's important to say.*

Once the trade in *toi moko* was up and running, it didn't take long for the Māori to realise they could exchange their unwanted heads for something they were very keen to get their hands on: guns.

\*

When Cook sailed into Iripiri (soon to be renamed 'Bay of Islands') on his first voyage, he unwittingly introduced the local Ngāpuhi *iwi* to the weapons that would wreak such havoc on the local Māori population in the following century. The *Endeavour* faced off against eight of the intimidating Māori *waka*. These massive boats required at least seventy-six warriors to paddle them. The aggressive greeting didn't come as any surprise to Cook, as his reception elsewhere in New Zealand had been almost universally combative.

The six hundred or so ferocious warriors on board the canoes in Iripiri lived in a permanent state of war-readiness. As far as they were concerned, Cook and his men were yet another bunch of enemies planning to attack them. The Māori brandished their

*A Maori, holding a gun,* Alexander Sinclair, 1842– 1853. The trade in muskets destroyed the existing balance of power between Māori tribes, redrawing boundaries established over centuries.
Bridgeman Images, BL3291426

weapons but didn't strike. Then, Cook gave the orders. He commanded his men to fire above the warriors' heads. It was a lightning-bolt moment for the Māori of the Ngāpuhi *iwi*. After they retreated, they planned to do whatever was necessary to get their hands on the British weapons, one way or another.

To some who first saw the awesome power of the British guns, it was a deeply affecting experience. Te Hōreta – who as an old man gave an account of meeting Cook – remembered the supernatural terror he and his friends felt when they saw the sailors shoot a bird.

> **TE HŌRETA TE TAHIWHA, Ngāti Whanaunga Tribe,**
> **Te Mateawa Hapū**
>
> *The goblins had walking-sticks which they carried about with them, and when we arrived at the bare dead trees where the shags roost at night ... the goblins lifted the walking-sticks up and pointed them at the birds ... thunder was heard to crash and a flash of lightning was seen, and a shag fell from the trees ... [we] handled the bird, and saw that it was dead. But what had killed it?*

But for the warriors in Iripiri, it was a transformative moment.

From the early 1800s when whalers began plying their trade in New Zealand, the Ngāpuhi began to exchange goods that the whalers needed, in order to build an almighty arsenal and settle scores with neighbouring *iwi*. Trading *toi moko* was the most effective and lucrative way of securing weaponry; two preserved heads could buy one gun. This started an arms race as the other Māori tribes rushed to accumulate their own weapons. So began the Musket Wars, which spread across New

Zealand and decimated the Māori population between 1818 and the early 1830s.

This intertribal warfare made it much easier for Europeans to exploit the turmoil and populate the land, and the conflict was encouraged by the agency of the whalers, who settled in and around Iripiri and ran the arms trade as a lucrative side business.

*

Today the Bay of Islands ranks as one of New Zealand's most delightful locations, which is no small claim in a country that enjoys an embarrassment of picturesque vistas. The Māori had always known this; when Cook arrived, Iripiri was one of the most densely populated areas in Aotearoa, its residents living in and around heavily fortified hilltop refuges, or *pahs*.

**KIHI HOWE-RIRINUI, Ngāpuhi ki Tauranga Moana Tribe, Tour Guide**
*It still is as beautiful as it was back in those days. Few more honey bees on the land and a few more houses. Before Cook came here, the land was just like the line where the sky meets the sea – that feeling, it was like the feeling of a sunrise ... the feeling of a sunset ... just calm and beautiful.*

Just twenty-two years after Cook's visit, the whalers who arrived in what they called the Bay of Islands weren't interested in its scenic qualities.

Cook could not have known of the eventual outcome of his activities in New Zealand. He might well have strenuously objected to what would occur in his wake. But the fact remains:

he was responsible for putting Aotearoa on the map – quite literally. The exceptionally accurate charts he produced provided a maritime pathway for the Western exploitation that followed.

The first whaling vessel to visit Kororāreka in the Bay of Islands, or Russell as it became known, was the *William and Ann* piloted by Captain Eber Bunker, which anchored in Doubtless Bay in 1791 while taking a respite from hunting sperm whales in the Pacific.

The amenity of the area and its capacity to accommodate many large sailing vessels drew whalers to Russell. The men who dedicated their lives to the rather messy and pungent hunt for whale blubber were not, as a rule, drawn from the more reputable corners of society. These were hard men – escaped convicts from across the Tasman Sea, deserters and adventurers amongst them. For a while in the first half of the nineteenth century, Russell had the dubious honour of being the biggest whaling port in the southern hemisphere.

Although it's impossible to give a precise figure for the number of whaling ships that visited New Zealand in the peak year of 1839, it's estimated that a hundred and fifty or so American vessels and over fifty belonging to other nations arrived during a twelve-month period.

### KIHI HOWE-RIRINUI

*Māori got involved in whaling because it was arranged work – just like the arranged marriages. Two of my great-great-grandfathers were a part of that. My first Pākehā ancestor was Captain John Howe, an American captain. He arranged to be with my great-great-great-grandmother, Heni Nuka. She was black as the ace of spades, and he was white with blue eyes with a pointy nose. That arranged marriage worked for my Māori ancestors because we had lost power and we needed to gain some. When they married, it was arranged to keep the land. The white man could look after us and provide all his goodies that he brought with him. When I see you, Sam, do I see a coloniser? Yes and no. Yes, I see a coloniser. But I see colonised when I look at me. When I look at you again, I see a great relationship building, or starting to build. With a conversation, we find a little bit more understanding. And I see someone who is trying to find the other piece of the story. My piece of the story.*

With so many seamen flooding Aotearoa's shores, there was feverish demand for female companionship, so prostitution became another means by which the Māori could acquire guns and ammunition.

**EDWARD MARKHAM, 1801–1865, Nineteenth-century English Writer and Traveller**

*Thirty to forty ships would come in for three weeks to the bay and four hundred to five hundred sailors require as many women, and they have been out [at sea] one year ... These young ladies go off to the ships, and three weeks on board are spent much to their satisfaction as they get from the sailors a fowling piece ... blankets, gowns.*

It didn't make for the most salubrious of settings. One visitor to Russell didn't mince words. To him, the town was '*Gomorrah, the scourge of the Pacific, which should be struck down by the ravages of disease for its depravity*'.

Given the enthusiasm with which marine mammals were pursued and slaughtered in New Zealand waters, it's not surprising to learn that within fifty years the industry became unviable. Before that happened, though, the chaos unleashed on the Bay of Islands and general lawlessness inflicted on the local residents had an unexpected consequence.

Fed up with the general nastiness that had become the norm in the Bay of Islands, a group of settlers and Māori prevailed upon the British government to enforce some law and order.

### EMERITUS PROFESSOR NGAHUIA TE AWEKOTUKU

*Colonisation has been blamed for the doom of so many indigenous peoples. I certainly would never defend what happened to us. But I also like to remind people that what took place here were conversations of encounter. People were reaching out to each other and trying to be friends. OK, there was conflict, fear and hostility. That's human. But in the context of the colonisation of Aotearoa – New Zealand – what makes us different is that we did have a treaty. It wasn't until after that we saw the horrors of what uncontrolled migration can bring with it. In 1840 at the time of the Treaty there were about three thousand Pākehā – non-Māori – in New Zealand, but by 1890 there were seven hundred thousand. For me, although Māori had agency until 1840, in a very subtle and sinister way that agency was being worn down. And that is when colonisation occurred. It's important to remember though that in those periods of first encounter we were friends and we were equals, and the Māori set the terms.*

Just across the bay in the settlement of Waitangi, the British consul took heed of the local residents' appeal and drew up a document. It is now known as the Treaty of Waitangi and regarded as New Zealand's foundational document.

**KINGI TAURUA, Ngāpuhi Tribe, Elder**
*I don't think we need a Treaty for our relationship. We worked together, we swore in Māori, we swore in Pākehā, in our own languages ... that's what we used to do here. We took one another into consideration. The British – the Pākehā – came here and they sweated for this country. We all sweated for this country. That relationship has always been there.*

At the time, the Treaty seemed simple enough. There were just three clauses written in both English and Māori. The English version was fairly straightforward; it ceded sovereignty to the British Crown, stating that Queen Victoria had 'all the rights and powers of sovereignty' over Māori land. But as is so often the case, the devil was in the detail. The Māori conceded *te kāwanatanga katoa* (complete 'government') over their land. But as there was no real translation for 'sovereignty' in *Te Reo* (the Māori language) the signatories, including Te Hōreta – now grown to adulthood – thought they had signed up for a cooperative partnership involving power sharing.

**TINA NGATA, Ngāti Porou Tribe**
*The records of the time show there was great debate over the Treaty, right up to the signing. Many were against it. But others felt that this was the best way to move ahead as*

*they knew that the tide wasn't able to be stemmed so it was best to work out an agreement to try and manage it. It is an interesting thing because we didn't write it, but it's often seen as a Māori issue. So one of the eternal struggles for us is to bring our Treaty partners to the table and honour it as their issue as well as ours.*

They never intended to hand over authority to a foreign governor. And yet that's exactly what happened when they signed the document on 6 February 1840.

In a testament to how things have changed, amongst the post-European settlement initiatives conceived to address wrongs inflicted upon Māori people is a concerted effort to repatriate the *toi moko* that were sent out of the country in the nineteenth century. Between 1820 and 1831, many hundreds of preserved heads were taken away from their ancestral home; over five hundred are still thought to remain outside New Zealand. The Museum of New Zealand, Te Papa Tongarewa, has been leading the campaign to repatriate Māori ancestral remains. Some – but, unbelievably, not all – international collecting institutions that hold Māori remains have agreed to repatriate them and send them home.

### SAM NEILL

*I have begun to understand why Cook's blamed for so much stuff. He was a precursor of so many things that turned out to be just horrible for those who were already here.*

*Captain James Cook, 1728–79*, Nathaniel Dance, 1776. Perhaps the best-known portrait of Cook, depicted in full dress uniform and holding his own chart of the Southern Ocean. Cook sat for this portrait before his final voyage to the Pacific.
*State Library of Victoria, H32508*

Sam Neill reading on a beach in New Zealand. Take a close look at the book in his hands. It can seem that Captain Cook is everywhere, and yet really, we know so little about him.
SAM NEILL: We don't get much from [Cook's] logs … But the fact he kept going back to the Pacific – he couldn't stay away – shows he was completely taken by the place. In the end, it wasn't just that he changed the Pacific … the Pacific also changed him.
*Photo by Kirrilly Brentnall, © 2018 Essential Media & Entertainment*

Sam Neill with Josiane Teamotuaitau, Tautira Bay, Tahiti. On arrival in Tahiti, Cook and his men formed friendships with the locals – although the give and take was not always equal.

JOSIANE TEAMOTUAITAU: Tahitians are very pragmatic … When Cook and the other Europeans arrived on the island they tried to make the best of it. They knew they couldn't fight guns. So this trade began: these exchanges, these friendships.

*Photo by Kirrilly Brentnall, © 2018 Essential Media & Entertainment*

*Venus Fort, Erected by the Endeavour's People, to secure themselves during the Observation of the Transit of Venus, at Otaheite.*

*Venus Fort*, after Sydney Parkinson, 1773. The fort was erected at Matavai Bay for Cook's observation of the 1769 Transit of Venus. In spite of this daunting construction, the Tahitians managed to distract the guards, get inside and make off with the quadrant on which the success of the measuring of the Transit of Venus relied.

*SP Lohia Collection, 5469_007*

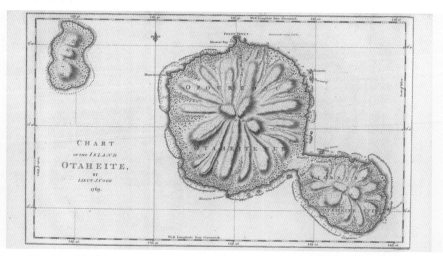

*Chart of the Island Otaheite*, Captain James Cook, 1769. Matavai Bay and Fort Venus can be seen at the northernmost point of the large island.

*David Rumsey Map Collection, David Rumsey Map Center, Stanford Libraries*

*Mr Banks Shows the Indians the Planet Venus on the Sun*, artist unknown, 1769 (engraved c.1771). For his part, Mr Banks is looking closely at the three women he will persuade to spend the night in his tent. Venus prevails. *State Library of NSW, c2856*

*Parkinson's Nose Flute Player*, after Sydney Parkinson, 1773. The model for this picture might have been Taiata, Tupaia's servant (and some say nephew) who accompanied him on the voyage and, like his master, died in Batavia. *State Library of NSW, D Q78/10, FL3746793*

*Utensils and Tools*, after Sydney Parkinson, 1773. Did ship's artist Sydney Parkinson realise he was recording a technology and artisanal way of life that would not survive exposure to the West? *State Library of NSW, D Q78/10, FL3746797*

*A Scene in Tahiti with Two War Canoes and a Sailing Canoe*, Tupaia, 1769. This painting, which also shows a longhouse, with pandanus, breadfruit, banana and coconut trees and taro plants, is one of eight existing paintings by Tupaia, the Tahitian priest and navigator. Until 1997 these paintings were cryptically attributed to the 'artist of the chief mourner.' Then a letter from Joseph Banks came to light where he wrote, 'Tupaia, an Indian, learned to draw in a way not unintelligible.' The young fop was not very woke – it's a remarkable work in a new medium for Tupaia.
*Bridgeman Images, BL3743002*

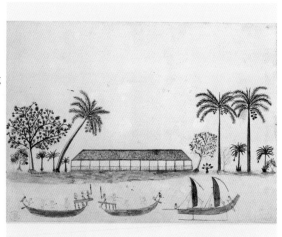

Filming on the beach in Tahiti. Originally, the *Pacific* television series planned to visit every Pacific nation seen by Cook – but the demands of Pacific flight schedules, film crews, and budgets meant some countries were regrettably omitted. Their stories are no less important, and will no doubt be told by others as the re-examination of Cook and the Pacific continues.
*Photo by Kirrilly Brentnall, © 2018 Essential Media & Entertainment*

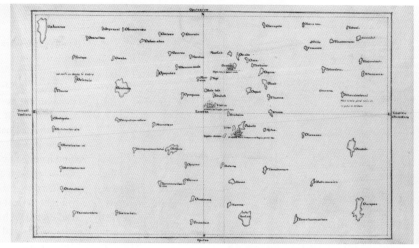

*Chart of the Society Islands*, with Otaheite in the centre, Tupaia, 1769. Tupaia's chart, drawn from memory, with the names of the islands inscribed by Cook. Two world views come together on the same page. *Bridgeman Images, BL3292585*

Sam Neill at Taputapuatea Marae, the hub of Pacific navigation and spiritual life for 1000 years.

SAM NEILL: Taputapuatea is the spiritual heart really of Polynesia. It's a very sacred place. It gives me the same sort of feeling I've had at the pyramids in Mexico or at Stonehenge … I don't really understand it, if I'm honest.

*Photo by Kirrilly Brentnall, © 2018 Essential Media & Entertainment*

*The Marae of Mahaiatea, Tahiti, or Great Morai of Oborea*, after Wilson, 1799. Designed and built under Tupaia's supervision after he was banished from Ra'iatea, it's reputedly the largest ever built. Today it lies in ruins.

*National Library of Australia, 919.6 W749*

GREAT MORAI of TEMARRE or PAPPARA in OTAHEITE.

Sam Neill with Moana'ura Walker, Humutu Valley, Tahiti.

MOANA'URA WALKER: The French missionaries put into people's minds if they go to their traditional places of worship they'll be visited and haunted by ghosts … Once we started worshipping just one god, everybody forgot the rest of them … And every god had a purpose that was linked to a specific cultural practice.

*Photo by Sally Aitken, © 2018 Essential Media & Entertainment*

This monument at the Tūranganui (Gisborne) River mouth marks the spot where Cook stepped ashore, bearing arms and, apparently, the best of intentions. 'Hints' issued by the Royal Society suggested Cook 'exercise the utmost patience and forbearance with respect to the natives … check the petulance of the sailors, and restrain the wanton use of firearms …' Things did not go to plan.
*Photo by Kirrilly Brentnall, © 2018 Essential Media & Entertainment*

Sam Neill greets a Māori performer with a hongi at the Waitangi Treaty Ground. Cook's hongi – the exchange of sacred breath – with a Māori warrior at Tūranganui brokered a peace of sorts. Without Tupaia as translator, there may have been no peace at all.
*Photo by Kirrilly Brentnall, © 2018 Essential Media & Entertainment*

*A War Canoe, of New Zealand*, engraving after Sydney Parkinson, 1770. A *waka toa*, Māori war canoe, crammed with warriors energetically expressing their contempt for the visitors, with many graphic expressions of what they plan to do with them as soon as they land.
*State Library of NSW, DQ78/10, FL3746802*

A War Canoe, of New Zealand.

*Head of Otegoongoon, Son of a New Zealand Chief, the face curiously tataou'd*, Thomas Chambers after Sydney Parkinson, 1773. Cook noted, 'The marks in general are spirals drawn with great nicety and even elegance … they have such a luxury of forms that of a hundred which at first appeared exactly the same no two were formed alike.'
*SP Lohia Collection, 5469_023*

Sam Neill with Emeritus Professor Ngahuia Te Awekotuku, Ship Cove, Totaranui/Marlborough Sounds.
EMERITUS PROFESSOR NGAHUIA TE AWEKOTUKU: *Moko* can be menacing and fearsome and ugly. But it can also be erotic … desirable … appealing. There's a mixed aesthetic. Even today people meet *moko* Māori, and they don't know quite where to look. It's very funny.
*Photo by Kirrilly Brentnall, © 2018 Essential Media & Entertainment*

*A view of a perforated rock in Tolaga Bay in New Zealand*, after Sydney Parkinson, 1773. Banks described this pierced rock as 'far superior to any of the contrivances of art'. To the Māori, it was known as Te Kotore e te Whenua – the anus of the land.
*David Rumsey Map Collection, David Rumsey Map Center, Stanford Libraries*

*A Maori bartering a crayfish with an English naval officer,* Tupaia, 1769. In his journal, Banks noted: 'The genius for caricature which all wild people possess led him to caricature me and he drew me with a nail in my hand delivering it to an Indian who sold me a lobster.' Of course Banks presumed he himself was not seen as wild.
*Bridgeman Images, BL3283459*

*Portrait of Sir Joseph Banks,* Benjamin West, 1788. Banks, an inveterate collector, wears a Māori flax cloak and is surrounded by objects from New Zealand and Polynesia.
*Alexander Turnbull Library, 22796842*

*Horatio Robley, Seated with His Collection of Ssevered Heads of Maori,* Henry Stevens, c.1900. Probably the most egregious example of a colonial collection. Horatio Robley served with the British Army in New Zealand in the nineteenth century. On his retirement back in England, he built up his collection of *toi.moko,* thirty-five heads in all. Their repatriation to New Zealand was finalised in 2014.
*Wellcome Library no. 664088i*

*Ship Cove, Queen Charlotte Sound*, John Webber, c.1788. Ship Cove (or Meretoto) became Cook's favourite anchorage in the Pacific – he described it as a 'very snug cove' – and he visited it on each of his three Pacific voyages. It was here that Cook's men first observed the Māori practice of cannibalism, and where the trade in *toi moko* began, Banks exchanging a pair of white linen undershorts for a preserved head.
*Museum of New Zealand, 1991-0005-1*

Kiley Nepia, Peter Meihana, Raymond Smith and Sam Neill at Ship Cove.
KILEY NEPIA: *Kaitangata*, or the eating of people, wasn't for protein or the eating of nutrients. It wasn't an everyday occurrence. It was very rare. You're talking about strict tapu rules, so a specific type of person would have carried out that ritual. Not everybody was permitted to do those things.
*Photo by Kirrilly Brentnall, © 2018 Essential Media & Entertainment*

Sam Neill at Ship Cove in the Marlborough Sounds, taking advantage of a welcome chance to relive the rowing exploits of his childhood holidays in these waters.
*Photo by Kirrilly Brentnall, © 2018 Essential Media & Entertainment*

*Map of the Coast of New Zealand*. A coloured version of Cook's New Zealand chart, produced to enhance one of the many publications of his voyages rushed into print in the early nineteenth century. The chart is remarkably accurate, with the exception of Banks Peninsula, shown as an island, and Stewart Island, shown as a peninsula – the hazards of doing a running survey from a ship offshore and not seeing some landform distinctions.
*SP Lohia Collection, 5469_027*

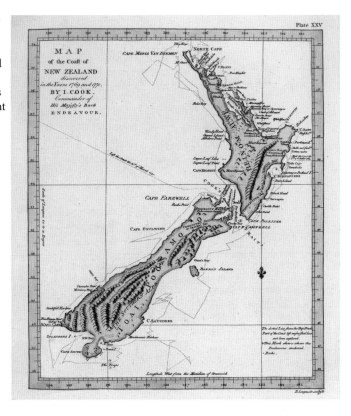

*The Warrior Chieftains of New Zealand*, Joseph Jenner Merrett, 1846. Hone Heke, his wife Hariata and Kawiti. Heke and Kawiti were the chief leaders of the rebellion in the Far North of New Zealand in 1844–46. This was the first serious resistance to British rule, two years after the signing of the Treaty of Waitangi. Heke is popularly remembered for cutting down the flagpole above Kororāreka (Russell) four times.
*National Library of New Zealand, 23153045*

*Landing of Captain Cook at Botany Bay, 1770*, E. Phillips Fox, 1902. A colonist's point of view. This iconic Australian painting depicts a noble Cook, hand raised to stay the action of his men, who point their weapons towards the Dharawal warriors in the distance – although in fact Cook himself was armed and shot twice at the warriors, wounding one in the legs.
*National Gallery of Victoria, Gilbee Bequest, 119-2*

Plate XXVII

*Two of the Natives of New-Holland, Advancing to Combat.*

*Two of the Natives of New Holland Advancing to Combat*, after Sydney Parkinson, 1773. This Parkinson image perhaps informed Fox's work (above). Of this incident Banks wrote: '[They were] shaking their lances and menacing, in all appearance resolved to dispute our landing … 2 more muskets with small shot were then fired at them on which the eldest threw one more lance and then ran away as did the other.'
*SP Lohia Collection, 5469_029*

Dr Shayne Williams, Sam Neill and Rod Mason at Botany Bay. Days before Cook's first landing, the Aboriginal peoples of southern New South Wales were observing his progress up the coast.

ROD MASON: They were asking themselves, what is this thing coming up the coast? The news travelled faster than a bushfire … My people were watching Cook for days, always wondering when and where they were going to land. We were ready. We were waiting for it.
*Photo by Kirrilly Brentnall, © 2018 Essential Media & Entertainment*

*Australian Aborigines Paddling Bark Canoes and Spear Fishing*, Tupaia, 1770. Tupaia's drawing reveals his acute awareness of Aboriginal body language, something Cook and Banks missed.
*Bridgeman Images, BL3283454*

Sir Joseph Banks left his name in Australia – or at least had it given to the iconic Australian woody shrub *Banksia serrata* by Linnaeus the Younger. This specimen was collected in Botany Bay.
*Royal Botanic Gardens and Domain Trust, NSW133651*

Sam Neill, Gemma Cronin and Badtjala Nation dancers on Fraser Island (K'gari), Queensland. As Cook sailed north, the people on land knew he was headed towards trouble.

GEMMA CRONIN: They saw the ship about seventy-five miles from here … The people got worried for the boat and ran up onto the headland to try and warn him about the shoal out there. They were trying to tell him to go back, but in his journal he thinks we were waving at him.

*Photo by Kriv Stenders, © 2018 Essential Media & Entertainment*

*A chart of New South Wales, on the east coast of New Holland.* Cook's chart marks the point from which the Badtjala people waved in warning as 'Indian Head'.

*David Rumsey Map Collection, David Rumsey Map Center, Stanford Libraries*

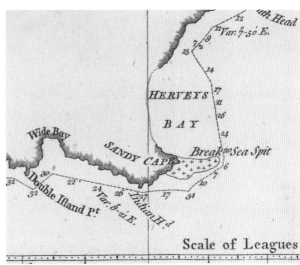

Sam Neill on K'gari. In 1851 'Indian Head' was the site of a massacre of Badtjala men, women and children.

SAM NEILL: There are terrible things that happened all over the Pacific in the wake of Cook's voyages. I've had to face up to this on my journey.

*Photo by Kirrilly Brentnall, © 2018 Essential Media & Entertainment*

*A view of the Endeavour River on the coast of New Holland, where the ship was laid on shore in order to repair the damage which she received on the rock,* John Hawkesworth, 1773. After striking the coral reef, the *Endeavour* was repaired at a river mouth which Cook named Endeavour River – the site of present-day Cooktown. To the Guugu Yimidhirr people, the site was known as Waymbuur. *David Rumsey Map Collection, David Rumsey Map Center, Stanford Libraries*

Sam Neill with Alberta Hornsby, Cooktown Re-enactment Association. ALBERTA HORNSBY: For the thirty-two tribal clan groups that make up the Guugu Yimidhirr–speaking nation, Waymbuur was a neutral zone. Cook and his crew could have been picked off at any time during their forty-eight days here, but the law dictated that no blood was to be spilt on this land … Cook was very fortunate that these laws – indigenous laws – protected them. *Photo by Kirrilly Brentnall, © 2018 Essential Media & Entertainment*

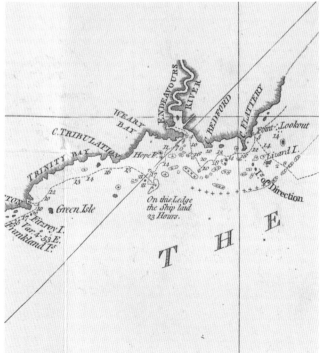

*A chart of New South Wales, on the east coast of New Holland.* Cook labelled the Great Barrier Reef 'The Labyrinth', and the point where *Endeavour* struck 'On this Ledge the Ship laid 23 Hours'. 'Endeavours' River can also be seen.
*David Rumsey Map Collection, David Rumsey Map Center, Stanford Libraries*

Sam Neill at a bush burn, Cooktown. Cook and his men could not comprehend Aboriginal land-management systems: the deliberate use of fire to open up hunting grounds and to ensure that edible plants and animals were not destroyed in out-of-control bushfires, thereby establishing a circuit of hunting and harvesting grounds. BRUCE PASCOE: Aboriginal people lost their ability to grow the crops because they lost the land. The hard-hoofed animals were destroying the soil by compacting it and drinking all the water. [Aboriginal people] were constantly harassed and driven off their land.
*Photo by David Alrich, © 2018 Essential Media & Entertainment*

Sam Neill with Bruce Pascoe. BRUCE PASCOE: We're talking about blaming Cook, but I blame his boss. I don't see Cook as the devil. I blame the Crown. I just see Cook as an Englishman with that mindset of the Englishmen – they believed they could possess anything the world had to offer.
*Photo by Kirrilly Brentnall, © 2018 Essential Media & Entertainment*

*A chart of New South Wales, on the east coast of New-Holland.* Cook's final act on mainland Australia was to raise the Union Jack on 'Possession Island' in the Torres Strait – known to the locals as Bedanug and home to the Kaurareg people. In his journal he wrote: 'in the name of His Majesty King George the Third took possession of the whole eastern coast from the above latitude down to this place by the name of New South Wales together with all the bays, harbours rivers and islands situate [sic] upon the same said coast.'
*David Rumsey Map Collection, David Rumsey Map Center, Stanford Libraries*

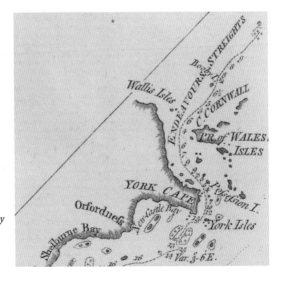

To date over four hundred ancestors have been returned to Aotearoa. Thankfully, the tattoos mean that some of the individuals' remains can be identified and returned to their families. But given the passage of time, most cannot.

For those remains, a resting place is reserved at Te Papa. It remains a sacred place for New Zealand's First Nation people; an important site for reverence and remembrance.

\*

As Cook progressed around New Zealand, he had no way of knowing what his work would mean for its Māori occupants.

### TINA NGATA

*If there's one thing that I want people to take away from this, it is that this is not a historical event to us. This is something that is still happening to us – every day.*

One thing still preoccupied Cook. Was New Zealand, or was it not, part of the Great Southern Continent? He knew there was only one way to find out for certain; sail right around it.

Using Tupaia as an intermediary, Cook had pursued the question with Māori elders who assured him that New Zealand comprised just three islands. Cook was intrigued by their geographic knowledge, but struggled to process Māori conflation of the physical and spiritual worlds. Te Hōreta described one of these encounters. As the Māori elders spoke of Cape Reinga at the northernmost tip of New Zealand's North Island, Cook suspected they might be describing the Cape Maria van Diemen charted by Abel Tasman.

**TE HŌRETA**

*This lord of these goblins ... took some charcoal and made marks on the deck of the ship, and pointed to the shore ... One of our aged men said ... 'He is asking for an outline of this land'; and that old man stood up, took the charcoal, and marked the outline of Te Ika-a-Māui.*

But the elders also explained the Cape's significance to the Māori people. Its name means 'the leaping-off place of spirits', and it was where Māori spirits plunged into the Pacific and migrated back to their ancestral home of Havaiki.

Cook was just searching for Tasman's Cape. As far as he was concerned, the Māori gave him spiritual mumbo jumbo; for someone who saw himself as a rational man of science, their explanation was meaningless. He probably nodded politely, smiled and shut them down – there was no bridge wide enough to cross that cultural chasm.

Although Cook was determined to see the northernmost point on Tasman's map, the weather was anything but cooperative. A series of brutal gales blew him out further into the ocean, and he sailed back and forth across the tip of the North Island without sighting Cape Reinga. At last, he had a lucky break and spotted it, marking it on his chart.

In a moment of serendipity, Cook was completely unaware that while he was tacking to and fro through the storm, the French navigator Jean-François-Marie de Surville passed by in the opposite direction. It was a literal crossing of ships in the night. This was the European story of the Pacific in a nutshell. These were contested waters. The original occupants of these lands were, as yet, unaware of the fate that competing European powers had in mind for them.

## TINA NGATA

*We had relationships that crisscrossed the Pacific basin. It was like a highway for us until it was cut up by explorers who claimed this area. Then there were borders that were set up and exclusive economic zones that ended our relationships with each other. It's like having your own family forcibly estranged from you and then, years later, hearing that they had been abused as well.*

That was yet to come. Cook's search for the Great Southern Continent – his charting of these Pacific islands – was, for want of a better term, a land grab. He was here for Mother England and planned to claim as much of what he found for her as he could. He certainly wasn't planning to lose ground to a Frenchman.

Having successfully circumnavigated the North Island of New Zealand, Cook headed south again. He was sceptical about the existence of the fabled Great Southern Continent. But in this he was at odds with Joseph Banks and most of the other learned gentlemen on board, who had arrived in New Zealand unwavering in their belief that here they would find it.

On 10 March 1770, the question was laid to rest. The *Endeavour* rounded South Cape and found nothing more than an expanse of ocean to the south. New Zealand was not and would never be part of a Great Southern Continent. Banks was bereft, realising this meant '*the total demolition of our aerial fabric called continent*'. The 'no-continents' celebrated by killing and roasting a dog – which had become quite the thing after their time in Tahiti. Tasted like lamb, by all reports. Banks might well have been nursing his dented pride, but he surely lined up for a slice of the roast.

Returning to Marlborough Sounds, Cook had travelled over 4000 kilometres, or 2500 miles, in just over six and a half months. Doing his calculations and measurements on board a listing ship's deck, he produced a chart of New Zealand that is still frequently held up as his most astounding cartographic achievement.

That was all well and good. But Cook wasn't done yet.

His instructions were to return home directly, either via Cape Horn or the Cape of Good Hope. But the *Endeavour* was no longer holding up to the rigours of open ocean travel. Knowing the ship would face a hammering if he followed the Admiralty's instructions, he had something else in mind. And it would allow him to pop another feather into his navigational cap.

By Cook's reckoning, the safest route back to England was via the port of Batavia in the Dutch East Indies. It was relatively close in proximity, and he knew he'd be able to find the materials in Batavia he required to repair the *Endeavour* before returning home across the Indian and Atlantic oceans. But there was one other thing that drew him eastwards. Something big.

Since 1606, navigators – most of them Dutch – had been charting the northern, western and southern coastlines of the continent known in the eighteenth century as New Holland. But the entire eastern shoreline was still a blank. When it was filled in on maps of the time, it was a malformed shape based on ill-informed conjecture and supposition. For someone who liked more than anything to fill in blank spaces on charts, it was too big a temptation to ignore.

**JOHN ROBSON, Map Librarian, University of Waikato**
*Cook's raison d'etre was chart making, and I think that really was his supreme skill. He saw it as his role, when he travelled, that he should make a chart of wherever he went so that it would be something future sailors could use.*

Cook proposed an audacious plan to his officers: they would cross the Tasman and explore the eastern coast of the continent we now know as Australia.

On the last day of March 1770, this man – notable for endowing places with the most prosaic of names – called the last piece of land he saw in New Zealand 'Cape Farewell'. It was a strangely sentimental gesture from a stoic man.

**EMERITUS PROFESSOR NGAHUIA TE AWEKOTUKU**
*James Cook? He's someone to whom we owe a great deal, and from whom we must demand a great deal. He was remarkably greedy, adventurous, and an extraordinary human. I can't hear myself completely agreeing with cousins from the other parts of our ocean when they say on hearing that name: venereal disease, despair, colonisation. Upheaval and catastrophe came with the* Endeavour. *But so, too, came some really good things. Not just economic and cultural change, but also the opportunity to extend, to explore and to understand.*

Cook also seems to be telling us something else. As he was farewelling a land he had grown to love, he was anticipating and, perhaps, dreading what lay beyond.

**KINGI TAURUA**

*I think Cook explored the world and we learnt a lot from him. It was all information, and I think we need to understand and learn about those things. Māori need to know. People like James Cook and Abel Tasman – I think that we understand that they have contributed to our culture.*

The unknown coastline and its people would not disappoint him. As for the Aboriginal people of Australia, after Cook's arrival, their lives – like those of the Polynesians – would never be the same again.

**SAM NEILL**

*I do really think of myself as a Pacific person. I was brought up in New Zealand. My family has been there for one hundred and fifty years. My grandchildren, who have Māori heritage, can trace their connections to the Pacific back thousands of years. But finding a way to understand my own relationship to this extraordinary place has been a challenge for me.*

# PART THREE

*SEVEN*

# WELCOME TO COUNTRY

*It behoves all of us to live in context with what's going on
around us ... to understand that context in a historical
sense and to understand where we live and understand
the people we live with.*

**SAM NEILL**

Recent evidence from the Madjedbebe rock shelter near Kakadu National Park in the Northern Territory shows that Indigenous Australians found their way south via Asia at least sixty thousand years ago. When Aboriginal people say they've lived in Australia forever, they're not kidding. It makes the two hundred years plus change since the British colonised Sydney Cove look pretty pathetic, doesn't it?

**SAM NEILL**

*What I was taught at school was so Eurocentric. The
Pacific was seen as a mysterious place that was gradually
discovered by people like Cook – a last frontier. But if you
look at it from the Pacific perspective, the people living here
were wondering who the people were who were coming*

*here wearing strange clothes, speaking strange languages,*
*and sailing strange ships. That's been a revelation to me –*
*seeing things from the other side of the beach.*

To put this in a global context, it's generally thought that the earliest *Homo sapiens* migrated out of Africa somewhere between seventy and a hundred thousand years ago. Sometime very soon after this, we find in northern Australia evidence of an Aboriginal presence on the continent in an impressive range of lithic – stone – technologies. Madjedbebe has yielded the world's earliest known example of a ground-edge axe, made by grinding – rather than chipping – down the stone to a sharp edge. In Palaeolithic terms, it was a technological breakthrough; the equivalent of a smartphone versus the 1980s analogue brick.

**BRUCE PASCOE, Boonwurrung Nation, Author**
*Most world cultures don't last for two thousand years and*
*here we are with a culture that is at least sixty thousand*
*years old. We should be so proud of what those old wizards*
*created on this country that we all want to be part of it too.*

The people living in Australia when James Cook arrived were custodians of the world's oldest multilingual and multicultural society, largely undisturbed by the cultural and social upheavals caused by the cross-continental migrations that shaped the Western world. But this wasn't a discrete population of people. Before settlement, a population of an estimated 750,000 Indigenous Australians occupied over two hundred countries, all speaking their own languages.

As the *Endeavour* ploughed into the unrelenting headwinds in its crossing of the Tasman Sea between New Zealand and Australia, Tupaia must have wondered what on earth the Englishman was doing. The Ra'iatean navigator and priest knew not to fight prevailing winds but to work with them as they changed with the season. Cook, the Enlightenment warrior, was fighting to outwit, outplay and outlast nature, while Tupaia, the star navigator, had learnt to work in concert with natural forces.

It's often said that Cook was sailing into unknown waters when he embarked upon his journey to the eastern coastline of the continent known in 1770 as New Holland. That's not strictly accurate, though. Armed with a 'hot off the presses' copy of Alexander Dalrymple's 1767 publication, *An account of the discoveries made in the South Pacifick Ocean, previous to 1764*, Cook had on hand the most up-to-date information about New Holland and its immediate neighbours.

Dalrymple himself is worthy of a short sidebar in Cook's story. As a fellow of the Royal Society, Dalrymple had harboured ambitions to lead the expedition to the South Pacific himself. But he had been rather sensibly passed over by the Admiralty in favour of a man who actually knew how to sail a ship. Dalrymple nursed a festering grudge that would explode to spectacular effect after Cook returned to England.

But at this point in the journey, Dalrymple's thorough academic survey of previous European expeditions to the Pacific was proving to be a great help. From his account, Cook knew of Tasman's exploration as well as Luís Vaz de Torres's 1606 navigation of the strait that now bears his name at the northernmost tip of the continent. Also covered in Dalrymple's

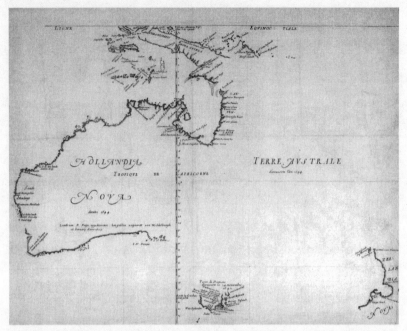

*Hollandia Nova detecta 1644 (New Holland discovered in 1644)*, published in
Melchisedech Thevenot's *Relations de Divers Voyages Curieux* (*Tales of
Various Strange Voyages*) in 1663. Although the north, south and western
coasts of Australia had been charted and Abel Tasman had contributed two
squiggles in Van Diemen's land, the eastern coast was a blank page on
European maps of the time. National Library of Australia, MAP NK 2785

book was the early charting of the southern and northern
coastlines of New Guinea and a number of the Melanesian
islands.

New Holland hadn't been completely ignored by the outside
world, of course. Besides the Dutch and other early voyages of
European exploration, there's extensive evidence, dating back to
at least the middle of the eighteenth century, documenting
regular visitations by Macassan fishermen along the northern
coast from the south-west corner of Sulawesi. They came to
Australia to harvest sea cucumbers and trade with the Yolgnu

people, leaving behind the remnants of processing plants and stands of imported tamarind trees.

A discovery in the Northern Territory's Wessel Islands hints at other, perhaps much more far-reaching contact between Australia and distant lands across the sea – a small cache of Arabic-inscribed twelfth-century coins from the medieval African sultanate of Kilwa, which have only twice been found outside Tanzania. The Yolngu people of north-eastern Arnhem Land also tell tales of men with white skin coming from the sea wearing 'mirrors', presumably armour, and beating stones on the beach to make metal. Ancient rock art on Marchinbar Island, where the Kilwa coins were discovered, shows ships under sail and figures thought to depict European sailors wearing hats and trousers.

That's without even touching on the contested theory that the Portuguese charted Australia's east coast in the sixteenth-century, reaching as far south as Warrnambool in Victoria, where one of the expedition's caravels is thought to have foundered and ended up lost in the sand dunes. To this day the locals tell of 'the Mahogany Ship' that periodically appears in the shifting dunes. Some believe that because Cook wrote in his journal that the harbour in Queensland where he would take refuge after grounding on the Great Barrier Reef was *'much smaller than I had been told'* it meant he had seen a copy of a map that purports to record the Portuguese discoveries and knew he would find an anchorage on the coast.

Even if we only accept what is known to be historical fact, Cook knew the continent was anything but unknown to the outside world when he arrived. The point he was headed for in New Holland was well documented in Dalrymple's book. As Cook sailed west, he was aiming for the land recorded by Abel

Tasman in 1642; the island we now know as Tasmania. But fierce winds drove the *Endeavour* off course. When land was sighted on 19 April 1770, it wasn't Tasmania; it was land near the promontory they named Point Hicks, which extended into the Tasman Sea.

Cook fought his way north, charting the Australian coastline as he went. His priority was to get it over and done with as quickly as possible. His ship was in terrible shape, and the sooner they arrived in Batavia, the better. But this was important work – he was laying claim to this land in the name of the King. To do that, Cook needed to chart it.

But the Tasman Sea wasn't going to make it easy for him. Towering waves and hideous weather kept the *Endeavour* at sea. Cook had to be happy with naming landmarks remotely and mapping from the deck of a ship that bucked and heaved in the fierce seas. But there was more to come. As the *Endeavour* travelled up the coast from Point Hicks, the men saw a series of waterspouts between the boat and the shore.

A fundamental Aboriginal belief is the connection between natural phenomena and the spirit world. As far as the locals were concerned, the waterspouts were messages from the spirit world, as were the impassable waves and angry winds that kept pushing the British ships away from land … 'Stay away.' But, of course, Cook didn't read the signals.

\*

It had been over five hundred kilometres since Point Hicks was sighted and all attempts to make it to shore had been foiled. Cook had had enough. Determined to set foot on land, whether the land and the locals wanted it or not, on Saturday, 28 April 1770

Cook dropped anchor two miles off the coast near Woonona, now a suburb of the city of Wollongong.

From the deck, the crew could see a group of four or five men walking briskly along the shore. Two of them carried a small canoe on their shoulders. Would this be the moment the locals decided to make contact?

But this was not Tahiti. This was not New Zealand. Here, there would be no grand reception or fleet of canoes, warriors and women paddling out to greet them.

Undoubtedly a little disappointed, Cook, Banks, Tupaia and the naturalist, Daniel Solander, climbed aboard the ship's yawl and made for shore to force the issue. But again, conditions were against them. The surf pounded the small boat, and the men were forced to retreat to the mothership.

Cook wanted to meet the locals, but it appeared the feeling wasn't reciprocated. He could see they were there – all the way along the eastern Australian coastline, Cook made frequent note of the fires he saw inland. He already knew the continent was inhabited and assumed the fires were for cooking. What he didn't, and couldn't possibly, realise was that to Indigenous Australians, fire meant something a whole lot more than a means to heat up dinner and keep chilly nights at bay.

The first hint of what was going on can be found in the *Endeavour*'s journals. Cook spoke of the 'woods' they could see on land as '*free from under wood of every kind*', and hills '*chequered with lawns*'. The voyage's artist, Sydney Parkinson, described the landscape as like a '*gentleman's park*'.

Similar observations were made by the early European settlers who marvelled at the 'tame' Australian landscape, thinking it a natural phenomenon.

As anyone who has spent any time in the Australian bush can confirm, the last word you'd use to describe it is 'tame'. The undergrowth is as dense and fractious as steel wool and stands of young saplings grow so close together that weaving between them is like trying to find your way through the teeth of a fine hair-comb. It's difficult to see these poetic descriptions of Australia's landscape as anything other than the delusions of a boatload of men who had spent way too long at sea. But that wasn't the case at all. They were describing exactly what they saw.

The men on board the *Endeavour* and those who came after didn't realise it, but they were describing a farm. They were seeing, without seeing. The entire continent was managed and maintained by the people living there.

**BRUCE PASCOE**

*They were trying to deny Aboriginal agency in the landscape, trying to deny Aboriginal possession of the soil, and probably trying to deny that Aboriginal people were intelligent enough to produce these systems. That was all so they could steal the land in the first place.*

The open land they described was anything but accidental. Ecology – the understanding of all living organisms and their relationship to each other – was a cornerstone of Aboriginal beliefs and governance.

And central to that was the use of fire to generate new vegetation, clean water, fresh air and manage hunting stocks.

**ROD MASON, Dharawal Nation, Cultural Teacher**
*Our number one law is fire; then wind and rain. They are the three laws of country. We believe we made this country. We create new country all the time through these practices.*

Aboriginal land management started with the first fires of the season, opening up the hunting grounds and laying the foundation for the control of food sources. Clearing the undergrowth meant that edible plants and animals weren't destroyed in out-of-control, wild bushfires of the sort known all too well in modern Australia; carefully set and supervised fires were used to hunt and lure game. The Aboriginal farmers used their knowledge to make resources abundant and predictable by establishing a circuit of hunting and harvesting grounds. It was a labour-intensive process that was highly specialised. Indigenous fire plans involved processes including burying leaves and grasses to create carbon potash and enrich the soil. It was hard work. But it created a land of great abundance.

Australia had grain crops, enormous tilled paddocks of yams, and permanent fish and eel trapping systems. The problem was that Cook and his men – and the British settlers who arrived after them to take possession of Aboriginal lands – were unable to recognise Aboriginal cultural practices for what they were because they were so unfamiliar to them.

**BRUCE PASCOE**
*Aboriginal people lost their ability to grow the crops because they lost the land. The hard-hoofed animals were destroying the soil by compacting it and drinking all the water. So the Aboriginal ability to continue managing the*

*land had been compromised. They were constantly harassed and driven off their land. It happened all over Australia. We're talking about blaming Cook, but I blame his boss. I don't see Cook as the devil. I blame the Crown. I just see Cook as an Englishman with that mindset of the Englishmen – they believed they could possess anything the world had to offer.*

Cook even saw Aboriginal fire setting and described it in his journal. But he couldn't understand its purpose.

**CAPTAIN JAMES COOK**

*They produce fire with great facility, and spread it in a wonderful manner ... We have often seen one of them run along the shore, to all appearance with nothing in his hand, who stooping down for a moment, at a distance of every fifty or a hundred yards, left fire behind him ... we saw him wrap up a small spark in dry grass, which, when he had run a little way, having been fanned by the air that his motion produced, began to blaze.*

Fire and burning to generate life and new growth? Really? To a European way of thinking, the fact that most Australian flora requires fire to regenerate and stay healthy would have been utterly incomprehensible.

The point is that Aboriginal people were not just wandering the countryside, exploiting natural resources as they found them. This was not 'hunter-gathering'. This was farming.

But how could Cook have missed something as obvious as effective land management practices on such a large scale? Was it because Cook and the other early arrivals landed in Australia with very low expectations of the people they expected to find there?

**DR PETER MEIHANA, Massey University, Ngāti Kuia, Ngāti Apa, Rangitāne, Ngāi Tahu Tribes, Tribal Historian**

*Cook was part of that generation of explorers who adhered to the Enlightenment model that placed societies on a scale, based on their means of subsistence. As Aboriginal people were deemed to be hunter-gatherers, they were at the bottom of that scale. Those involved in agriculture were higher on the scale because everything was measured by European standards. The aim was to move from hunter-gatherer to agriculturalist to industrialist.*

First-time European visitors to lands that were unfamiliar to them tended to place more stock in the accounts of other Western travellers than they did their own observations. Just as most modern tourists expect flamenco dancing and paella in Madrid and berets and baguettes in Paris, more often than not, early European navigators like Cook arrived on foreign shores with a firm idea of what they'd find and what to expect from the local inhabitants when they got there. Whether or not that tallied with the multi-faceted and complex reality of the cultures they encountered had little bearing on their perceptions – they arrived with a fairly unshakeable, and often utterly inaccurate, preconception of the place and people they were visiting. And the only account Cook had of the Indigenous inhabitants of Australia came from the English privateer, William Dampier, who had visited the western coastline in 1688 and described the local inhabitants as 'the miserablest people in the world'.

**WILLIAM DAMPIER (1651–1715), English Explorer and Privateer**

*Setting aside their human shape, they differ but little from brutes ... The colour of their skins, both of their faces and the rest of their body, is coal-black ... They all of them have the most unpleasant looks and the worst features of any people that ever I saw, though I have seen a great variety of savages.*

Unfortunately we don't have a record of what the Dampier Peninsula's Bardi people thought of him. But considering he was a sallow-skinned and wispy-haired man who had been at sea for two years, it would be nice to think their assessment of him was just as uncharitable.

Whatever the reasons for the wilful blindness towards Aboriginal Australians and their connection to and custodianship of the land, it's a great deal easier to justify dispossessing a people if you don't think they have much attachment to the land you're taking.

\*

Although the Dharawal people of Botany Bay couldn't have known what Cook's arrival on 29 April 1770 would mean for their country, they did know he was coming.

**ROD MASON**

*They were asking themselves, what is this thing coming up the coast? The news travelled faster than a bushfire ... My people were watching Cook for days, always wondering when and where they were going to land. We were ready. We were waiting for it.*

Because in Australia, the other thing fire was useful for – besides farming – was smoke signals. As Cook tacked to and fro along the coast, he was being watched. For days, the clans communicated with each other using a method not dissimilar to Morse code.

**DR SHAYNE WILLIAMS, Dharawal Nation, Senior Cultural Knowledge Holder**
*We were sending messages to one another with smoke, using different kinds of leaves to produce different colours. The Aboriginal people here knew that the vessel was on the way well before it got even halfway here.*

This method of communication was a specialised art – only elders initiated in the practice could make and translate the messages.

The Dharawal language group extended from the southern end of Botany Bay – or Kamay – as far south as Jervis Bay and inland along the Georges River. It was to the clan's 'safe camp' near Campbelltown on the Georges River that most of the community retreated when it became clear the *Endeavour* was entering the bay. Hidden from view, the community leaders watched the ship sail past from caves set in the cliff at Tabbagai.

**ROD MASON**
*There were different jobs for different people within the clan; those who were hunters, those who were gatherers, tradespeople, fire men ... But we sent our warriors down to the beach that day. They were our 'policemen'. They shouted, 'Warra Warra Wai!' They were explaining ... 'We have been watching you! Go away!'*

Deciding to take a different tack from the one he employed on his first landing in New Zealand, Cook resolved to avoid the shore where the locals seemed determined to oppose his landing. He chose to head for the opposite side of the bay instead. As the *Endeavour* passed the south head of the bay, four small canoes paddled past, each navigated by a single man spearing for fish. Like the men Cook and his crew had encountered further down the coast, these fishermen pointedly ignored the new arrivals.

### DR SHAYNE WILLIAMS

*They believed that the Aboriginal people weren't actually looking at them but we do have ways of looking at people without looking at them directly. So, they were being watched when they came in.*

Anchoring opposite a small village, an old woman bereft of clothing accompanied by three children stepped out of the forest. Watching them through his telescope, Banks saw that they looked at the ship but didn't appear at all concerned about its presence. Reassured that the people here seemed to be, at worst, disinterested in their arrival, Cook decided to try again. But the lukewarm welcome quickly heated up. Two men confronted the new arrivals, brandishing woomera and spears. They made their feelings fairly clear, screaming out in a '*harsh sounding language*'. Most disturbingly, Tupaia understood not a single word the Aboriginal men were saying. Whatever advantages Tupaia had given Cook in Polynesia would amount to nothing in this new land.

**SIR JOSEPH BANKS (1743–1820), 1st Baronet,**

**Naturalist and Botanist on Cook's first voyage**

*[They were] shaking their lances and menacing, in all appearance resolved to dispute our landing … 2 more muskets with small shot were then fired at them on which the eldest threw one more lance and then ran away as did the other.*

After absorbing a volley of small shot, the two warriors ran into the bush and were deemed '*rank cowards*' by Banks.

Cook resorted to the sure-fire icebreaker that had served him so well at other anchorages in the Pacific – surely some little knick-knacks would capture the locals' interest? He scattered an offering of sorts around the campsite. Pieces of cloth. Looking glasses. Beads. Combs. Nails.

Imagine Cook's surprise when that peace offering was rejected. This was totally unexpected. The Aboriginal people of Botany Bay weren't following the rules. Their refusal to cooperate must have been confusing and frustrating to Cook; his journal entries certainly suggest he was, at the very least, disappointed by his failure to establish a line of communication with the locals.

**CAPTAIN JAMES COOK**

*We could know but very little of [their] customs as we never were able to form any connections with them.*

Australia was refusing to give Cook anything. Everything he saw was unfamiliar and unsettling. And when the politicians and lawmakers back in Old Blighty found out how thoroughly Cook and his men had been flummoxed by this continent and its inhabitants, it played right into their hands. As they were mapping out their plans for their island prison, the powers-that-be would have been quite happy for word to spread about Australia's perceived shortcomings. Nothing was more effective than the threat of banishment to a bleak and brutal continent on the other side of the world to strike mortal fear into the hearts of would-be criminals and encourage them to keep on the straight and narrow.

The continent would continue to baffle Cook and his men with a parade of unfamiliar and remarkable flora and fauna. Later in the voyage, when they asked an Indigenous man the name of a pouched creature they saw bounding through the bush, they were told it was a *gunguuru* ... which Cook's naturalists recorded as 'kangaroo'.

### CAPTAIN JAMES COOK

*An animal something less than a greyhound, it was of a mouse colour very slender made and swift of foot ... the full size of a greyhound ... with a long tail ... I should have taken it for a wild dog, but for its walking or running in which it jumped like a hare or a deer ... its progression is by hopping or jumping 7 or 8 feet at each hop upon its hind legs only, for in this it makes no use of the fore, which seem to be only designed for scratching in the ground. Excepting the head and ears which I thought was something like a hare's, it bears no sort of resemblance to any European animal I ever saw.*

But *gunguuru* was the name given by the locals to a specific species of kangaroo. Aboriginal people had different names for different species of kangaroo, and other names for male and female animals.

**SAM NEILL**

*The name this fantastic beast has carried with it since the time of Cook comes to us from the local Aboriginal language. And that our national symbol – on the Australian coat of arms – has its basis in Indigenous language says something about the potential for much greater integration of our shared histories and languages than we have done otherwise.*

Still, the name stuck. One of the kangaroos was shot and eaten by the officers and gentlemen, and declared 'fine fare'. Meanwhile,

*A Singular Animal Called Kanguroo Found on the Coast of New Holland*, engraving after George Stubbs, c.1773. Considering all he had to go on was Cook's fanciful description, Parkinson's sketches and one dried skin, Stubbs made a reasonable fist of illustrating the kangaroo for an eager audience.
National Library of Australia, 7412 #S1700

Banks had grand plans for its skin. When Banks returned to England he commissioned George Stubbs, one of the foremost Georgian painters, to produce a portrait of the peculiar animal from the skin. The artist inflated it in an attempt to understand the animal's anatomy; this explains its rather unconvincing posture in Stubbs' painting. Along with the partner painting, *Portrait of a Large Dog*, which shows a dingo that looks suspiciously like a fox, these are the first known depictions of these two animals in Western art.

*

For Cook, the eight days in Botany Bay yielded only frustration. He had failed in his attempts to connect with the locals and initiate trade for the supplies they so desperately needed. But not everyone on board was so forlorn. The *Endeavour*'s scientists were having an absolute field day. For Joseph Banks and his fellow scientists, this place was a veritable Garden of Eden.

**PROFESSOR DARREN CRAYN,**
**Australian Tropical Herbarium**

*When they arrived on these shores no European had ever been on the east coast of Australia and certainly no men of science. They'd never seen anything like most of these plants. Prior to this voyage it was usually just the ship's surgeon that did the natural history. When they weren't hacking off gangrenous limbs and treating scurvy, they were collecting molluscs and plants. But they were usually only trained in a very rudimentary way in the natural sciences. But Banks was able to bring a team of eight on the voyage – himself, Daniel Solander and another naturalist and two illustrators, two servants and two assistants. Together they comprised almost 10 per cent of the entire crew. That was unheard of at that stage.*

It's important to remember that the voyage of the *Endeavour* was more than just a naval venture; it was a true Enlightenment pleasure cruise. This was the first time Britain sent out a voyage of exploration carrying a full entourage of naturalists and artists to classify and record the things they saw. One of the illustrators, Sydney Parkinson, painted ninety-four watercolours and sketches in Botany Bay, while Banks and Solander collected and classified innumerable botanical samples.

Banks' efforts were prodigious. Over the course of the first voyage, he collected specimens of 110 genera and 1400 species that were unknown to science. The tally of the world's known plant species increased by 10 per cent after the *Endeavour* returned to Britain. Once he returned to London, Banks set to work trying to lose the paradise he had found on the other side of the world. He became the principal lobbyist for establishing a British penal colony in Australia, and it's widely accepted that without his efforts the First Fleet would not have set sail.

Unfortunately for the poor souls who first landed in New South Wales, the man who was largely responsible for sending them there was a scientist, not a chef. While he was gathering botanical samples in and around Botany Bay, and tagging and classifying them as scientific curios, he had no idea that to the locals, many of these plants were culinary staples.

**JODY ORCHER, Ularai/Barkandji Nation, Educator**

*I ask people, what's your favourite fruit and vegetable? And they'll give me a list. Then I'll ask what their favourite Australian fruit and vegetable is and they don't know. But there's probably a plant that's been in their yard all their life and they don't know they can eat it and cook it.*

Each time Cook dropped anchor he was looking for three things: water, food and grass – the latter to feed the mobile menagerie on board. His experience around the Pacific had been that the locals were generally open to trade for all the things he needed, but in Australia they were left to their own devices. So Cook and his men hunted and fished for whatever they could get. And, intending to improve conditions for future European visitors to these shores, in far north Queensland Cook set loose a brace of pigs to breed. Needless to say, they did what Cook – and nature – intended and bred like ... pigs. To excess. The creatures descended from those imports continue to cause environmental chaos in the rainforest.

Banks was scathing about Australia's culinary offerings, declaring it *'a country where we had not the least reason to hope for subsistence ... so barren had we always found it'*. How did he think the Aboriginal people kept themselves going if it was so difficult to find food?

**JODY ORCHER**

*A traditional lifestyle wasn't like having breakfast, lunch and dinner. It was more of having a little bit of what you might still have left over from the night before and then foraging. So you'd be looking for those little fruits – lilli pillies – or looking for those sweet grevillea nectars, things to give you energy bursts until you had your next meal.*

When the First Fleet anchored in Botany Bay, Joseph Banks made sure they brought with them all the agricultural comforts of home. Rather than making the most of what they found growing naturally, the first settlers tried – and failed dismally – to cultivate European grains, fruits and vegetables, and were driven to the point of starvation. The men and women of the First Fleet stripped the land of anything deemed edible or useful, destroying in months an ecosystem that had allowed the Dharawal people to subsist for generations.

Unfortunately for Botany Bay's resident bird life, one of the favourite dishes on board the *Endeavour* was lorikeet pie. Why just admire nature when you can eat it, too?

**SYDNEY PARKINSON (1745–1771), Scottish Botanical and Natural History Illustrator on Cook's first voyage**
*[S]aw a great number of birds of a beautiful plumage; among which were two sorts of parakeets, and a beautiful lorikeet ... we shot a few of them, which we made into a pie, and they ate very well.*

Rainbow lorikeets are rather sleek birds, so it's difficult to imagine them yielding much edible meat. They're certainly no plump-breasted pigeon. One little fledgling amongst them got lucky that day. It was rescued from the pot by Tupaia, who adopted it as his pet. And that wasn't the end of this extraordinary creature's story.

Having polished off their lorikeet pie, the men turned their hungry eyes to the waters. The original name for Botany Bay, Kamay, is the Dharawal word for the stingray's barb. No surprises, then, to find an abundance of stingrays in the clear waters. For their final fresh feed in the bay, the men were served stingray with a side order of the one local green they deemed edible: warrigal greens, which Banks likened to spinach. The greens were particularly important to the *Endeavour*'s crew as a means of staving off the dreaded scurvy. With no idea how long it might be between Botany Bay and a plate of greens, the seamen must have tucked into the vegetables with gusto.

Scurvy is a horror. The potentially fatal disease, caused by severe vitamin C and B deficiency, was for many centuries the scourge of long-range European maritime voyages. A vivid description of the symptoms was written in the mid-1770s, listing blackened skin, shedding of teeth, ulcers, difficulty breathing and, most hideously, a sudden eruption of gum tissue in the mouth that rotted away. Although many mariners knew that fresh fruit and vegetables – particularly citrus fruit and greens – would keep scurvy at bay, they were too perishable to be useful on long voyages. As maritime powers extended their reach around the globe, finding a way to treat the disease became a high priority.

Cook had been instructed by the Admiralty to test the efficacy of fermented malt and wort and sauerkraut as a means of warding off scurvy. He attributed his apparent success at keeping the disease at bay to regular doses of fermented malt, but it's more likely that it was due to his attention to hygiene and keeping the ship clean and his men warm and well rested. That, and the fact that he made the most of any opportunity to ply his men with fresh greens. In Botany Bay, the warrigal greens made this easy. But as the journey progressed, it would become more challenging.

\*

Seeds from the warrigal greens would eventually find their way back to London via Joseph Banks' agency, where a taste for the Australian vegetable became quite the thing in fashionable London circles. By then, Banks had other things on his mind, foremost amongst which was protecting and promoting Cook's legacy. Banks would become Cook's most passionate champion. In a way this is peculiar, because throughout the voyage of the *Endeavour* their relationship, although largely cordial, was not without its issues. Cook and the other naval officers were not accustomed to sharing their space with so many civilians who were unfamiliar with the ways of the navy. Given his social standing, Banks could be high-handed, and for Cook it must have been challenging to share the Great Cabin with him and the naturalist Daniel Solander.

Without the agency of Joseph Banks, it's quite possible that James Cook would have remained a footnote in Australia's history. But that wasn't to be. In white Australia, Cook would eventually assume mythical status. And without any consultation, the Indigenous Australians who had called the continent home for tens of thousands of years, found themselves lumbered with a brand-new, British founding father.

# EIGHT

# LARGER THAN LIFE

*I really underestimated how strongly people felt about*
*Cook. I guess I knew he was unpopular in some parts.*
*But I hadn't realised there was such anger. On the one*
*hand, I vaguely understand that anger. But on the other,*
*I'm not sure how fair it is to blame Cook.*
**SAM NEILL**

Australia can't get enough of its 'big' things. The big pineapple. The big koala. The big lobster. The big banana. There are even big potatoes complete with big forks. So it should be expected that Australia would also put in an order for a big foundation myth.

What any fledgling nation needs more than almost anything else is an uplifting genesis story – all the best countries have them. When Australia decided to let go of mummy's hand in 1901 and step forward into the world with head held high as an independent nation, it needed its own mythology.

Sure, the beliefs of the Aboriginal people had sustained them for tens of thousands of years. Not to mention, their origin story was pretty spectacular. But that wasn't much help to white Australia.

> **WARWICK THORNTON, Kaytej Nation,**
> **Filmmaker/Director**
> *There was something bigger here in Australia. There was*
> *an existence that was sustainable and a culture with laws*
> *and a religion that covered much bigger concepts of life,*
> *humanity and connectedness. Pre-Cook, this place was*
> *bigger than Europe ... bigger than Asia in a way. What has*
> *happened is that we've lost a lot of that through this bloke*
> *rocking up.*

The leaders of this great land fished around in their nation's embarrassingly short history to find a worthy founding father. And in Captain James Cook, the unmoored British colony found its made-to-measure saviour – the brave, steadfast British explorer who risked life and limb to cross the oceans and discover this wide brown land and claim it for the Crown. He even came pre-packaged with a suitably tragic end. Perfect!

Captain Cook discovered Australia in 1770. Got it? Good. Because that's exactly what all children who went through the Australian school system prior to the 1980s were taught.

> **DR SHAYNE WILLIAMS, Dharawal Nation, Senior**
> **Cultural Knowledge Holder**
> *We went to school and all they ever taught us was how*
> *Cook discovered Australia. Well, this country was occupied*
> *by us well before 1770. If anyone discovered this country,*
> *it's us. But we were never told that side of the story in*
> *history classes in school.*

History lesson done and dusted. Cook 'discovered' Australia just as Columbus 'discovered' America.

It must have occurred to more than a handful of students to ask how it was possible to 'discover' a land already inhabited by human beings, but such insolent questions most likely earnt the inquisitive soul a swift backhander or trip to the principal's office.

## WARWICK THORNTON

*The Captain Cook I grew up with is from the textbooks, so in a strange way I grew up thinking that he found Australia. The only thing I had a conflict with was the idea that there was nobody here. But you can't put your hand up in class and go, 'No, we were here first, sir.' But when you see other people putting a person up on a pedestal as the perfect explorer ... the perfect human, the great saviour ... you really do start to hate him. I think that's what created the antagonism towards him. But he was a patsy. He was doing the dirty work of something much bigger, and much darker.*

There's a spot deep in the heart of Melbourne's Fitzroy Gardens that embodies the fabrication of Captain James Cook's myth. In 1933, a wealthy philanthropist, Sir Russell Grimwade, acquired a quaint Georgian cottage in the village of Great Ayton, Yorkshire, and transported it, brick by brick and at enormous expense, to Melbourne. This was not just any cottage; this was, according to local legend, Captain Cook's home. There is a catch, though, as there so often is. Yes, this had been 'Cook's' cottage – Cook senior, that is. As in, James Cook's father. Although James may have visited his parents there once or twice, no amount of creative licence could justify saying he lived in the house.

That this furphy took root in a corner of Australia that Cook never even visited is symptomatic of the Cookmania that took hold in the country after Federation. What was happening to Cook was an early, and very effective, example of what's known today as 'spin'. In the utopian era before PR agents and marketing executives became ubiquitous, Cook was trimmed, plucked, bleached and blow-waved into shape to give the nascent nation the daddy figure it was looking for.

The Cook we know from primary historical sources was a fiercely ambitious man. He certainly wanted to make a mark. But he was also remarkably modest and not one to blow his own trumpet. Witness, for example, the fact that unlike most other navigators, he didn't name anything much after himself. The places around the world that now bear his name – Cooktown, Cook Strait, Mount Cook and Cook's Bay amongst many others – were named by others. It's not unreasonable to think that he would have been fairly embarrassed by all the fuss.

As an unassuming man, Cook would have had good reason to blush. Every spot along Australia's eastern coast that can claim to even the slightest association with him is graced by at least one memorial to commemorate the fact. There's even a town in Queensland called 1770.

*

Even decades before Federation, the legend of Cook had already been growing exponentially as Australia began to morph from a colonial offshoot of Great Britain into an independent nation.

**WARWICK THORNTON**

*The British Empire was basically built on stealing everyone else's resources. But they basically obliterated some of the kindest, most beautiful cultures in the world to create this nation we call Australia today.*

When a statue of Cook was unveiled in 1879 in Hyde Park, Sydney, more than sixty thousand people went along for a stickybeak – a figure that's all the more remarkable because it amounted to 10 per cent of the population of the entire colony of New South Wales.

This statue is instantly recognisable. Standing atop a mighty granite plinth with one foot tipping over the edge of the base as if he has been interrupted mid-stride, Cook is depicted as a resolute and determined man of action. He holds his telescope in one hand and raises the other in a gesture of … is it pride? Is Cook acknowledging the silent applause of his people? There's a sense of self-importance in his stance and outlook that seems at odds with what we know of him (or what we think we know of him, anyway). This haughty figure bears little resemblance to the portraits made of Cook by artists who knew him. Those likenesses captured a reflective and restrained man who almost seems to recoil from the viewer. Cook's piercing brown eyes gleam with keen intelligence but in most cases he looks away from the viewer, deep in contemplation and apparently a little discomfited by the attention. Compare these with the portraits of Cook's partner in crime, Joseph Banks, who leans towards his audience and locks the viewer in his gaze, giving us the sense he'd do anything to be able to burst out of the picture frame.

But verisimilitude was not of much concern to the burghers of Sydney town. The Cook they stuck on a plinth in the middle of the city's most important public park had a job to do. In his speech at the unveiling of the Hyde Park memorial, the governor, Sir Hercules Robinson (yes, his name was really Hercules), described Cook as a 'humane, just and God-fearing man' and urged Australia's youth to 'imitate his nobility of character'.

In Australia, the appetite for all things Cook was insatiable. Even his failures were commemorated. His thwarted attempt to land at Woonona was honoured by a memorial erected by the local Rotary Club. Surmounted by a stern portrait of Cook in profile flanked by twin copies of George Stubbs' *Kongouru*, it's inscribed: 'Near this spot Captain James Cook first attempted landing in Australia 28th April 1770.' It's a miracle we don't also have a memorial or two recalling: 'Near this spot in 1770, Captain James Cook sneezed.'

Of course, the site that looms the largest in Australia's narrative about James Cook is the place he first set foot on the continent, just twelve hours after weighing anchor and turning his back on Woonona. Botany Bay or Kamay is deeply meaningful for Indigenous and non-indigenous Australians, although the reasons couldn't be more different.

**DR SHAYNE WILLIAMS**

*This place is very special to Aboriginal and Torres Strait Islander people right across the nation because this is where the country was annexed to the British Empire and where dispossession began.*

From the British perspective, Botany Bay was where modern Australia was born. It was also the place where the post-settlement myth-making machine groaned into action. What's often forgotten is that even though Joseph Banks identified it as being the perfect spot to lay the foundations of the first British settlement in Australia, he was there in May after autumn rains. Which meant there was water. When the commander of the First Fleet, Captain Arthur Phillip, sailed into Botany Bay on 18 January 1788 with his eleven ships, it was mid-summer and fresh water was in short supply. For a fledgling settlement, it was quite an oversight.

Phillip immediately set about finding an alternative location and very quickly happened upon what's widely regarded as the most stunning harbour in the world. Sydney Harbour was also, thankfully, blessed with an abundance of potable water. Cook had sailed right past Sydney Heads and although he noted its potential at the time, he had no real reason to investigate because he had fully restocked his ship in Botany Bay. Phillip relocated the first settlers to Sydney Cove on 26 January, which is why that date is now celebrated as 'Australia Day'. The colony's false start on 18 January was relegated to the dustbin of history.

Botany Bay wouldn't be forgotten, though. It would retain its standing thanks to Cook. His landing there was a symbolic moment signifying the birth of the colony that would morph into modern Australia. Preserved in the visual memory of most of the children who were taught that Captain Cook 'discovered' Australia in 1770 is the iconic painting by Emanuel Phillips Fox, *The Landing of Captain Cook at Botany Bay, 1770*, painted in 1902, just one year after Federation. This is Cook as described by Governor Hercules Robinson – leading his men from the front with a sense of justice and humanity. Rather than raising a gun to shoot at the Dharawal people on the distant hill, he lifts his hand to reassure his nervous crew and commands them to hold their fire.

To commemorate the landing in Botany Bay, from 1899 until the 1950s this momentous occasion was re-enacted each year in official ceremonies. Dignitaries would hop aboard a steamship and cut through the waves to Kurnell where they would halt over the spot where the *Endeavour* anchored before landing to hoist the flag and make the requisite toasts and speeches. Why, you may well ask, was this deemed necessary?

The hoisting of the flag was an important eighteenth-century European maritime practice as a means of laying claim to a land. All along the eastern Australian coastline, Cook planted the flag in the earth when he managed to reach the shore and brandished it in the air where he could not. By recording this in his journal, Cook was claiming the eastern coast of Australia in the name of King George III. When he reached the very top of the continent, he considered the job done.

**TINA NGATA, Ngāti Porou Tribe**

*Flag raising and the Doctrine of Discovery ... It's one of those things that you think – how did someone in France ... somebody in Spain ... somebody in England ... somebody in Holland ... all happen to have the same idea that we raise a flag and this is what that means? It was the ceremonial enactment of the Discovery doctrine. It was certainly understood to be something that forfeited the sovereign rights of the people of that land.*

The replication of the ritual in Botany Bay each year was a way of reinforcing possession of the land.

*

Needless to say, Aboriginal Australians have always seen these events in a completely different light. Cutting to the heart of the matter is a painting by contemporary artist Daniel Boyd. Its title is fairly unambiguous: *We Call Them Pirates Out Here*. In a scathing parody of the original painting, Boyd's Cook steps ashore wearing an eye patch and brandishing a skull and crossbones where Phillips Fox's Cook carries the Red Ensign. The eye patch is also deeply symbolic. Yes, it signifies piracy, but it also stands for the 'one-eyed' perspective European settlers brought to Australian shores, declaring as 'unoccupied' the territory they seized. Boyd gives us an unambiguous view of the beach from an Aboriginal perspective and shows this moment for what it was – a land grab.

For the Dharawal people, the appearance of the *Endeavour* in Botany Bay was a significant moment. Oral histories tell us that they thought Cook's ship was a floating island. At first they believed the men on board were spirits returning from the afterlife.

**ROD MASON, Dharawal Nation, Cultural Teacher**
*It was believed in the camps that when a black man dies he goes over to the other side and comes back white. So when Cook and his men arrived here, we thought they were ghosts. When we die, the arm of a cabbage tree palm takes us across to the other side – the water to the east ... and we walk across to another world.*

It was no surprise, then, that the Dharawal did everything they could to avoid the spectral new arrivals. Visitors from the afterlife? Under what circumstances would that be a good thing? The only reason the spirits could have for being there was to carry the Dharawal into the next life. Leaving behind peculiar objects didn't help the British case and of course the Dharawal refused to touch the trinkets Cook left in their campsite. Why would they go anywhere near things that came from these ghouls?

As they watched the sailors climb the rigging, the Dharawal began to doubt their first impressions. Perhaps these creatures weren't spirits after all, but *goomeras* (possums) scrambling up and down the ship's masts. Whether they were spirits or possums, the Dharawal people weren't going to let these strange creatures land without opposition. And here we find another example of the Cook myth-making apparatus at work. Because it has long been claimed that when the *Endeavour* arrived in Botany Bay it encountered no resistance at all.

Even without drawing upon local oral traditions, there's no shortage of evidence that reveals the opposition Cook faced from the locals when he attempted to land.

**DR SHAYNE WILLIAMS**

*The warriors were already painted up as they arrived. I doubt it was coincidence. They painted themselves up in anticipation that the vessel was on its way. In particular ceremonies you use particular colours – white is usually used for serious occasions – either punishments or to repel intruders.*

Banks speaks of warriors threatening them with 'crooked' weapons shaped like the curved blade of a scimitar – his description of boomerangs. He also recalled the warriors wielding spears and woomera – an Aboriginal innovation that improved the spear's speed and accuracy. Until the invention of the self-loading rifle, the woomera and spear were the fastest weapons in the world.

**SIR JOSEPH BANKS (1743–1820), 1st Baronet, Naturalist and Botanist on Cook's first voyage**

*[A]ll … were armed with long pikes and a wooden weapon made something like a short scimitar. During this time a few of the Indians who had not followed the boat remained on the rocks opposite the ship, threatening and menacing with their pikes and swords …. Each of these held in his hand a wooden weapon about 2 feet long, in shape much resembling a scimitar; the blades of these looked whitish and some thought shining insomuch that they were almost of opinion that they were made of some kind of metal, but myself thought they were no more than wood smeared over with the same white pigment with which they paint their bodies.*

These people could spear kangaroos and wallabies bounding through the bush. They wouldn't have missed a cluster of sailors bobbing about in a boat. If they had wanted to hit the interlopers, the sailors would have ended up with more holes than a colander.

**DR SHAYNE WILLIAMS**

*Our people are so skilful with the spear, that if they really wanted to hit them with the spear, they would have. These were warning shots.*

*

The tweaking of the history of Aboriginal resistance happened just as Cook was assuming his position at the summit of white Australia's secular pantheon. Prior to Federation, there are illustrations of the resistance put up by the Dharawal that day, described as the 'Battle of Botany Bay'. But after that? Nothing. This ties in with the myth that when Cook arrived, Aboriginal people had no concept of land ownership but were just wandering around enjoying a hunter-gatherer lifestyle, eating whatever they found lying around the place, with little or no connection to the land. The story was that they didn't fight to defend their turf because one piece of bush is as good as the next when you're a hunter-gatherer, right?

Wrong. We now know this to be complete bunkum. Although Aboriginal Australians didn't mark out boundaries in a way that would have been obvious to a European eye, they did, and still do, have strong connections to traditional lands bounded by geographic markers and preserved in oral records. As in Tahiti, the problem arose because Aboriginal and British conceptions of 'ownership' and territoriality are at odds.

### DR SHAYNE WILLIAMS

*We don't feel like the land is separate from us. Spiritualism is in everything – in other life forms, in inanimate things like rocks and stones as well as in mountains and hills. It's about being in unison with country.*

Just because something wasn't written down doesn't mean it didn't exist. But the lack of a tangible record or any visual markers – fences, signposts – does make it much easier to take something that you don't think belongs to anyone else.

Possession Island's name tells you everything you really need to know. It is a tiny dot of land at the northern tip of Cape York Peninsula. When Cook stepped ashore just before sunset on 22 August 1770, he climbed to the top of the highest hill to get a view of the surrounding islands and confirm he had passed the northernmost point of the eastern coastline. He acknowledged in his journal that the land to the west had already been charted by the Dutch and so belonged to them. As an afterthought, he struck that line out. Why admit anything in writing that could give England's maritime competitors an advantage? While the Union Jack was hoisted, the marines on the hilltop fired three volleys that were answered by guns on the *Endeavour*. Cook had charted the entire east coast – as far as he was concerned, that gave him the right to claim these lands, despite their occupation by Indigenous Australians.

### CAPTAIN JAMES COOK

*[I]n the name of his Majesty ... I now once more hoisted English colours and in the name of His Majesty King George the Third took possession of the whole eastern coast from the above latitude down to this place by the name of New South Wales together with all the bays, harbours rivers and islands situate upon the same said coast.*

Hence, Possession Island.

Of course Cook knew these lands were occupied. Although Possession Island is deserted today, in 1770 the place known to locals as Bedanug was home to the Kaurareg people. Cook had passed a group of them as he climbed the hill.

What's difficult to understand is the contradiction we find between what actually occurred and the instructions Cook was given by the Admiralty:

> *You are also with the consent of the natives to take possession of convenient situations in the country in the name of the King of Great Britain: Or: if you find the country uninhabited take possession for His Majesty by setting up proper marks and inscriptions, as first discoverers and possessors.*

There was no ambiguity in the 'hints' the Earl of Morton had given Cook at the beginning of the voyage as guidelines for playing nicely with the locals. Just a reminder here – he declared all indigenous inhabitants *'the natural, and in the strictest sense of the word, the legal possessors of the several regions they inhabit'.* But that wasn't all. *'No European nation has a right to occupy any part of their country, or settle among them without their voluntary consent'.*

Yet occupy Aboriginal land they did.

**ERNIE DINGO, Yamatji Nation, Actor**

*There's a lot to be angry about. But rather than be angry about what's been done towards blackfellas in this country ... well, you'd be up all night. These places had traditional names. Now they're all desecrated by giving them a new name, even to the stage where out of hundreds of major languages, now there's less than eighty spoken on*

> *a daily basis. You wouldn't do that to Europe. Get the*
> *whole of Europe with all of their different languages to*
> *speak one language. They're all going to jump up and*
> *down … 'Ooh that's my heritage!' Well, this is our*
> *heritage. We all had to stop speaking our native tongue to*
> *speak whitefella.*

The logical conclusion from all this is that Aboriginal people were dispossessed and marginalised by Cook and those who came after him because they didn't govern themselves by the same rules of social hierarchy that were familiar to Westerners.

In Tahiti and New Zealand, there were chieftains – kings and queens. That was easy for Cook to understand. But everything else about Indigenous Australian society – from their relationship to the land to their social hierarchy – was so strange and unfamiliar to him that he couldn't fully comprehend the highly ritualised interactions that existed between the people who lived there. Even Tupaia struggled to understand the Aboriginal way of life.

Meanwhile, the (deservedly) much-maligned Doctrine of Discovery underpinned the early European voyages of exploration. Issued as a papal edict in 1452, it held that as Christian nations were favoured by God, they were expected to observe the rule of law when interacting with other sovereign Christian nations. But when it came to lands that were populated by 'heathens', the gloves were off. These places were deemed to have been 'discovered' by Christian explorers because the people who lived there were classified as subhuman. Why else do you think Indigenous Australians weren't permitted to vote in

Federal elections until 1962, and until 1967 weren't counted in the national census? They were lumped in with the native flora and fauna.

> **DR SHAYNE WILLIAMS:** *When Rod and I were born in 1960, for the first seven years we weren't classified as humans.*
> **ROD MASON:** *I'll never ever get rid of that way of feeling, until someone or something comes together and tries to sort this out.*
> **DR SHAYNE WILLIAMS:** *1770 was a real precursor to all of that.*

Regardless of the justifications given, hubris and greed would see the entire continent of Australia deemed *terra nullius*. Nobody's land.

> **WARWICK THORNTON**
> *Terra nullius said 'they're all nomads – the missing link …*
> *We'll do some studies – then we'll decide they're actually subhuman, so they don't really have any idea about owning anything. So we'll just claim it all and if they object, we'll just shoot the shit out of them.'*

It was the Governor of New South Wales, Sir Richard Bourke, who came up with this idea. When the upstart would-be founding father of Melbourne, John Batman, attempted to purchase land from the Aboriginal people living along the Yarra River, he wanted to establish a settlement. But Bourke stymied his plans by issuing a proclamation on 10 October 1835 that declared as trespassers all people occupying land in Australia without the express consent of the government. The idea underpinning this was that nobody had owned the land before the British Crown claimed it – therefore, apparently the Wurundjeri people had no right to sell any land to Batman.

Times, they are a-changin', though. When Eddie Koiki Mabo and four other Meriam people embarked on their campaign to reclaim their traditional lands in the Torres Strait, it took many years of determined social, political and legal action before a ruling was passed down in the favour of the plaintiffs. Eddie Mabo himself didn't live to see the 1992 law passed that became a landmark precedent, sending 'terra nullius' back into the dark ages where it belongs. Under what's now known as the Mabo Case, the Australian High Court determined that common law as it stood violated international human rights and denied the historical dispossession of Australia's first occupants. The doctrine of native title was enshrined in law, acknowledging that Aboriginal people have a prior claim to the lands taken by the Crown in 1770.

### DR SHAYNE WILLIAMS

*We might have won some little battles here and there, but in terms of the reconciliation process, we're way behind other parts of the world. There's a lot more soul-searching that needs to be done on behalf of the non-Aboriginal people who actually govern this country.*

*

While myriad Aboriginal nations were dispossessed of land in the wake of Cook's journey, they certainly didn't go quietly. It's a fight that continues today.

### ROD MASON

*We've been displaced from what we once were responsible for, and all we want to do is to belong again. It's not given to us – we can't be given back something that always belonged to us. All we want is to be repositioned in this universe again.*

The battle is often fought through art. This has become a way for Aboriginal people to reclaim land and territory, and to assert ownership and connection to country.

### WARWICK THORNTON

*Today, Indigenous people have to prove their connection to country, even though we've just had two hundred years of people trying to obliterate our existence as Indigenous people. In the court of law we have to prove after 250 years that we are still part of the country and have cultural practices and spiritual connections with the land, and that we still hunt and live traditionally on country even though they've spent the last 250 years stopping us from doing anything. It's hypocritical, and it's disgusting.*

Aboriginal culture sings and performs to the land, deepening the ties of a mutual relationship – just as all those re-enactments of the landing at Botany Bay were a way of asserting the British claim to the land. Though the latter was a rather pathetic attempt by comparison.

## WARWICK THORNTON

*There are many beautiful human beings out there who are really interested in a different version of Australia's history and they're getting it through art, literature, and film. That's where it's all coming from – the different point of view ... the first voice. So it's a very exciting time.*

To many contemporary Aboriginal Australians, Cook symbolises the end of Indigenous sovereignty and self-determination. Artists including Daniel Boyd, Jason Wing, Christian Thompson, Gordon Bennett, H.J. Wedge, Vincent Namatjira and Paddy Wainburranga have drawn on the Cook story to present an Indigenous perspective on invasion, colonisation and dispossession.

## WARWICK THORNTON

*Is Cook friend or foe? I think he was a pawn. He was tasked to claim Australia, which he did. But the foundation of the nation? That falls on Britain – the empire that was built on the back of other cultures ... other peoples. They obliterated a shitload of culture. But a shitload of culture still remains, and we're celebrating it. And it seems like the rest of Australia has started celebrating it too.*

## ERNIE DINGO

*James Cook? He don't mean nothing to me other than the fact that he was a so-called bloke who discovered something that wasn't lost.*

But throughout much of Australia, Cook still has a larger-than-life status.

**WARWICK THORNTON**

*Do I blame Cook? I think we all do. But is it fair? Well, if you need to point the finger, he's the guy. But it's those who came after him that were the real bad guys. Cook is like the footy coach who cops the blame for the team performance. We know that. But he's become a useful metaphor. Art is also a way to deconstruct the myth of Cook and grapple with the potency of his story to reframe and reinterpret the first encounter.*

Looming over the northern Queensland city of Cairns is a reminder of just how enormous – and disconcerting – the myth of Cook can be.

Yes, to go with all the big animals and produce, Australia has a Big Captain Cook. A very big Cook who appears as if he's giving a Nazi salute. The intention of the statue's creators, though, was to render an oil painting on a monumental scale – in this case, as depicted by Emanuel Phillips Fox in *Landing of Captain Cook at Botany Bay*.

Even if we put aside the goose-stepping Cook in far north Queensland, the Cook we think of in Australia today bears little resemblance to the man who came ashore in Botany Bay. He has come to represent so many different things.

**JOHN ROBSON, Map Librarian, University of Waikato**

*I think he was a great man and had many admirable qualities. He wasn't perfect but he was placed upon a pedestal in the nineteenth and early twentieth centuries, especially in New Zealand and Australia – both countries that were looking for a hero. I think he himself would have hated to have been in that position .... A lot of the negativity that surrounds him now is not so much about him, himself, but more to do with what Europeans brought to the Pacific and the indigenous people of the Pacific afterwards.*

The person you see when you look at Cook is not just an eighteenth-century navigator who was the first man to chart the east coast of the continent. He is also a reflection of who you are: your personal history, your perceptions and your prejudices. For all Australians – Indigenous and non-indigenous alike – Cook is a whole lot more than the sum of his parts.

### WARWICK THORNTON

*I'm looking forward to Australia's future. We can only get better, because we've been pretty terrible for quite a while.*

James Cook, the man, is long gone. What Australia is left to grapple with is Captain Cook, the myth.

### ERNIE DINGO

*I like to think about history 'BC' – Before Cook.*

# NINE

# DANGEROUS SHORES

*You can't reverse things. You can't put things into reverse.*
*It is a new Pacific and we make what we can of it and*
*make the best we can of it. And you see glimmers of really*
*wonderful things happening all over the place.*
**SAM NEILL**

There are days you should just stay in bed. You're out of milk. Your bar of soap is the size of a water cracker. The seam that's been threatening to pop on your pants finally gives up the ghost. You catch every red light. The lid of your takeaway cup is askew and after one sip your lap is swimming in hot coffee. Mid-text, you drop your mobile phone and it ends up in the inaccessible crack between the driver's seat and the chassis. OK, you shouldn't have been texting while you were driving – not the point. Some days it seems like the world's got it in for you.

For James Cook, Australia was that day. As he departed Botany Bay on 6 May 1770 without making the local connections he had so desperately wanted to establish, he could only hope things would be easier as the *Endeavour* headed north. The ship was low on supplies – and given it had been a year and a half since they'd left Plymouth, that was a fairly frequent state of affairs. Replenishing stores was never straightforward, but Cook was a persistent man: up until his arrival in Australia, he had been able to negotiate with the locals to get what he needed.

**JOHN ELLIOTT (1759–1844), Midshipman,**
**Cook's second voyage**

*No man could be better calculated to gain the confidence of savages than Capn Cook. He was brave, uncommonly cool, humane – and patient. He would land alone unarmed, or lay aside his arms, and sit down, when they threatened with theirs, throwing them beads, knives, and other little presents, then by degrees advancing nearer, till by patience, and forbearance, he gained their friendship.*

The one thing we can be fairly certain of is that even in the face of adversity James Cook refused to turn his back on a challenge. Accounts written by crew members on all of his three Pacific voyages spill over with evidence of Cook's resolve and unstinting praise for his character.

**JAMES TREVENEN (1760–1790), Midshipman,**
**Cook's third voyage**

*This indefatigability was a leading feature of his character. If he failed in, or could no longer pursue, his first great object, he immediately began to consider how he might be more useful in prosecuting some inferior one. Procrastination and irresolution he was a stranger to. Action was life to him & repose a sort of death.*

But, still. Charting the east coast of the continent of New Holland was not in his brief. It wouldn't have been at all unreasonable for him to break out into the open ocean and head straight to the safe harbour of Batavia. Once he had committed to a course of action, though, he saw it through.

Before he left England the Admiralty and Royal Society had set Cook a series of tasks to be undertaken on the South Seas expedition. He had ticked them all off the list. So what was motivating him as he fought the winds and currents while he traced his way north, charting as he went? Was he just having a stab at empire building and laying claim to yet another distant land for the British Crown? Or was Cook inspired by something more? Perhaps this was symptomatic of his ambition and hunger – the steely resolve of a lowborn country boy determined to make a mark. Australia wasn't going to make it easy for him, though. This land had a few nasty surprises in store for him.

When Cook sailed the *Endeavour* past the island of K'gari (later named 'Fraser Island' by the British) on 20 May, its Badtjala inhabitants knew he was headed for trouble. A stunningly beautiful place encircled by powdery white beaches and swathed in rolling sand dunes and towering rainforest, at 120 kilometres in length and about twenty-five kilometres wide K'gari is the largest sand island in the world. It's also a botanical peculiarity because it's the only place on earth where sand sustains a large rainforest canopy. To the Badtjala people it is – quite literally – paradise.

**GEMMA CRONIN, Badtjala Nation, Linguist and Performer**
*There's absolutely everything here. There's an abundance of food and water ... shelter. It's a paradise.*

The Indigenous name for the island is taken from the Badtjala creation story. The goddess K'gari was tasked with finding her way down to earth to make the mountains, rivers and sea. Having fallen in love with her creation, K'gari didn't want to leave, and so the messenger god, Yendingie, transformed her into a heavenly island.

As they enjoyed another day in paradise, the Badtjala were surprised to see Cook's ship appear on the horizon.

### GEMMA CRONIN

*They saw the ship about seventy-five miles from here, down on Hook Point on the bottom end of the island. And they started walking because it was tacking, to and fro, off the beach. They followed it for a whole day but they weren't really sure what it was.*

As the ship sailed past the island's eastern shore, the Badtjala tracked it, following it along the beach. They scrambled to the best vantage point on the island to get a better look – the headland they called Dhokki Wurru.

### GEMMA CRONIN

*The people got worried for the boat and ran up onto the headland to try and warn him about the shoal out there. They were trying to tell him to go back, but in his journal he thinks we were waving at him.*

Cook saw the assembled Badtjala people watching the ship, and so fell back on the ubiquitous, catch-all term for anyone other than a European and called it 'Indian Head'.

Today, Indian Head is one of Fraser Island's most popular tourist destinations. Making the most of the same stunning vantage point used by the Badtjala to watch Cook sail on by, visitors to the island take selfies overlooking the crystalline tropical waters below. But these days, Badtjala people stay away from the lookout point. It evokes too many grim memories.

**GEMMA CRONIN**

*They brought the black trackers, the native police up here, and ... drove my people off this headland. All the women and children and old people that were hiding behind Indian Head ... they drove them up with horses and shot them. So this is a major massacre site, for Badtjala people. Women and children and old people killed – the ones who were supposed to be protected.*

This massacre occurred during the settler wars, as European arrivals began to exploit the island's sand and timber resources. It was just one of many tragic events in the sad history of British colonisation that played out across the continent.

**SAM NEILL**

*Another unseemly chapter of Australian history is the many, many massacres of Aboriginal people that took place here. There are terrible things that happened all over the Pacific in the wake of Cook's voyages. I've had to face up to this on my journey.*

Since 1770 and in keeping with oral tradition, the Badtjala people have preserved a record of Cook's swift passage past the island. A song, still performed by Badtjala dancers today, recounts the *Endeavour*'s arrival and the local response to its appearance.

> *Strangers are travelling with a cloud, Areeram!!*
> *It has fire, inside must be a bad water spirit.*
> *It's stupid maybe? It's going directly to that rainbow serpent*
>     *place,*
> *This is the truth that I bring*
> *It is breathing smoke rhythmically from its rear, must be*
>     *song men and sorcerers*
> *Coming up and going back with the wind at its rear, like a*
>     *sand crab*
> *The sea carries this ship here, why?*
>
> *Gabrin wuna'la yaneen, Areeram*
> *Ngun'gu'ni wiinj gung'milung*
> *Nyundal wun'yamba dhali dhak'kin'bah, Gebeer barine*
> *Moomoo gumbir'l'im bundi burree, Yauwa dhan*
>     *man'ngur*
> *Yuang yangu moomoo gumbir, Billi'ngunda*
> *Tin'gera dan'da gung'mungalum minya?*

Clearly the locals saw it as an event worth commemorating.

### GEMMA CRONIN

*Most indigenous people have that painful past no matter where they come from in the world. It was that change for us as a people, and that's what that song's about – a foretelling of what was coming, and our old people were intuitive enough to realise something like that in the last line ... 'the sea brings this ship here – why?' They knew something big was coming.*

In the early 1900s a phonograph recording was made of the song. In 1923, an Irishman who was admitted to the island's Wide Bay clan, Edward Fitzgerald Armitage, translated and published two Badtjala songs; the one that describes Cook's arrival, and another that relates to Matthew Flinders' visit to Fraser Island in 1802. Armitage's translations were published in 1944.

\*

In May 1770, if Cook had known what the Badtjala had to say about where he planned to travel next, the final chapter of his voyage up the eastern coastline might have had a happier ending for him and his crew. They knew Cook was navigating his ship towards a dangerous shoal known as Thoorvoor, later named Breaksea Spit. It was a precursor to the 2300 kilometre-long labyrinth of coral reefs that make up the Great Barrier Reef.

As he navigated past Fraser Island, Cook had sailed over 1200 kilometres since leaving Botany Bay and had yet to find a suitable place to make landfall. Restocking his ship's dwindling supplies was a high priority as the dreaded scurvy began to raise its rancid head on board. But he was also still determined to become the first man to chart this coastline. What he didn't – and couldn't – know was that the entire continent had already been charted by its inhabitants; in song.

## GEMMA CRONIN

*Songlines are like a big web that sits over the whole of Australia. They all interconnect. In the old days when we walked the trails – the Dreaming trails – you'd have to sing the songs of all the land that you went past – of that tree, that rock, that lake, that creek. It's all a picture in the land. We don't need a map, and we don't even need to use the stars to guide ourselves through country. They link us up, from this side of the country, to the other side of the country. Every songline runs into another songline. The practice of song is connected to the Dreamtime story. In this story, the serpent that created land started singing up people and places, when he gets to the end of the song people know where their country begins and ends. Song was also a significant part of exchange between clans. New songs were brought when women from other clans joined the tribe. Some of the songs and stories match up from places as far away as Arnhem Land and the Gold Coast – it's a vast network of exchange and interconnected communication traversing the country.*

Australia is crisscrossed by a network of songlines, or Dreaming tracks that tell of the creation of the land by the Aboriginal ancestors. One songline crosses all the way from Port Augusta in South Australia to Arnhem Land in the far north of the country. Another runs from the coast of Western Australia to Central Australia. The songlines are shared by clans and pass from one tribe's country to another, recording waterholes, hunting grounds and rivers. Custodians of the country have ownership of the songs and it was, and still is, their duty to pass each song on to the next generation.

**GEMMA CRONIN**

*Songs are part of our bloodlines. When we teach our children we teach them first about their body parts, because each part of the body corresponds to a part of the land. Our songs tell about our fingers and hands, which are mangroves coming up out of the mud. Our body is a map for the land.*

Songlines are deeply spiritual. But they also perform a practical function. By memorising the ancestors' journeys and the landmarks they made as they travelled, Aboriginal people commit to memory the paths that lead them safely through country.

The first Europeans who travelled into the interior of Australia were led by Aboriginal guides who followed their songlines and showed the new arrivals the easiest and safest routes with stops at waterholes and hunting grounds. Eventually, these became stock routes, then roads. Today, as travellers take off along Australian highways armed with GPS and Google Maps, most of them are unaware that the roads they're following are quite often songlines.

*

As the *Endeavour* sailed up the coast, Cook had no idea he was also following a songline – the migration route of the whales that cruised along the same currents that were carrying the ship north. Not that this would have been any use to Cook if he had known. Things were going from bad to worse. A brief landing at Bustard Bay on 23 May (near what would one day be the site of the town known as 1770) yielded some water and a serve or two of fish and birds felled by some accurate marksmanship. But little was found in the way of fresh fruit and vegetables. They pushed on, and the pickings became slimmer still. Just south of present-day Mackay on 30 May, Cook was unable to find fresh water. He was getting desperate and gave the barren place a rather forlorn name – 'Thirsty Sound'.

The men on board were getting tetchy. When Cook's clerk, Richard Orton, fell into bed in what can only be assumed was a state of dead drunkenness, person or persons unknown relieved him of his clothes and cropped his ears. Cook was livid, as much for the perceived insult to his authority as for poor Orton's misfortune.

### CAPTAIN JAMES COOK

*[T]he greatest insult that could be offered to my authority in this ship, as I have always been ready to hear and redress every complaint that have been made against any person in the ship.*

Despite threats, entreaties and inducements, nobody fessed up.

By this point, Cook must have been thinking things couldn't possibly get any worse. But he was wrong. When he passed Fraser Island, the Badtjala people knew he was navigating into some of the deadliest waters on the planet.

Cook and his ship had managed to escape relatively unscathed up to this point. But he was about to meet his match.

Beginning halfway up the eastern coast of Australia and running all the way to Torres Strait, the Great Barrier Reef is the world's largest deposit of coral. It's a mass of over 2900 individual

*The Endeavour on the reef, Australia, 1770,* artist unknown (1886). An imaginary impression of the *Endeavour* marooned on the Great Barrier Reef. Once the ship was freed, Cook sent out longboats to recover his anchors – but one was not reclaimed until the twentieth century.
Getty Images, Hulton Archive, 1218507

reefs dotted with nine hundred islands, and it's also the largest structure on the planet made by living organisms. Cook was caught up in what he described in his journal as an '*insane labyrinth*'.

### CAPTAIN JAMES COOK

*A reef such as one speaks of here is scarcely known in Europe. It is a wall of coral rock rising almost perpendicular out of the unfathomable ocean, always overflown at high water generally 7 or 8 feet, and dry in places at low water. The large waves of the vast ocean meeting with so sudden a resistance makes a most terrible surf, breaking mountains high.*

There's a very good reason it's called a 'Barrier' – for sailors who harbour a desire to make it safely to shore, the reef is a daunting obstacle.

It was 11 p.m. on 10 June. Cook had issued his final orders for the night before retiring. Banks and some of the officers were having supper when, as Cook put it, *'The ship struck and struck fast.'* Cook raced up to the deck in his underwear. The mate shouted, *'Up every soul nimbly, for God's sake, or we all perish!'* The crew rolled out of their hammocks and stumbled up into the tropical air. They were eight leagues – about forty-five kilometres – from shore. The men were terrified. No one on board could swim. And even if they survived, if the ship was wrecked beyond salvation and they managed to make it to land, their prospects were less than fantastic.

### SIR JOSEPH BANKS (1743–1820), 1st Baronet, Naturalist and Botanist on Cook's first voyage
*[They were] debarred from a hope of ever again seeing their native country or conversing with any but the most uncivilised savages perhaps in the world.*

Cook's first order was to bring in the sails and make sure the ship was driven no further into the coral. The tide was on its way out and, as the water receded, the *Endeavour* was marooned high and dry on the reef. Cook ordered his men to hoist overboard all but the absolute necessities.

### ALBERTA HORNSBY, Guugu Yimidhirr Nation, Cooktown Re-enactment Association
*They were stuck fast in the coral reef and you can see all the barrels being thrown overboard. They've also thrown over*

*cannons and everything else they could spare – even their*
*food – to make her lighter. The pumps couldn't keep up*
*with the emptying of the water. It would have been a very*
*horrible time for the crew because none of them would*
*have known how to swim, and they knew their lifeboats*
*could only hold a certain number of people.*

About fifty tons of equipment including six cannon, decayed stores and oil jars were thrown into the sea. After the cannon were salvaged in the twentieth century, one of them found a home at the James Cook Museum in Cooktown, along with one of the Endeavour's anchors.

It was remarkable that Cook had managed to navigate so far along the Great Barrier Reef without coming to grief. Of course, this would have been cold comfort to Cook and his men as they attempted to lever the *Endeavour* off the coral.

### DAVID PRYCE, Sailor and Adventurer

*By the time Cook arrived at the Great Barrier Reef, he'd*
*covered a lot of miles. He had learnt a lot of things. But the*
*Great Barrier Reef provides one of the most challenging*
*environments to navigate a ship. To press forward into the*
*reef at night without charts is like Russian roulette. Poor*
*old Cook had no chance. It's remarkable that he got as far*
*as he did. When you approach unknown shoals you've got*
*to be on your toes. That's what Cook was doing everywhere,*
*but when he gets to the reef it's different – it's a network of*
*shoals that just goes on and on and on! He couldn't use the*
*tactic of approaching, negotiating and anchoring offshore*
*somewhere safe, he just had to keep ploughing through.*

*And this is day and night, through the dark. He would have been running a line, listening for breaking water ... trying to suss out the situation every inch of the way.*

Even today, in an era of sat navs and depth sounders, sailors attempting to negotiate the reef call on the expertise of professional pilots who have intimate knowledge of these waters. Although the Indigenous Australians who lived on the coast were intimately acquainted with the perils and potential hazards of the reef and were adept at negotiating their way in and around it, Cook was the first European known to have tackled it, and he had still managed to travel 1700 kilometres from Fraser Island without coming to grief. He was just a few hundred kilometres from Torres Strait and the terminal point of the reef. From there he could have turned the ship westward past the northernmost tip of Australia and headed for the relative safety of Batavia.

It was quite an achievement.

Not that this was any help as the ship rocked and groaned on the coral. Things were desperate.

**SIR JOSEPH BANKS**

*Our situation became now greatly alarming ... The officers however behaved with inimitable coolness void of all hurry and confusion ... All this time [s]he continued to beat very much so that we could hardly keep our legs upon the quarter deck; by the light of the moon we could see her sheathing boards &c. floating thick round her.*

The wholesale evacuation of the ship's stores had done little to improve the *Endeavour*'s prospects. Anyone who's ever had the misfortune of standing on coral in bare feet can imagine what it does to a weighty timber vessel grinding down on its razor-sharp pointy bits.

The longer the ship remained on the reef, the greater the chance it would disintegrate. Banks and others readied to abandon ship.

Then, things began to go their way. After hours of back-breaking work on behalf of every man on board, the Whitby collier proved its mettle. The *Endeavour*'s flat bottom made the ship ungainly and slow, but it also saved the day. At last, the boat floated free of the reef.

But the ordeal wasn't over yet. As the ship broke away from the coral, a breach opened in its timbers and water began to flood the hold. All hands worked the pumps – even Banks and his fellow scientists. Never one to give up when the going got tough, Cook instructed the crew to make a 'fother' – a sail coated with a nasty mix of dung, frayed rope fibres and wool.

**DAVID PRYCE**

*It was a beautiful example of Cook's leadership. One of the junior officers comes up with the idea of fothering – he'd used it before to save a sinking ship. And Cook takes up the recommendation. It probably is the key to the ship's survival.*

The fother was slung beneath the ship's hull over the hole like a giant diaper, then lashed onto the deck. It worked, and Cook was able to negotiate the *Endeavour* to shore.

Cook didn't know just how lucky they were until the crew beached the grievously damaged boat. He then realised that a great chunk of coral had broken off in the hull breach and acted as a plug. Without it, no amount of pumping would have helped and the *Endeavour* most likely would have sunk.

Cook had averted disaster, but he gave the bulk of the credit for the ship's survival to the swift action and discipline of the crew.

### CAPTAIN JAMES COOK

*During the whole time of this distress I must say for the credit of our people that I believe every man exerted his utmost for the preservation of our ship, contrary to what I have universally heard to be the behaviour of seamen who have commonly as soon as a ship is in a desperate situation begin to plunder and refuse all command.*

But a good team requires a good leader, and that's exactly what the *Endeavour* and its crew had. In the many journals written by members of the crew during Cook's three Pacific voyages, there are many laudatory passages praising Cook's stoicism under fire.

### ALEXANDER HOME (c.1739–1823), crew member, Cook's third voyage

*In the midst of the greatest jeopardy [Captain Cook] could judge and reflect calmly and always had the skill and good fortune to extricate himself and his people … By degrees a habit grew upon us of placing such confidence in him, that although surrounded with dangers in shallow seas, fogs and storms we could go calmly to rest placing our safety in the skill and fortune of our leader.*

Cook was the man you wanted at the helm when things went wrong.

*

After the *Endeavour* had limped to shore, Cook feared they might be stranded on the mainland for a year as they attempted to make the ship seaworthy again and find their way back out to the open ocean. Still, he had little choice. On 17 June 1770, the men – accompanied by a menagerie of sheep, pigs, dogs, ducks, hens and a goat – stepped ashore on the southern bank of Waalumbaal Birri, the river that would later be named the 'Endeavour'.

The British ships had found a safe haven when they needed it the most. Cook declared it more than adequate and ordered tents set up on shore for the men who were suffering from scurvy, Tupaia amongst them.

After tucking into the local fare – fish, birds, shellfish, wild bananas and taro – the men who had been feeling somewhat peaky recovered quickly.

As their one means of escape was sitting high and dry with a great hole in its side, the first order of business was to repair the *Endeavour*. After the ongoing struggle to restock provisions along the coast, it must have been a relief to have landed somewhere with a freshwater stream and no shortage of things to eat. The men harvested greens and stocked up on birds, fish and turtles. Within ten days, the necessary repairs to the ship had been made. But the tides and winds worked against them, and it would be over a month before Cook could give the order to depart.

There's no doubt Cook knew how lucky he was to escape disaster on the reef, but he would never know the true extent of his good fortune. He'd unwittingly escaped another potential calamity when he landed on these riverbanks and managed to find the one spot on this part of the coast where local clans forbade the spilling of blood.

According to the Guugu Yimidhirr people, Waalumbaal Birri was made when a coloured python rolled across the landscape and created the river and reefs. The place Cook landed – Waymbuur – was where the clans met to conduct ceremonies and settle disputes.

**ALBERTA HORNSBY**

*For the thirty-two tribal clan groups that make up the Guugu Yimidhirr speaking nation, Waymbuur was a neutral zone. Cook and his crew could have been picked off at any time during their forty-eight days here, but the law dictated that no blood was to be spilt on this land. Women went there to give birth. They settled their disputes. They performed their initiation ceremonies. They had celebrations there. They all shared in the resources of that area. Cook was very fortunate that these laws – Indigenous laws – protected them.*

Because of the spiritual significance of the land where Cook set up his camp, the Guugu Yimidhirr allowed him to go about his business. They didn't make contact with him until 10 July 1770 – three weeks after his arrival.

Over a period of ten days, there were six meetings between Cook and his men and the Guugu Yimidhirr people.

And it was only the men. Although Cook and the crew saw women on the northern shore of the river, they never came over to the British campsite. Forced to focus their attentions on something other than the local womenfolk, the scientists made good use of their time on shore and their brief interactions with the Guugu Yimidhirr men. While Banks and the naturalists collected floral and faunal samples, a twenty-five-year-old artist, Sydney Parkinson, began to write down words from the local language. He also noted that the locals whistled when surprised.

This list of words became part of the first written account of an Aboriginal language. Thanks to Cook's first voyage, over one hundred Guugu Yimidhirr words were brought back to England. When Governor Arthur Phillip embarked with the First Fleet, he carried the list with him. Of course, Phillips was oblivious to the fact that there were hundreds of Aboriginal languages in use across the continent, and so the words would only be useful if he happened to bump into a local from Guugu Yimidhirr country.

*

As their time on shore drew to a close, the British found another way to highlight the chasm that existed between their view of the world and the belief systems of the indigenous people they'd encountered across the Pacific. Under Aboriginal laws, all land and all forms of life are sacred. The right to exploit natural resources is governed by rules that, in part, ensure sustainability. So when the men on board the *Endeavour* helped themselves to twelve turtles from a spot now known as Boulder Reef, the Guugu Yimidhirr were apoplectic.

### ALBERTA HORNSBY

*It was the first time our men had been on board the* Endeavour. *What they saw didn't make them happy at all. There were twelve turtles, all weighing between two and*

> three hundred pounds, and they were taken off a reef that
> Cook called Turtle Reef. But it was not the right time to
> hunt turtles – it was actually a time for breeding, and at
> that time it was so rough and windy that our mob couldn't
> get out to the reef ourselves. They didn't do anything on the
> first day, but the next day they came back with a group of
> ten men. They left their spears with some young boys and
> went on board the Endeavour to try and reclaim two of the
> turtles.

The reef itself is a sacred place and an important part of a creation story shared by five clans. When Cook arrived, it was also a shared fishing and hunting ground, so strict rules and protocols controlled the use of the area. The reef is a long way from the river mouth, and the Guugu Yimidhirr could only bring one or two turtles back to shore in their canoes. This, along with the fact that it was forbidden for the locals to hunt turtles during the breeding season, ensured the turtle population was never over-hunted. That Cook took twelve turtles during the breeding season was beyond the pale. A delegation of local men boarded the *Endeavour* and made their displeasure known, asking Cook to return the turtles to them. He refused and the men stormed off the ship.

When they reached shore, one of the men set fire to the grass around the British camp.

### ALBERTA HORNSBY

> In his journal, Cook says they became angry when they
> were stopped from taking the two turtles. They couldn't kill
> or spill blood on this land. So they went over and grabbed a

*firestick from around the campfire and set fire to the grass*
*around the British camp. It was a sign of frustration – a*
*way to tactfully get rid of the intruders without physically*
*hurting anyone. In this way our people were still following*
*our lore. I could imagine the frustration of Cook as well, I*
*mean they're ready to go – they just want to get out of here.*

Cook prepared to retaliate. And just when a violent confrontation seemed inevitable, something truly extraordinary happened. An elder stepped forward holding a spear without a point.

### ALBERTA HORNSBY

*Out of the scrub came a Waymbuur elder who has the*
*authority to speak for this country. He comes forward and*
*performs a ritual. He collects sweat from under his arms*
*and blows it in the wind. It's a way of asking his ancestors*
*for protection. It's also giving him courage to resolve this*
*conflict. He carries with him a spear that has a tip*
*broken. Although Cook could not understand what he*
*was saying, by his gesture he knew that this man was*
*making an attempt to resolve this conflict. Cook himself*
*calls this 'reconciliation'. When we talk about*
*reconciliation today, you know they set an example in*
*1770 of what can be done.*

The elder was performing a ritual known as *ngaalangun daama*. It was a way of calling for protection while demonstrating a willingness to be friends. Of this moment, Cook wrote: *'I handed the spears back to him which reconciled everything.'*

It was Australia's first reconciliation.

**ERNIE DINGO, Yamatji Nation, Actor**

*If you have a disagreement between a friend over years and years and it festers to a point where you don't even know what the truth is anymore, and you go up to that person and say, 'mate, I'm sorry for all this stupidity – we used to be friends – we could have been better friends but we've wasted all this time bickering and not understanding' ... if we could start a new day right here and now, think of all the positives that could happen. But I don't really understand reconciliation, either. I mean, we didn't do anything wrong. Why should we reconcile? Why is reconciliation an Indigenous thing? It should be a non-indigenous thing.*

Another disaster averted – this time thanks to the magnanimity of the locals – Cook confronted his next challenge. After climbing a hill, he looked out over the reef to try to find a passage back out to the open ocean.

All his survey did was to emphasise the difficulty of what he had to do next.

On 5 August 1770, the *Endeavour* departed the river, surrounded by shoals and reefs in all directions. Cook's nautical skills were stretched to the limit. After narrowly managing to avoid grounding the ship on numerous occasions, he took ten days to find his way out to the open sea.

As Cook sailed away, a fire was set to cleanse the land the British had occupied and chase away any bad spirits they might have left in their wake.

**ALBERTA HORNSBY**

*Joseph Banks noted that all the hills surrounding the Endeavour River were put on fire, and they could see this blazing at night and he said it made a beautiful sight. But for us, it means that they were glad this mob were going. The smoke would have represented a cleansing of their land. That's what the fires tell us about what our people thought of Cook as he was leaving ... you had a nice visit, but it's time for you to go.*

This ritual would be repeated across Australia after European settlement. Decades later in the Kimberley, locals set fire to the land after they saw the first cow walking out of the desert.

Of the Indigenous Australian attitude to the *Endeavour* and its strange occupants, Cook couldn't have said it better than when he observed in Botany Bay that '*All they seemed to want was for us to be gone.*' Who could blame them? And that was before what was to come in Cook's wake.

**GEMMA CRONIN**

*So much of our history is hidden. I remember sitting in a class one day and having a teacher talking about Aboriginal people and how we were dirty and lazy and how you could never get us to work 'cause we went on walkabout. I don't think I even really realised it was me she was talking about.*

From the hill on Possession Island on 22 August 1770, Cook went through the motions and claimed Australia's east coast for the British Crown.

**WARWICK THORNTON, Kaytej Nation,**
**Filmmaker/Director**

*Do I see you as a colonist? No ... God no! Indigenous people grew out of that a long time ago. But we still need someone to blame. It could have been anybody. We could have been here going, 'That dickhead Columbus.' Different continent, but same shit really. It's about empires and the Mother Country. It's much bigger than Cook.*

To the British, the Aboriginal connection to the continent amounted to nothing – despite their tens of thousands of years of occupation and songlines that documented and traced the geographic features of the land.

**SAM NEILL**

*I can't fathom it – but mine are the eyes of a modern man. What possessed Cook, you might ask? Well, the Admiralty's instructions for one. But, their advice also said 'with the consent of the natives'. I don't know how Pacific peoples could agree to a mystifying act in a foreign language made in the name of a king and country they didn't know. But we do know one thing: they weren't asked.*

In the eighteenth century, only marks on paper counted.

**AARON LEGGETT, Dena'ina Tribe, Historian**

*In the Western sense, it's not enough to talk about a place. To write it down – to draw maps – that's how the power of the written word overshadows the oral tradition.*

In the four months Cook had spent travelling along the Australian shore, he had executed thirteen landings. Just one of these was in the territory now bounded by the modern state of New South Wales. The rest fell in Queensland. Cook renamed 120 landmarks, none of which he named for himself. And the coast he mapped today supports over 80 per cent of Australia's population. When all was said and done, Cook should have regarded it as a successful expedition.

But Cook was a man who liked to be in control. Perhaps that's why he struggled with Australia's ambiguity. He didn't really know what to do with it. After he left Possession Island he never set foot on mainland Australia again despite two more voyages to the Pacific and a passing flirtation with the island that would one day be called Tasmania. It's not that he left the continent with a negative assessment of the locals and their circumstances – quite the opposite, actually. He described Aboriginal people as *'timorous and inoffensive ... no ways inclinable to cruelty'*.

And Cook directly contradicted William Dampier's scathing assessment of Indigenous Australians.

**CAPTAIN JAMES COOK**

*[T]he natives of New Holland ... may appear to some to be the most wretched people upon Earth, but in reality they are far more happier than we Europeans; being wholly unacquainted not only with the superfluous but the necessary conveniences so much sought after in Europe, they are happy in not knowing the use of them. They live in a tranquillity which is not disturbed by the Inequality of Condition: The Earth and sea of their own accord furnishes them with all things necessary for life; they covet not*

*magnificent houses, household stuff etc. They live in a warm and fine climate and enjoy a very wholesome air, so that they have very little need of clothing and this they seem to be fully sensible of, for many to whom we gave cloth etc. to, left it carelessly upon the sea beach ... as a thing they had no manner of use for ... they seemed to set no value upon anything we gave them, nor would they ever part with anything of their own for any one article we could offer them; this, in my opinion argues that they think themselves provided with all the necessaries of life and that they have no superfluities.*

\*

As Cook approached the Dutch colony of Batavia, he had many reasons to be fairly pleased with himself.

**DAVID PRYCE**

*There are plenty of people who can sail a ship. But to be able to sail a ship well, and exhibit the leadership skills required to keep everyone together on board for several years in really trying conditions, never knowing whether you're going to survive till the next day or what sort of hazards are going to present themselves ... it's pretty impressive.*

By the measure of the day, Cook had achieved most of what was expected of him when he set out in the *Endeavour*. He had charted the entirety of New Zealand – almost four thousand kilometres of coastline – and was the first Westerner to give shape to Australia's east coast on a European navigational chart. The conditions under which he'd worked were far from ideal. More often than not he had made his measurements and surveyed the coastlines from the dipping and swaying deck of the *Endeavour*. The speed with which Cook had drawn his charts and the accuracy of his work was, in retrospect, remarkable.

When he arrived in Java, the thing that pleased Cook the most was the fact that he had managed to get there without losing a single man to scurvy during the voyage.

His men docked in good health, so much so that despite the fact they had been at sea for over two years, thanks to their captain's strict regime of good hygiene, warm cabins and fresh food the crew of the *Endeavour* arrived in a much better physical state than most of the people who lived permanently in Batavia.

But Cook's delight was short-lived. Once they made it off the ship, the *Endeavour*'s crew succumbed to the grim conditions in the Dutch outpost. One-third of the men who arrived there hale and hearty died between the Dutch East Indies and England. They had circumnavigated the world, only to be felled by disease. Artist Sydney Parkinson, aged just twenty-six. Surgeon William Monkhouse, who had bared his bum at the Māori in New Zealand. The ship's master, Robert Molyneux. The astronomer, Charles Green.

Joseph Banks made it home, of course, although in Batavia he too suffered terribly from the dysentery that carried away so many of his shipmates, writing on 27 October 1770, '*me so weak as scarcely to be able to crawl downstairs*'. But apparently not so weak that he couldn't find time to write in his journal.

After his recovery, Banks returned to England on the *Endeavour* carrying a remarkable companion. In Botany Bay,

Tupaia had saved a young lorikeet from the pot. He'd kept it with him as he travelled up the Australian coastline. When Tupaia, like so many of his shipmates, died of dysentery in Batavia and was buried in an unmarked grave, Banks adopted the orphaned bird.

On Cook's second voyage, as his ship approached New Zealand, the Māori hailed Tupaia. They assumed he was on board the ship they had believed was his. When the Māori in Tolaga Bay learnt of his death, they wrote a mourning lament: *a koe mate auē Tupaia*. 'You have died, alas, Tupaia.'

Tupaia's parrot would outlive him by many years. In England, it became the first Australian bird to be depicted by a European artist. It was painted twice – once by Moses Griffith in 1772 and again by Peter Brown in 1794, when the lorikeet had reached the ripe old age of twenty-four. This means that the bird outlived most of the men who sailed on Cook's first voyage, including its captain.

As for James Cook, after that first voyage he returned to his home in Mile End. An embarrassment of professional recognition followed. He was presented to King George III and promoted to commander. Despite this, in a letter to the Admiralty and demonstrating characteristic modesty, Cook declared that '*the discoveries made in this voyage are not great*'.

Alexander Dalrymple – fellow of the Royal Society, Great Southern Continent cheerleader and confounded would-be commander of the expedition to the South Pacific – agreed with Cook's choleric assessment. When Cook announced that he had cast about and found no evidence of an unknown continent, Dalrymple was scathing. He decided to write to John Hawkesworth, who had written the account of the first voyage. In a letter unambiguously titled 'Letter from Mr Dalrymple to Dr Hawkesworth occasioned by some groundless and illiberal imputations in his account of the late voyage to the South', Dalrymple aired his grievances. He was not a man to pull any punches.

'*The point is not yet determined whether there is or is not a SOUTHERN CONTINENT? although four voyages have been made … at the same time I dare appeal … that I would not have come back in ignorance,*' he wrote. Yes, SHOUTY CAPS were a thing even in the eighteenth century.

Sounds like a challenge, doesn't it? And Cook, as we now know all too well, was never one to walk away from one of those.

# PART FOUR

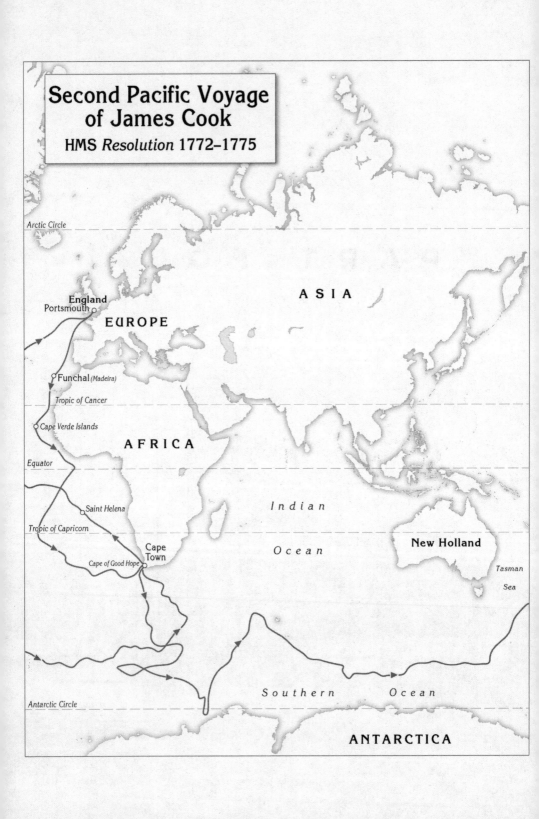

# Second Pacific Voyage of James Cook

## HMS *Resolution* 1772–1775

Arctic Circle

ASIA

England
Portsmouth

EUROPE

Funchal *(Madeira)*

Tropic of Cancer

Cape Verde Islands

AFRICA

Equator

Indian

Saint Helena

Tropic of Capricorn

New Holland

Ocean

Cape Town

Cape of Good Hope

Tasman

Sea

Southern        Ocean

Antarctic Circle

ANTARCTICA

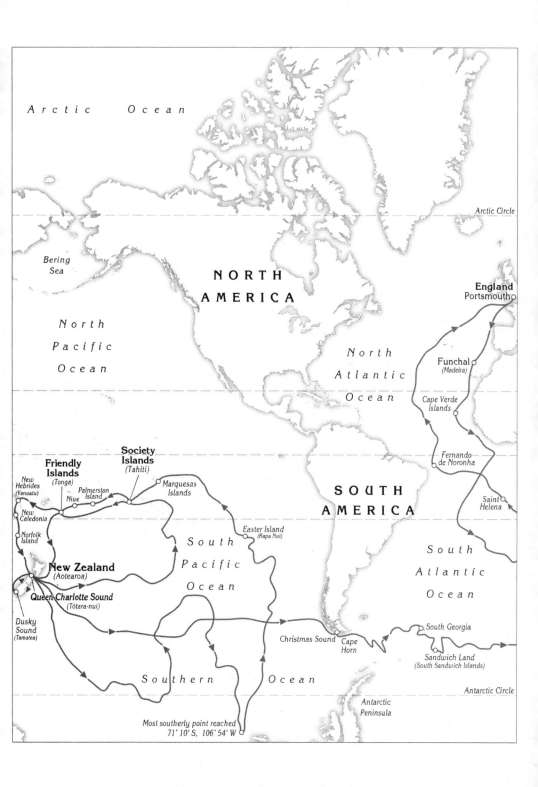

Arctic Ocean

Bering Sea

North Pacific Ocean

NORTH AMERICA

Arctic Circle

England
Portsmouth

Funchal
(Madeira)

North Atlantic Ocean

Cape Verde Islands

Friendly Islands
(Tonga)

Society Islands
(Tahiti)

New Hebrides
(Vanuatu)

New Caledonia

Palmerston Island

Niue

Marquesas Islands

SOUTH AMERICA

Fernando de Noronha

Saint Helena

Norfolk Island

Easter Island
(Rapa Nui)

South Pacific Ocean

South Atlantic Ocean

New Zealand
(Aotearoa)

Queen Charlotte Sound
(Tōtara-nui)

Dusky Sound
(Tamatea)

Christmas Sound  Cape Horn

South Georgia

Sandwich Land
(South Sandwich Islands)

Southern      Ocean

Antarctic Circle

Most southerly point reached
71° 10′ S, 106° 54′ W

Antarctic Peninsula

# TEN

# ENDS OF THE EARTH

*It's becoming clear to me that Cook found the perils of the
sea far less daunting than those on land. Out here amidst
an immense ocean, most of the time he was in full
control. But, still ... what greater adventure would there
be than being on one of Cook's voyages?*

**SAM NEILL**

You've just sailed into port after years at sea. You've cheated
death, seen things no Westerner before you has ever seen,
circumnavigated the globe and changed the course of history.
You'd be forgiven for taking some time out. But you're not James
Cook, are you?

As he dropped anchor, he was already planning his next
voyage.

It's occasionally been suggested that Cook's eagerness to
avoid home may have been caused by a less-than-stellar domestic
situation. But given that Cook and his wife, Elizabeth, were on
opposite sides of the world for thirteen of their seventeen years of
married life and they still managed to chalk up six offspring, this
does hint at what might politely be described as an affectionate

relationship. Cook's commitment to amorous pursuits with Elizabeth and his demonstrated fecundity may also have been assisted by the fact that he – reputedly – never indulged in the sexual exploits pursued by his men. His abstinence in the face of temptation is evidence of the deep love and sense of loyalty Cook felt for his wife. After years at sea, it must have been with considerable relief that he found comfort in her arms.

What seems a more likely explanation for Cook's itchy feet than marital discord is that he knew he still had a fair bit to do in the Pacific. He had barely dipped his big toe into its vast waters and, as far as he was concerned, his work there had only just begun. His prolific record of procreation leaves not a skerrick of doubt – Cook was not a man who liked to leave a job unfinished. Not to mention, his profession was a calling and one he relished, although he was not blind to the hardships of life at sea, writing, 'Were it not for the thrill of discovering even so much as a sand bar, this service would be insupportable.'

Before Cook headed south again, he had to get official backing. Not surprisingly, it was the floral and faunal treasures and anthropological curiosities that Banks had brought back that captured the public imagination – a mighty-tailed, bounding creature the size of a greyhound outshone a painstakingly drafted chart. Whether consciously or not, Banks trumped Cook.

If the men and women on the streets of London were more impressed by Banks' cabinet of curiosities than Cook's prodigious gifts, the same could not be said of Cook's masters at the Admiralty. They appreciated the scale of his achievements and had no qualms about sponsoring another voyage to the Pacific. He must have been relieved. The successful observation of the Transit of Venus and his detailed charting of New Zealand and the east coast of Australia were achievements to crow about. But it rankled that he'd failed to discover the elusive Great Southern Continent – or, for that matter, blow belief in its existence out of the water.

Although he had successfully shown there was no mega-continent lurking in the tropical waters of the Pacific, Cook had yet to venture into the daunting waters of the Southern Ocean where there was still much virgin sea to explore.

After Cook added the east coast to what the Dutch had already recorded of western, southern and northern Australia, he knew the continent wasn't 'Great' enough to qualify as the Great Southern Continent – he was looking for something much more impressive, geographically speaking.

To prove, or disprove, the theory, Cook had to venture into the forbidding waters of the Antarctic Circle. He had the Royal Society's full support. If the Crown was truly to 'Rule Britannia! Britannia, rule the waves', then an Englishman would have to be the one to put the myth of the Great Southern Continent to rest.

**CAPTAIN JAMES COOK**

*Whether the unexplored part of the Southern Hemisphere be only an immense mass of water, or contain another continent, as speculative geography seemed to suggest, was a question which had long engaged the attention, not only of learned men, but of most of the maritime powers of Europe. To put an end to all diversity of opinion about a matter so curious and important, was His Majesty's principal motive in directing this voyage to be undertaken ... to go beyond former discoverers; and continue to Britain the reputation of taking the lead of nations, in exploring the globe.*

But it wouldn't be easy. His experience of the terrifying seas off the tip of Cape Horn as Cook had passed the tip of South America on the first voyage left him in no doubt about the dangers of the undertaking and the brutal conditions he would encounter in the southernmost reaches of the Pacific.

Cook had barely escaped catastrophe on the first voyage and this time round he intended to take a different approach. If the *Endeavour*'s near-disaster on the Great Barrier Reef had taught him one thing, it was that when blithely sailing into unknown waters, it was unwise for him to put all his maritime eggs in just one floating basket. So as he planned the second voyage, Cook outfitted a companion ship, the *Adventure*, to accompany his own, the *Resolution*.

As it happened, the *Adventure* was to live up to its name and chalk up an extensive rollcall of exploits under the oversight of Lieutenant Tobias Furneaux. Furneaux was no stranger to the Pacific. He had accompanied Captain Samuel Wallis on his 1767 journey to Tahiti aboard the *Dolphin*, and had won plaudits when he assumed command during Wallis's protracted bouts of illness on that voyage. With the commander confined to his cabin, Furneaux was the first Englishman to set foot on Tahiti. However, his mission to pilot the 'lifeboat' for Cook and his crew on the *Resolution* was to end rather less successfully.

The two ships sailed from Plymouth in July 1772, heading for the tip of South Africa via the island of Madeira.

The day before he sailed from Cape Town, Cook wrote to his former master, the Quaker sea captain John Walker of Whitby. *'I should hardly have troubled you with a letter was it not customary for men to take leave of their friends before they go out of the world.'* For Cook, this was uncharacteristically fatalistic. It was also a fairly pragmatic – and realistic – perspective.

\*

As the *Resolution* and the *Adventure* steered south, things got very cold very quickly. This made difficult manoeuvres at sea all the more challenging. Cook described the fast-deteriorating conditions on board, writing: *'Our ropes were like wires, sails like board or plates of metal and shivers froze fast in the blocks so that it required our utmost effort to get a top-sail down and up.'* He couldn't do much to alleviate the conditions, but he could help the crew a little. And what better way to keep a frosty company of sailors happy than to ply them with grog? Ignoring the naval regulations that strictly controlled the frequency and volume permitted, Cook gave orders to issue a tot of spirits at any time of the day.

The British Navy – and military forces the world over – recognised the importance of serving up alcohol to its troops, not only in order to boost morale and provide a good dose of Dutch courage, but also as a way of overcoming the soul-destroying boredom and monotony that went hand in hand with long sea voyages. In Cook's time, the daily ration was half a pint of spirits. The sailors were allowed to down half their allocation at noon and were given the rest at six in the evening. Give or take, that amounts to a quarter of a litre of rum a day. To fully appreciate the impact that this might have had on the crew's sobriety, you need to understand that it was 94 per cent proof alcohol. That's right: a quarter of a litre of grog strong enough to topple an elephant, each day. And that doesn't count the lashings of wine

*The Resolution and Adventure Taking in Ice for Water,* William Hodges, 1773–4 (watercolour). William Hodges, official landscape artist on the *Resolution,* was the first professional painter to depict the icy seas of the Antarctic. SLNSW, Mitchell Library, SAFE / PXD 11, IE1006576

and ale. No wonder Cook's journal frequently included the observation, *'More or less drunk all day.'* It wasn't until 1970 that the Royal Navy ended the tradition. As the English privateer Woodes Rogers observed in 1712, *'good liquor to sailors is preferable to clothing'.*

Rogers had been more accustomed to sailing in the Bahamas than the conditions Cook's men were confronting. In the frigid polar climes where clothing was significantly more important than in the tropics, Cook's sailors might well have disagreed with Rogers' assessment. But the extra tots of rum did calm the anxieties of those on board the *Resolution* and *Adventure.* It's unlikely they did anything to alleviate Cook's concerns, though, as massive floating mountains of ice loomed out of the fog, threatening to smash his two timber boats into rafts of matchsticks.

### RICHARD PICKERSGILL (1749?–1779?), Lieutenant, Cook's first and voyages

*[T]he masts sails and ropes were all caked with ice and it constantly snowed which froze as fast as it fell ... Towards the evening we saw a prodigious number of ice islands and before morning the sea was so thick with them that it was with the utmost difficulty we could steer clear of them – good God!*

But icebergs did come in handy for one thing. They provided a way for the men to harvest fresh water, an absolute necessity as they pushed further into the Southern Ocean.

On 17 January 1773, Cook became the first navigator known to have crossed the Antarctic Circle.

### SAM NEILL

*It took another hundred years after Cook crossed the Antarctic Circle for the first explorers to finally walk on this continent. Not hard to see why ... There's no question this is the last place on earth anyone could hope to reach. Many don't even want to ... but being here ... it's immense. It's overwhelming and terrifyingly beautiful.*

Cook recorded the moment in his journal: 'we crossed the Antarctic Circle for at noon we were by observation four miles and a half south of it and are undoubtedly the first and only ship that ever crossed that line'.

**TIM JARVIS AM, Adventurer**

*It was an amazing notion that there was this continent down there and he had the audacity to try and find it in the kind of vessel that he was in. He gets all the way down to seventy-one degrees south, which is further south than modern vessels typically go even today. A couple of years ago we had a steel hull vessel with nuclear power get stuck in the ice further north than Cook achieved in his flimsy thirty-three metre sail-driven vessel. It was incredible, really.*

Soon after, on 8 February, the *Adventure* and the *Resolution* lost sight of each other in Turkish-bathhouse-thick fog. Cook fired his cannon into the soppy gloom but heard nothing in response other than the cracking of ice. It must have been a desolate moment, both for him and for Furneaux, who would sail on to the rendezvous point in New Zealand via a sojourn along the eastern Tasmanian coast first charted by the Dutch explorer Abel Tasman in 1642.

Cook's 'lifeboat' was gone, but he pressed on. There was no improvement in the conditions the men and his boat had to endure.

**CAPTAIN JAMES COOK**

*[With] all the rigging covered with ice and the air excessive cold, the crew however stand it tolerable well, each being clothed with a fearnought jacket, a pair of trousers of the same and a large cap made of canvas & baize, these together with an additional glass of brandy every morning enables them to bear the cold without flinching.*

The more he saw of what lay below the Antarctic Circle, the more convinced Cook became that if there was a hidden continent in the Pacific's southern waters, it wouldn't be a particularly inviting place to set up shop. With the southern winter fast approaching, Cook pulled the pin. There wasn't enough grog on earth to justify continuing. Any further exploration inside the Antarctic Circle would have to wait until summer. After 122 days at sea, his sailors were spent, and the *Resolution* in not much better shape. He turned the ship north and sailed for the rendezvous point in New Zealand.

### SAM NEILL

*[Antarctica is] still the last frontier, much as it was for Cook. And there's a purity that is hard to find anywhere else on the planet. But for how much longer, I wonder?*

\*

It had been three years since Cook had seen the islands known to their Māori inhabitants as Aotearoa. He had made no secret of his affection for New Zealand on the first voyage, and in the journal entries written as he sailed once again into its waters, there's an undertone of giddy euphoria. Or as close as Cook would ever come to being 'giddy', anyway.

### CAPTAIN JAMES COOK

*The weather was delightfully fair and genially warm when compared to what we had lately experienced ... We had long and eagerly wished for the land and its vegetable productions, and therefore could not but eye the prospect before us with peculiar delight, and with emotions of joy and satisfaction.*

During the first voyage, when Cook had passed the place the Māori called Tamatea on the remote south-western tip of New Zealand's South Island, Cook had given it a new name: 'Dusky Sound'.

### SAM NEILL

*[N]othing prepares you for waking up to dawn in Dusky Sound. It's still almost as hard to get to as it was in Cook's day, and it's almost unchanged since the* Resolution *anchored here. This place is one of New Zealand's – indeed, the world's – great treasures.*

When they sailed past on board the *Endeavour*, Banks had made a valiant effort to convince Cook to make a diversion and head into the Sound for a bit of a look around but he was out of luck because Cook had other things on his mind. Not to mention, the prevailing south-western winds meant the captain knew the ship could find itself locked into the fiords with no way out. The naturalist's nose was put out of joint because he suspected that the fertile and remote fiord would offer a plethora of natural delights.

At this early stage of the second voyage, Cook still had the luxury of time, so he decided to explore the Sound he'd been forced to neglect on his previous visit to New Zealand. As the *Resolution* sailed into Dusky Sound in 1773 to the noise of bird song so deafening the men could hardly hear each other speak, Banks's suspicions about the natural wealth of the region were proven correct.

In the autumn of 1773, during the six weeks the *Resolution* spent in the Sound, Cook directed his men to undertake essential repairs and maintenance. They cleared an acre of forest for taking astronomical observations; the stumps of trees they felled on what's now known as Astronomer's Point are still visible today. They cut wood for fuel. They filled casks with fresh water. They repaired torn sails and fired up a forge to mend damaged ironwork. But most importantly, they set up the one thing that every homesick Englishman needs: a brewery. All that was required was a sheltered anchorage, a running stream and some fresh greens. Although the men's favourite tipple was rum, without a ready supply of sugar cane, they were restricted to beer.

### CAPTAIN JAMES COOK

*We also began to brew beer from the branches or leaves of a tree, which much resembles the American black-spruce. From the knowledge I had of this tree, and the similarity it bore to the spruce I judged that, with the addition of … juice of wort and molasses, it would make a very wholesome beer and supply the want of vegetables.*

This alcohol was more than just a distraction and a diversion for the sailors. As explained by the first lieutenant, Robert Cooper, in Dusky Sound the beer was *'intermixed with the tea plant'*, being manuka, or *Leptospermum scoparium*. When incorporated into the brewing process, it was thought that fresh greens like manuka contributed to the fight against scurvy. The other benefit of alcoholic beverages is that they stay fresh a great deal longer than water, which has a nasty habit of stagnating. If you've ever fished a full water bottle out of your gym bag and taken a swig before realising that it's been in there for a month, you can imagine what fresh water tasted like after an extended period in a wooden cask stashed in a ship's hold.

**SAM NEILL**

*The geography here means it's a hard region to access. Neither Māori nor later Europeans ever made permanent settlements here. Cook saw perhaps twenty Māori at most here. His only contact was with a small extended family including an older man and a woman (who was either his daughter or young wife) and who eventually came on board. The man was intensely curious about the* Resolution's *construction and muskets while the young girl struck up with a pretty midshipman. But it was a case of mistaken identity. She thought he was a girl and he thought she was flirting.*

During a period of such intensive activity on land, it might seem surprising that Cook and his men encountered only twenty or so Māori in the Sound. The locals that made the biggest impact on the *Resolution*'s crew while they were anchored in Dusky Sound were the fiord's avian residents, if only because the cacophony of their singing was so deafening that the sailors could barely hear themselves think.

Geographically speaking, little has altered since Cook visited in 1773. But the same can't be said for the bird life. Cook got the extinction ball rolling when the *Resolution* sailed into the Sound. Sadly, it wasn't just the two-legged mammals that found their way to shore. Rats took advantage of the situation and abandoned ship, scampering into the undergrowth where they found themselves in rodent heaven with an abundance of freshly laid eggs and vulnerable fledglings to feast upon.

**SAM NEILL**

*Now the birds are gone, thanks to the early European settlers who introduced rabbits then stoats to control the rabbits. The stoats made their way here to predator-free paradise. A vast forest supporting millions and millions of birds, whose eggs could be eaten with little effort. Stoats are little buggers who can also swim ... several kilometres. So they got around.*

\*

With the *Resolution* repaired, supplies replenished and the crew rested, Cook gave orders to set sail and head north towards his favourite anchorage in the Pacific. Queen Charlotte Sound was the designated rendezvous point where Cook hoped to locate his misplaced support vessel. As the *Resolution* entered the Sound, its cannon were fired as Cook crossed his fingers. With what must have been tremendous relief, he heard a volley of shots in reply. Furneaux shared his commander's relief. '*Both ships felt an uncommon joy at our meeting after an absence of fourteen weeks,*' he wrote in his journal that evening.

From Queen Charlotte Sound, Cook and his men wisely decided to head further north to warmer climes for winter. Both ships sailed to Tahiti, then on to Tonga. But Cook hadn't given up on *Terra Australis*, even if it was proving to be just as *Incognita* as anticipated.

In October 1773, as the southern hemisphere summer approached, the *Resolution* and *Adventure* turned towards New Zealand again, intending to pause there before resuming their mission to the Antarctic Circle. On their approach to Queen

Charlotte Sound, a fierce storm whipped up mountainous seas and destructive winds, battering the two ships and pummelling the unfortunate crews. Once again, Cook lost sight of the *Adventure*. Furneaux's recurring inability to keep track of his commander might have looked deliberate, if not for the fact that given what was about to transpire, the *Adventure* could have done with a companion ship of its own.

Left to his own devices, Furneaux dropped anchor in Ship Cove with the vain hope Cook might once again be able to track him down. Being a responsible captain, Furneaux made good use of this downtime and set his men to work replenishing stores. Ten men set off on board a small cutter in search of wild greens in Whareunga Bay, named 'Grass Cove' by Cook.

When the foraging sailors failed to return to the ship, a search party was dispatched. Finding a clutch of food baskets bound up on shore, the would-be rescuers cut them open. Inside was packed fresh meat and fern root, ready to roast in the *hangi* (pit ovens) that were smoking on the beach. The crewmen hoped against hope it was dog flesh, but a human hand tattooed 'T.H.' confirmed their worst fears – in Tahiti, sailor Thomas Hill had got himself a tattoo.

Horrified, the rescue party took their launch to Grass Cove. After shooting volleys of gunfire in an effort to disperse hundreds of Māori people gathered on the shore, the sailors stepped onto the beach. They were greeted by what Lieutenant James Burney described as *'such a shocking scene of carnage & barbarity as can never be mentioned or thought of, but with horror'*. Dogs were gnawing at the slain sailors' entrails while body parts – livers, heads, eyes, hearts and lungs – were sizzling on the coals of open fires.

**JOHN MARRA, crew member,**
**Cook's first and second voyages**

*The lieutenant, not thinking it safe to trust the crew in the dark, in an open boat, within reach of such cruel barbarians, ordered the canoes to be broken up and destroyed; and after carefully collecting the remains of our mangled companions, they made the best of their way from this polluted place.*

The human remains were buried at sea, before the *Adventure* turned tail and returned to Britain, arriving home in July 1774.

Things might have turned out differently if Cook and Furneaux had managed to join forces again in Queen Charlotte Sound. As it happened, Cook had been there but left just four days before the *Adventure* arrived. He must have spent the rest of the voyage wondering – and, surely, worrying – about what had happened to his consort vessel. For all he knew, Furneaux and his men had ended up at the bottom of the Pacific. Although it was surely quite a relief to the generally unflappable commander to find that Furneaux had found his way back home, the grisly encounter in Grass Cove would have grim repercussions for Cook's third voyage.

\*

As Cook cut through the waves, he couldn't have imagined the fate that lay in store for the men on the *Adventure*. If he had, he may well have delayed his departure. But 'Resolution' was more than just the name of his ship. With the onset of more clement weather, Cook headed south again, determined to put the myth of the Great Southern Continent to rest. On 30 January 1774, he reached a latitude of 71°10'S. It was the furthest south ever reached by any European voyage of exploration.

> ### TIM JARVIS AM
>
> *You can't really blame him for wanting to go out in search of new things and pursue his spirit of adventure. He was so driven that he couldn't resist. I think in life you're always trying to navigate your way through by pushing to see what's out there. It doesn't matter what the discipline is, you know the journey of exploration is something that we all do and sometimes not finding something teaches you something as well.*

A Swedish naturalist, Anders Sparrman, and midshipman George Vancouver – who would go on to make quite a mark in North America – both claimed they were at the southernmost point of the *Resolution* when it got there.

Despite a close encounter with an errant iceberg, Cook pushed on. Over the course of the second voyage, Cook would cross the Antarctic Circle twice more, before he confidently reached the conclusion that the South Pacific was not hiding a large body of land. Yes, there was Antarctica, a continent that – in a journal entry written on his return journey – he would later confidently predict existed. He was certain '*there is a tract of land near the pole, which is the source of most of the ice which is spread over this vast Southern Ocean*'. But thanks to his rigorous search, Cook knew that any land at the South Pole was too small and far too cold for anyone to worry about.

Antarctica's isolation and desolation would prove to be its greatest blessing. It is the only continent without a resident indigenous population, and no single country claims sovereignty over it. It's one of the few places on earth that has never seen war and where the interests of science are prioritised above all else. The Antarctic Treaty of 1959 calls for it to be preserved as *'a natural reserve, devoted to peace and science'*. Maintaining that status has, until recently, been relatively easy. Few people have shown much interest in Antarctica other than scientists and those addicted to extreme sports. But with the onset of global warming, Antarctica's climate is less daunting than it once was, and rapacious global powers are eyeing its untapped mineral wealth.

In the eighteenth century, Antarctica was the world's greatest uncharted wilderness. Pushing through the pack ice, navigating through the fog and avoiding icebergs was about as difficult as you could get from a nautical perspective. Cook had pushed his men to the outer limits of endurance. Food was running out, and the crew was ailing. Cook himself was also suffering. Although his cast-iron constitution was a thing of legend, by the time the *Resolution* departed the Antarctic Circle, he was in bad shape.

It was naturalist Johann Forster who saved the day. He suspected that what Cook needed was fresh meat. At that point, the only livestock on board was Forster's own, favourite, dog. Dog was a much sought after delicacy in Polynesia, and it had become a staple on board Cook's ships, generally flavoured with garlic. When he returned to Europe, Forster himself championed the idea of Europeans tucking into dogs – and cats. And despite the fact that the relationship between Cook and Forster had been fairly frosty, he willingly surrendered his pet to the cooking pot. Happily, the dog didn't die in vain: a canine casserole proved to be just the remedy Cook needed.

Feeling less peaked, Cook directed the men to turn eastwards to the outer reaches of Polynesia. On Rapa Nui, named Easter Island in 1722 by the Dutch explorer Jacob Roggeveen, Cook was astounded to realise that the people living on this incredibly remote island were also Polynesian.

### SAM NEILL

*Recognising the inhabitants as Polynesian, Cook was astonished that the ancient seafarers made it this far east. Today it's thought they reached the coast of South America and back. How else to account for the sweet potato – a staple in the Polynesian diet but native to the Americas?*

Cook and his men felt that they had also been to the ends of the earth. And they decided it was an occasion worth commemorating. On the first voyage, the crew of the *Endeavour* had been fascinated by the Polynesian tradition of tattooing. When the *Resolution* dropped anchor on Tahiti later in the second voyage, they got themselves a star tattoo. They were marking themselves as members of an exclusive group – a brotherhood of men who had seen and done things together that no other could understand. It was an expression of their camaraderie and evidence of their shared experience.

### JOHN ROBSON, Map Librarian,
### University of Waikato

*If your daughter brought one of Cook's crew home to meet the family, you'd probably have been appalled. They were not necessarily the cream of the crop of English or even European manhood. They were young men, most of whom were not particularly well educated, who had been cooped up in a cold and wet ship for months at a time. But Cook did manage to win his crew's trust. They saw him as a man who had risen from the ranks, so if he sent them up the mast to do something, they knew he himself had done it at one time. He knew it was a frightening experience. He would have built up a lot of trust that way.*

As one midshipman wrote at the end of the voyage:

*I will here do them the justice to say that no men could behave better, under every circumstance than they did, the same must be said of the officers; and I will add that I believe there never was a ship, where for so long a period, under such circumstances, more happiness, order and obedience was enjoyed.*

As captain, Cook must be credited – in part, at least – with establishing an environment on board in which happiness and order reigned.

# ELEVEN

# THWARTED AMBITIONS

*This is an ambitious man who wants to leave his mark on the world. Every distant latitude he charted added to the map of his ambitions. He would not yet admit this but his actions speak volumes. Cook wished to make his own name synonymous with the name of the Pacific Ocean. There is no question that he achieved that.*
**SAM NEILL**

Cook's second voyage was underpinned by one thing – ambition. And the thing about ambition is that it's not at all unusual for it to be frustrated, not to mention frustrating. Although Cook might have liked to discover the Great Southern Continent, he got the next best thing. As he sailed away from the Antarctic Circle for the final time, he knew he had confirmed once and for all that this continent was nothing more than a cartographer's pipe dream. But as one imaginary continent vanished from the hypothetical horizon forever, Cook also understood that he was shedding light on another important and very real, if also very watery, world. You win some, you lose some.

The maritime possessions of the Polynesian residents of the Pacific would become a crucial bridge for Britain's expansion into Asia. Although Cook, cut off from the homeland, was quite unaware of the renewed sense of urgency in Westminster, the lands he was charting would be the British Empire's saving grace, filling in for the American colonies whose time was fast drawing nigh. In December 1773, as Cook turned his attention to Antarctica for the second time, Boston was having its Tea Party. Considering that the War of Independence kicked off about a year and a half later, Britain's control of its American colonies was on borrowed time. And that made the Pacific all the more important to Mother England.

That doesn't mean that the well-established Pacific nations were planning to give in without a fight. They harboured their own ambitions. Anchored in the shadows cast by the hundreds of monolithic stone statues looming above the barren landscape of Rapa Nui, Cook could be in no doubt that the race of determined and brave people – who had settled this island at the furthest edge of their world – would have their own, very clear, ideas about how their future should look. This was true of all Polynesians, including those in the 170-island-strong archipelago of Tonga.

The first European encounter with Tonga occurred in 1616 when Willem Schouten and Jacob Le Maire, sailed by the Niua Islands. In 1643 Abel Tasman visited the island of Tongatapu and bestowed upon it the name 'New Amsterdam Island'. With nary a canal, a windmill or a clog in sight, the poor man must have been suffering severe homesickness. Tasman warmed to the Tongans, describing the locals as *good and peaceful people*.

These early visits made quite an impact on the locals. Today the Tongan word for white-skinned foreigners is *pālangi*, a term recorded by Cook in a phrase he transcribed, *'towacka no papalangie'*, and interpreted to mean 'cloth ships', referring to the billowing white sails that carried European vessels to Tongan shores.

When the Europeans began crisscrossing the Pacific, Tonga was a local superpower, and the island of Tongatapu its capital and home to its supreme leader. Blessed with fertile volcanic soils and cooperative prevailing winds that allowed its navigators to journey across the Pacific with ease, Tonga established itself as a wide-ranging maritime chiefdom reaching as far Uvea Island (named Wallis Island by the Europeans), Fiji's Lau Islands and Samoa. Tongan naval might was so impressive that its tentacles extended across almost three thousand kilometres of open ocean to strike fear into the hearts of the Melanesian inhabitants of the Solomon Islands.

### PRINCESS KALANIUVALU – LADY FOTOFILI,
#### Tongan Royal Family

*It's a story that's told from one generation to the other. It is a significant thing that Cook came here, because his encounter with Pau proves that our history was actually here ... it was a fact that there was a Tu'i Tonga here and this is something we're proud of.*

Cook was to visit Tonga three times – twice on his second voyage, and once on his third. On this, his second voyage, he stopped by the islands in 1773 after his sojourn in Dusky Sound, and then followed up with another quick visit in 1774.

Both times Cook was concerned principally with restocking his depleted ships with water and fresh food, of which there was no shortage on Tonga. Cook was so impressed by the fertility of the islands that on his third voyage in 1777 he decided to stick around a little longer, parking his ships on Tongatapu for two and a half months.

**CAPTAIN JAMES COOK**

*I thought I was transported into one of the most fertile plains in Europe, here was not an inch of waste ground, the roads occupied no more space than was absolutely necessary ... Nature, assisted by a little art, nowhere appears in a more flourishing state than at this isle.*

His men were also much taken by Tonga and its inhabitants, with the surgeon David Samwell falling back on the well-worn trope of likening the tropical islands to the mythological paradise of ancient Greece.

**DAVID SAMWELL (1751–1798), Welsh Naval Surgeon on Cook's third voyage**

*Nothing can be more agreeable than the enclosures in which their houses stand, round which the breadfruit & plantain trees grow & extend their friendly shade over the natives ... Such enchanting prospects does this little isle afford that it may be said to realise the poetical descriptions of the Elysian Fields in ancient writers, it is certainly as beautiful a spot as imagination can paint.*

Cook formed quite an attachment to the archipelago, naming it the 'Friendly Isles' because, as he put it: *a lasting friendship seems to subsist among the inhabitants and their courtesy to strangers entitles them to that name*.

> **PRINCESS KALANIUVALU – LADY FOTOFILI**
>
> *Captain Cook named us the Friendly Islands, and as all those years passed and centuries passed we are still referred to as the Friendly Islands and we live by that and everyone is proud of being friendly.*

Compare that with the name Cook came up with for Niue – 'Savage Island'. He must have been in a very uncharitable mood that day. But he certainly viewed Tonga most favourably and reciprocated what he thought of as the locals' friendship with generous gifts, including – according to local legend – a giant Madagascan tortoise. He gifted the lumbering beast to Tonga's paramount chief, or Tu'i Tonga. It was named Tu'i Malila (King of the Residence), and it's said to have survived to a ripe old age, wandering around the palace grounds until its death in the 1960s of natural causes.

> **PRINCESS 'OFEINA-'E-HE-LANGI, Tongan Royal Family**
>
> *The tortoise was brought here by Captain Cook. It ended up with the King and was brought over to the palace in the 1920s. I grew up seeing that tortoise outside. And it was brought out when Queen Elizabeth came over, and it was presented to her. He went through a lot. He's been through a fire, was hit by a horse, and I think he was blind when he died.*

Today Tu'i Malila's remains are preserved in the Tongan museum.

Cook was blissfully unaware that while he was basking in the convivial hospitality of his newfound Tongan acquaintances, the chieftains of the 'Friendly Isles' were planning to become decidedly less friendly. Cook had laid the seeds for this turnabout himself. The standard approach when meeting a new group of locals was to impress upon them the superiority of British weapons.

**CAPTAIN JAMES COOK**

*The best method in my opinion to preserve a good understanding with such people is first to show them the use of fire arms and to convince them of the superiority they give you over them and to be always upon your guard; when once they are sensible of these things, a regard for their own safety will deter them from disturbing you.*

This may well have been an effective way to discourage a futile attack on a British vessel in the short term. But it had the potential to have another, less positive, outcome they certainly didn't foresee. Imagine you're a fierce and proud warrior standing on the beach. The peculiar pale-skinned strangers who've just landed on your island put on a display of military might featuring an assortment of weapons more powerful than any you've seen, even in your wildest fantasies. You're left in no doubt about their capacity to do colossal damage. What are you going to do? Do you doff your cap, turn tail and succumb? Of course not! Ambition will out. You'll find a way – any way – to get your hands on those weapons of mass destruction. And that's exactly what happened.

During his extended stay in Tonga in 1777 during his third voyage, Cook accepted an invitation from the great chief, Finau, to attend a celebration on the island of Lifuka. It was a right royal knees-up, and Cook and his fellow officers enjoyed the entertainment immensely. Cook lavished praise on the Tongan performances, acknowledging they would have 'met with universal applause in a European theatre'. He had no reason to suspect that anything was amiss. Having delighted in a lovely evening of fine food and entertainment, he and his men retired for the night.

What they didn't know – and, in Cook's case, never would – was that they had narrowly escaped a plot to murder them while they were distracted by the delightful dinner and show.

We now know this thanks to the misadventures of a young British sailor, the aptly named William Mariner. At the tender age of fifteen, Mariner took to sea aboard the British privateer ship *Port au Prince*. A privateer was basically a pirate with a letter of sanction from the British Crown, so such ships were armed to the gills. When the *Port au Prince* anchored in Tonga in 1806, the captain was clubbed to death, the crew murdered, and the ship relieved of its cannon and ironwork. This was what had been planned for an unsuspecting Cook and his men. The cannon were then used in the intertribal wars raging across Tonga and, legend has it, today reside at the former residence of the British High Commission in Tonga.

The man leading the Tongan charge was Finau, the son of the man also known as Finau, who Cook had befriended, and he gave the order to save Mariner's life – because the Tongans knew they needed someone to show them how to work the cannon. Along the way, Finau became fond of Mariner, who reminded him of a deceased son. He gave the young Englishman his son's name –

Toki 'Ukamea (Iron Axe) – and adopted him as a member of his household. During the four years Mariner lived on Tonga, he became fluent in the local language, and was given his own estate on the islands. He remained there until a passing ship offered him passage back to England, and Finau permitted him to leave. Upon his return to England, a book was published that recounted Mariner's experiences and revealed the fate Cook had narrowly escaped.

When Cook left Tonga in July 1777, he wrote: '*took leave of the Friendly Islands and their inhabitants after a stay of between two and three months, during which time we lived together in the most cordial friendship*', and concluded that '*the advantages we received by touching here were very great*'. He had no idea what Finau intended to do to him, which is probably for the best.

### PRINCESS 'OFEINA-'E-HE-LANGI
*Was it good that Cook came here? Probably … I mean eventually somebody would have turned up, and I'd rather have Cook than somebody else who came with a gun and took us by force. So, yes, I would say it was a good thing.*

\*

After departing Tonga on his second voyage in 1774, Cook set sail for a group of islands first spotted by the Spanish navigator Pedro de Queirós, who meandered about the Pacific in 1605 and 1606 in search of – you guessed it – *Terra Australis*. Affected by the quixotic optimism that characterised so many early explorers, Queirós landed on Vanuatu's largest island in 1606 and declared it part of the Great Southern Continent. The next European visitor in 1768 was the navigator Louis Antoine de Bougainville – the Frenchman who had felt Tahitian sand between his toes prior to Cook.

In 1774, Cook carried with him the charts these first visitors had drafted on their voyages. Over a period of six weeks he sailed past or visited nearly all the islands in the archipelago he named the New Hebrides. This name would persist on Western maps until Vanuatu won its independence in 1980.

### JOHNNY KOANAPO, Vanuatu Politician

*After Cook, Europeans realised you could travel beyond the horizon without falling into a bottomless pit. And so they started to come here. They found a lot of resources on the islands and took them to their own countries. But I don't think we can blame any explorer for that.*

Cook's attempts to land on two islands – Malekula and Eromanga – were unsuccessful by any measure.

### SAM NEILL

*Cook's contact with the people of Vanuatu was equally volcanic. At Eromanga, it's as bad as it gets. Threatened by men with darts and bows and arrows, Cook aims at one with his musket. It doesn't fire so he orders the rest of his men to shoot. Perhaps the extreme state of nature in which the people of Vanuatu lived brought out something raw in Cook. Whatever the reason, he is in dangerous territory. He's at risk of being overwhelmed and this time gets away with it.*

Heavily armed locals kept Cook's men at bay, as the brandishing of wooden weapons was answered by cannon fire and lead shot. Cook was at a loss. This was new territory, figuratively and literally. The first people who settled Vanuatu arrived 3300 years or so prior to Cook, and they were the ancestors of the people Cook encountered when he arrived there in 1774. They were Melanesian and, like the Aboriginal people Cook encountered in Australia, they had no cultural relationship whatsoever with the Polynesian Pacific Islanders. They spoke different languages and had different customs. So unfortunately for Cook and his men, when they dropped anchor in Vanuatu their storehouse of cultural and linguistic knowledge was useless.

### SAM NEILL

*Travelling west from Tonga, Cook was leaving the familiar zone of Polynesia for an entirely new world. Reaching Vanuatu he was desperate for water. Meeting with fierce resistance at the first two islands he reacted as always with musket fire, leaving wounded islanders – some fatally. Then, surprisingly, here at Tanna things went well. One lone man paddled out to the* Resolution *with a gift of coconuts. Cook's luck persisted but only because, unbeknownst to him, he was fulfilling a prophecy.*

Cook, true to character, persisted. On 5 August 1774, he steered the *Resolution* towards the island of Tanna and the flame-spitting, smoke-billowing cone-shaped summit of its resident and very active volcano, Mount Yasur. It put on quite a show against a soundscape of ominous rumbling as it propelled molten lava into the air. Cook couldn't resist. He tacked along the coast until he found a likely harbour, dropping anchor in Uea, which he promptly renamed for his trusty vessel: '*I named the harbour, Port Resolution after the ship as she was the first whoever entered it.*'

As Cook clambered down into his launch with an escort of men armed to the teeth, the islanders watched from the shore in complete silence. The locals were naked, other than some curious genital embellishments that were impressive enough to inspire an extensive journal description from Cook.

### CAPTAIN JAMES COOK

*The men go naked, it can hardly be said they cover their natural parts, the testicles are quite exposed, but they wrap a piece of cloth or leaf round the yard [nautical slang for the penis] which they tie up to the belly to a cord or bandage which they wear round the waist just under the short ribs and over the belly and so tight that it was a wonder to us how they could endure it.*

Eventually a handful of canoes approached the *Resolution* cautiously and an old man threw a coconut towards the British. This wasn't just an offering of food to a starving boatload of sailors – it was a tribute. Traditional cosmological beliefs on Tanna hold that the world is a sea scattered with islands capped off with a domed sky; the world beyond the horizon line belongs to the spirits. So when white-skinned creatures appeared over the horizon, they assumed they were spiritual beings.

The coconut was a ritual gesture, and the man who made it, Paowang, would become Cook's envoy on Tanna. As Cook reciprocated with gifts from the *Resolution*'s stores, seventeen outrigger canoes surrounded the launch and the islanders set to trying to strip everything they could from the boat, including the anchor buoys and the British ensign from the launch's bow.

Apparently being a spirit didn't mean that living human beings left your stuff alone. Shots were fired, and the warriors fled into the forest.

The sun rose the next day and revealed a daunting sight. Journal accounts from that day estimated that nine hundred or so armed locals stood on the shore divided into two distinct groups. It didn't look good for Cook and his men.

**CHIEF SAM USUA ESKAR, Tanna Traditional Owner**

*When Cook landed there were two different tribal groups who came down to the beach. My tribe were coastal people and their beliefs were tied to the sea. We were accustomed to visitors and accepted and welcomed Cook. But the other tribe, the Enkahi, came from the hinterlands and were fierce warriors who practised cannibalism and traded in human bodies. During his stay Cook was warned to stay within the safe zone defined by my tribe. The volcano in particular was off limits.*

But Paowang again approached the *Resolution*, bringing with him another offering for the pale-skinned visitors: yams, sugar cane and coconuts. In exchange, Cook gave him a red Tahitian outfit that must have made him the envy of his peers. After Paowang left the ship, Cook decided to go with him. He ordered the marines and a group of well-armed sailors to attend him as he went to shore. As the two groups of warriors from different worlds faced off against each other, Cook stepped onto the beach, then Paowang and two other men gestured towards a pile of taro roots, yams and bunches of plantains, a traditional welcoming gift. The old man had laid out a path with reeds on the beach leading from the water to the offering, and he beckoned for Cook to approach.

With one group of warriors clearly hostile and the other apparently benign, and both advancing towards the British despite Paowang's admonitions that they stay back, Cook ordered his men to fire shots above the heads of the aggressive group on their right. The men ran away, other than one foolhardy warrior who bared his backside at the strangers, proving that 'mooning' is a universal gesture of contempt. He copped a buttock full of lead shot for his trouble.

Tribal divisions on the island were numerous and they were strong. The passive group on the beach that day were coastal people whose beliefs were tied to the sea. The other tribe were the Enkahi who lived inland and were fierce warriors and cannibals who ran a hot trade in human bodies. Paowang warned Cook not to venture away from the relative safety of the beach. The volcano, in particular, was out of bounds, which to an inquisitive soul like Cook must have been almost unbearable.

**CAPTAIN JAMES COOK**

*These people are yet in a rude state; and, if we may judge from circumstances and appearances, are frequently at war, not only with their neighbours, but among themselves; consequently must be jealous of every new face. I will allow there are some exceptions to this rule to be found in this sea; but there are few nations who would willingly suffer visitors like us to advance far into their country.*

\*

During the two weeks they stayed on Tanna, Cook and his men were impressed by the fertility and beauty of the island. The naturalist Forster wrote that: '*Quiros had great reason to extol the beauty and fertility of this country, it is indeed in appearance one of the finest in the world.*' Forster was also responsible for the misnomer that stuck: Tanna. Pointing at the ground, he asked a villager what its name was. A helpful islander gave him the word *tanna*, meaning 'earth' or 'ground' in one of the local languages. If it had a name at all it was Ipari, which it was called by the residents of the neighbouring islands. But the people living on Tanna itself had no sense of the island having a separate identity that required a name.

A relationship of sorts developed between Cook, his men and the locals. As would happen at other times on Cook's voyages, music was the one language the two groups of people had in common. The villagers called upon the crew to sing for them, enjoying the German and English ditties but transported to ecstasy by naturalist Anders Sparrman's Swedish songs. For their part, the men on board were transfixed by the beauty of the local songs and the melodious playing of reed flutes. When they left Tanna, Forster wrote of the bonds he believed had been formed: '*In a few days they began to feel pleasure in our conversation, and a new disinterested sentiment of more than earthly mould, even friendship, filled their heart.*'

In a moment of quiet contemplation, Cook expressed a more rational view of the nature of the relationships they were building with the people of the Pacific and the imbalance of power inherent in their encounters. It's a telling insight into the thinking of a fair-minded and circumspect man. Cook was beginning to see the Pacific and its people through different eyes.

### CAPTAIN JAMES COOK

*We found these people hospitable, civil, and good-natured, when not prompted to a contrary conduct by jealousy; a conduct I cannot tell how to blame them for, especially when I considered the light in which they must view us. It was impossible for them to know our real design; we enter their ports without their daring to oppose; we endeavour to land in their country as friends, and it is well if this succeeds; we land, nevertheless, and maintain the footing we have got, by the superiority of our firearms. Under such circumstances, what opinion are they to form of us? Is it not as reasonable for them to think that we are come to invade their country, as to pay them a friendly visit? Time, and some acquaintance with us, can only convince them of the latter.*

As for the locals, the restrictions they imposed on trade tell us much more about their attitude to the uninvited guests than a German naturalist's sentimental reflections.

Early on in the piece, Paowang presented Cook with a small pig. The men would have been thrilled because there was only so much salted meat and hard tack they could stomach. Imagine their horror, then, when they realised that in Melanesia the sacred status of the pig meant it was shared with an ally in anticipation of a gift of equal or greater value. But all Cook brought to the table were mirrors and 'trinkets'. Aside from the novelty value of these bits and bobs, which was slim at best, the locals had no interest in them. And so that would be the last pig Cook and his men would see on Tanna. In desperation, Forster attempted to trade an axe for one, but as he put it: *'they were deaf to this proposal, and never sold us a single hog during our stay'.*

When the white-skinned creatures had first arrived, the locals had treated them with superstitious awe because of their belief that these creatures were ancestor spirits.

### JOHNNY KOANAPO

*When Captain Cook landed here, people looked at him – obviously he looked different, and he came in with a much bigger boat than the canoes people were using at that time. They were amazed but they also wanted to chase him out. But Captain Cook eventually came into the bay and came ashore. It's the way people talk about it here – the arrival of a white man who was different from the way they look. So they began to imagine that there were people in other parts of the ocean who looked different from us.*

Paowang and those of his brethren who welcomed Cook to their shores nonetheless avoided touching the strangers, and if they accepted an object from them, they received it between two leaves and refused to touch it with bare skin. But as time passed, the islanders realised the men on board had very human failings – they got hot, they got tired and they got hungry, and they didn't understand the local language. The Tannanese then knew they were mere mortals. It must have been quite a disappointment. They had been expecting that these spirit beings would respond to their meagre offerings with vastly superior and sacred gifts.

\*

In the Pacific, Cook had become accustomed to a ritual of exchange that was far more complicated in Vanuatu. Paowang gave Cook's men permission to cut down wood and fill two casks of water, but he warned them off the coconut trees. Territoriality was a powerful motivator for the indigenous people of Vanuatu – and that was a problem for Cook. Obtaining fresh supplies was an absolute necessity, whether by trade or by force.

By 1774 Cook figured he had the process down pat, as did his men. And the barter system extended to more than just daily necessities. The crew worked out very quickly that what they needed to accumulate were the red feathers that were sacred in Polynesia. There was nothing more enticing to a Tahitian woman – even the high-born ladies who had scorned iron nails were happy to exchange their affections for red feathers. The crew knew this all too well. And when the *Resolution* sailed into Tahitian waters again on Cook's second voyage, the men were hanging from the rigging as they waved bunches of red feathers to the women who came out in canoes to greet them. The men on board all deserted their posts as the ship was swamped by a tidal wave of women clambering on board. With no hands on deck, the *Resolution* smashed into the coral reef that ringed the lagoon.

Cook was livid. He did so much jumping up and down and stamping that the crew memorialised it with a name. *Heiva* – the ceremonial Tahitian dance.

**JAMES TREVENEN (1760–1790), Midshipman,
Cook's third voyage**

*Heiva the name of the dances of the Southern Islanders,
which bore so great a resemblance to the violent motions
and stampings on the deck of Capt Cook in the paroxysms*

*of passion, into which he often threw himself upon the slightest occasion that they were universally known by the same name, & it was a common saying among both officers & people 'The old boy has been tipping a heiva.'*

Besides satisfying their mundane needs and earthly appetites, Cook's crew members were also desperate to acquire cultural artefacts. It would be nice to think they had developed an affection for the remarkable people they were meeting across the Pacific and wanted to collect some souvenirs to remember them by. No such luck – it all came down to cold, hard cash. After Cook's first voyage, London had been aflame with an insatiable appetite for South Seas treasures, and the men on Cook's ships knew they could turn a tidy profit if they fed that hunger.

### SAM NEILL

*An enduring commodity in Tonga and other Pacific islands is* tapa *cloth. It's as significant now as it was in Cook's time. We do know that* tapa *worked its charms on Cook.*

Amongst the things they brought back home were lengths of the ubiquitous *tapa* cloth. The crafting of the cloth is a deeply symbolic pastime on the part of Polynesian women. They use the paper mulberry tree that the early navigators carried with them on their journeys and transplanted in their new island homes.

### PRINCESS KALANIUVALU – LADY FOTOFILI

*Every day we get together and make* tapa *cloths. It takes half a year to produce these. Tapa is important because it signifies the work of women and portrays their strength,*

> *their skills, and their pride. Most importantly, it shows the*
> *value of women in Tongan society. In our society tasks are*
> *divided, so men work outside and women produce the*
> *tapa. Tapa has a cultural and social significance. It's used*
> *for all occasions: for weddings; to make the bedding of a*
> *newly wedded couple; it is used as an offering; it is a carpet*
> *for royalty; it is used as a reciprocated exchange between*
> *families. In recent times it's become important because we*
> *use it to help with our economy – people sell it as a form of*
> *income.*

Cook himself gave a gift of *tapa* to his wife, Elizabeth. It would become a tragic postscript to his life story.

However, the people living on Tanna were not interested in engaging in the system of exchange Cook had initiated across the Pacific, no matter how much he and his men tried to force the issue. Their sense of territoriality was new to him. '*[Never] did we touch any part of their property, not even wood and water without first having obtained their consent,*' Cook wrote. This mutual respect gave birth to a warm accord that was unique amongst his Pacific encounters.

*

As in a remarkable number of other places across the Pacific, the arrival of Captain Cook on Vanuatu had been foretold in prophecy. Uea – the bay Cook renamed 'Port Resolution' – has special significance on Tanna. It means, quite literally, 'small door to the world'. From this place, the sea merged with the world. And it's believed that the ancestors departed through this gate and will one day return to Tanna, bringing with them harmony and peace. That's why Cook's arrival in Uea was so significant – he was seen as one of the gifts that returned. Westerners dream about taking off to see the world. In Vanuatu, the world comes to you.

In Vanuatu today, formal ritual exchanges still take place, and the belief in ancestors bringing gifts and blessings from the spirit world is alive and well.

### SAM NEILL

*The people, their culture and their view of these strangers were starkly different from anything Cook had encountered before. Centuries since Cook's incursion have passed this place by, and yet today people live here as they did then. They have a continuous connection to the sea and their past. They remember Cook's visit as if it was yesterday.*

Islanders in remote regions await the return of an American god bringing with him refrigerators, jeeps, televisions and crates of Coca-Cola. These are the 'cargo cults' known across Melanesia. They evolved as a way of defending *kastom* – the Pidgin expression for traditional values – against the determined incursions of Christianity and Western culture.

### JOHNNY KOANAPO

*This is a very interesting island, where people talk about* kastom *and they want to live in* kastom *... they want to do things in* kastom *– in the* kastom *manner. It's different from what modern civilisation is teaching. Kastom, according to the people here, is the established ways of doing things,* *whether it's marriage, whether it's development of young people, the way the tribes are structured in the villages, the way these villages are connected together, and the way we interact with each other. Kastom is the established protocols of how things were in the past.*

Imagine how American troops and the Western military machine were received when they arrived in Vanuatu during the Second World War. The locals had never seen anything like it: aeroplanes, radios, individually wrapped sweets – without any understanding of mass production and modern technology, the islanders logically assumed these were the work of the gods. When the troops disappeared at the end of the war, so did their 'cargo'. In desperation, the islanders cut mock landing strips into the jungle and built timber lookout towers in the hope they could bring the cargo back. On Tanna, the most persistent cargo cult is the 'John Frum' movement.

### JOHNNY KOANAPO

*You know, here in Tanna, this is where the south-easterly wind comes from. Its name in our language here describes it as a very good wind. It brings a lot of opportunities with it – in terms of the potential for development coming from outside the island. So we believe very strongly that many more good things will come with this wind, from the south-east. A lot of old people here, particularly those in the John Frum cult, believed that something good was going to come from the east. So here in Tanna, Cook's ship came from the east, and it's so significant to the history and modern development of the island.*

Why the name? He would have been an American soldier who brought cargo to Vanuatu. 'John from America' – abbreviated to John Frum.

Tanna is also home to the truly extraordinary 'Prince Philip Cult'. Yes, *that* Prince Philip. For centuries, villagers recounted an ancient tale about the son of Tanna's mountain god crossing the seas in search of a powerful woman to wed. Unlike the islanders, the spirit had pale skin. When villagers visited the local post office or police station and saw the official portrait of Queen Elizabeth with her consort, they were certain they'd found their man. Or spirit, as the case may be.

### SAM NEILL

*The most vivid day of all for me was when I spent time with some people who live in the* kastom *way, as they call it – they live as they have always lived, eschewing T-shirts and jeans ... The way they live is a reminder of how material possessions are absolutely of no consequence when it comes to the index of happiness. A group of these blokes were taken to England as part of a BBC program on the Prince Philip movement a few years ago. When I asked them their main impressions of England, they told me two stories. The first once was about standing on a bridge over the Thames where they watched people go to work. As they put it, 'We watched people going to work for two hours' ... they said for two hours they watched people cross that bridge to go to work and not one person looked happy. They couldn't believe it. I thought it was a fantastic observation. The second thing they told me was that during their stay in England they stayed in a lot of old-money houses. What struck them the most in these manors was how many things people owned. Now these people from Vanuatu own virtually nothing at all. And they were so worried about these people who owned so many things because it was so much work looking after the things that they owned. They believed they were enslaved by the objects they owned.*

Recruitment for the movement went through the roof in 1974 when Prince Philip and the Queen visited Vanuatu aboard the royal yacht *Britannia*. As foretold, their ancestral spirit had returned to them to show off his bride. The movement's elders sent Philip a ceremonial club, and he sent them a signed photograph in return. In 2007, five Tannanese flew to England to meet him in person at Windsor Castle.

**SAM NEILL**

*The beauty here is obvious. What impresses me more is how the Tannanese insist on being themselves. They've wrenched the past back into the present. They've taken back everything the West took away from them. And they believe they've done this by magic ... the magic inherent in this, their land.*

James Cook has also left his mark on the island. He was the first white man to land on Tanna, and although the locals didn't rate him at first, after a Russian navigator visited the island thirty years later and asked its inhabitants about Cook's visit, they began to re-evaluate their relationship with him. Although centuries have passed since he landed there, Kapan Cook is now a common *kastom* name on Tanna.

**CHIEF SAM USUA ESKAR**

*Cook's memory on Tanna remains in the things he named – Port Resolution and Tanna itself. This is the first time my people have ever been contacted about the story of Captain Cook on Tanna.*

# TWELVE

# ON THE EDGE

*Wherever the white man went in this world they were*
*always treated with some trepidation. After all, only dead*
*people – cadavers – are white. I get the sense that Cook*
*was walking a fine line in his Pacific encounters. The*
*grand narrative had its dark side.*
**SAM NEILL**

One of the most enduring themes in the grand narrative of the Pacific is that of control – both winning it and losing it.

Tonga, which claims to be home to the oldest monarchy on earth, is not a place where losing control is an option. The first Tu'i Tonga was appointed in 900AD. That was a hundred and sixty-six years before William the Conqueror, also known rather deliciously as William the Bastard, crossed the Channel and set the Norman conquest rolling across England. There are more than a hundred and fifty islands in Tonga, and although the political machinations that shaped the archipelago's history haven't always been straight forward, by virtue of the language they share and the religious beliefs they hold, the people of Tonga have been culturally unified for over 1000 years.

And this is one thing that distinguishes Tonga from its Polynesian neighbours. It is the only island group in the Pacific that has never been colonised by a foreign power.

> **PRINCESS 'OFEINA-'E-HE-LANGI, Tongan Royal Family**
> *Tonga is the only kingdom here to survive that long. It's quite unique in itself. And as I say, it's mostly to do with our structure of the way we live. I think we survive because we depend on each other for most things.*

Legend has it that the first Tu'i Tonga, who went by the name 'Aho'eitu, clambered down a casuarina tree from heaven along with his five brothers. 'Aho'eitu was appointed paramount chief.

'Aho'eitu's brothers drew the short straws and became his attendants. What grew from this was a hierarchical society that was labyrinthine in its complexity. No two Tongans held the same rank, and the Tu'i Tonga presided over them all. He had at his disposal an enormous navy stocked with canoes over thirty metres in length and packed to the gills with fierce warriors. Paulaho, who was the paramount chief Cook encountered, might well have cast a covetous eye across the British weaponry, but he was unimpressed by the paltry scale of Cook's 'fleet', comprising just two ships. If a man's power was to be judged by the number of boats and warriors under his command, then Cook was sadly lacking. And the Englishman's reputation was not boosted when he spurned the amorous advances of Tongan women. He was most likely motivated by fidelity to Elizabeth waiting back in London – but as far as the Tongans were concerned, his behaviour reflected poorly on his manhood. And they weren't afraid to let him know it.

This was a peculiar state of affairs for Cook. During his travels he had become accustomed to being treated with reverence and awe at best, and fear at worst. But he enjoyed no such elevated status on Tonga. His standing on the island was dealt another body blow when, just prior to his departure from the islands, the Tongans learnt that Cook was not a nobleman, as they had imagined, but just a commoner who had risen through the ranks to reach a position of authority. Something that might be an admirable achievement in European circles counted for nothing in Tongan society. If Cook was a commoner and answerable to a king and higher authorities, he was consigned to the lowest rungs of the social ladder. Worse, this status meant he had no soul. As if they didn't have enough to worry about on earth, commoners and slaves in Tonga didn't have much to look forward to after death either. Only chieftains and the nobility ascended to the afterlife: everyone else just turned to dust.

Although Cook had no idea of his standing on the Tongan social ladder or what that meant for his eternal soul – or lack of one – he was comfortable with the rigid stratification of islander society. It mirrored the British hierarchy he had grown up with and in this aspect of life, if no other, Cook and the Tongans were speaking the same language.

### SAM NEILL

*Cook related to the Pacific societies that were hierarchical. He was from Britain, and he understood that. In Tonga, you know, they still talk about the 'aristocracy' and the 'commoners'. Cook got that. It was familiar.*

In both civilisations, the ruling class could exert control over the populace because everyone knew their place and was content to occupy the position assigned to them at birth.

When it came time for the Tongans to modernise their islands in the mid-nineteenth century, it wasn't at all surprising that they looked to Great Britain as a template for reforming Tongan high society. In 1845, after the tribal wars that ripped through the archipelago in the early nineteenth century, Tāufa'āhau I unified the islands and established a constitutional monarchy with himself as king. Tāufa'āhau adopted the name 'Siaosi' – a phonetic interpretation of the name 'George' – and became King Tupou I.

### PRINCESS 'OFEINA-'E-HE-LANGI

*The founding father of modern Tonga was His Majesty Tupou I. He conquered and bought all of the other factions together. There's a saying here in Tonga that everybody's related to the King somehow, and it's because of the structure of our society – we have His Majesty the King, obviously his family, then we have the nobles, and then we have the commoners, or the people.*

Tonga's nobility were given brand-new, Western-style titles.

But King Tupou wasn't finished with his reforms. Paganism was out; Christianity was in. He consigned his subjects' immortal souls to the stewardship of the Wesleyan Church. For those Tongans who, until that point, had no soul, it must have been a relief to learn there was a heaven waiting for them after death. To complete his universal reforms, Tupou commissioned the two things a fledgling nation can't do without – a flag and a national anthem. He then warned all foreign governments to keep their sticky noses out of Tongan business.

Today, Tonga remains the most rigidly stratified Polynesian society. The royal family still exerts enormous control over the islands, and Christianity is a cornerstone of the community, so much so that it's enshrined in the Constitution. Sunday is God's day, and His alone.

### SAM NEILL

*Tonga prides itself on never being colonised by the West. However, it enthusiastically adopted one of its instruments – Christianity. So much so that it is enshrined in the constitution. On Sundays it's illegal to work, shop, do chores, play sport and even swim. So what's to do? …*
*Go to church.*

\*

Another Pacific archipelago that proved difficult for the Europeans to control was Vanuatu.

When Cook visited the islands on his second voyage, he butted up against some of the obstacles that stood in the way of would-be settlers. But where Tonga's strength came from unity, Vanuatu's saving grace was its disunity. Even today, the population of a quarter of a million people speak 130 languages, and tribal beliefs differ from village to village. Try governing that as an outsider. The place is – and was – like quicksilver, and controlling it was next to impossible. No single warlord or chieftain ever managed to unite the tribes.

**JOHNNY KOANAPO, Vanuatu Politician**

*Before Captain Cook came in, people organised themselves in tribes, and those tribes are all connected to other tribes through marriage and other ways. So as a Tannese, I have a different tribe, and I feel that and nobody is going to take it away from me. So even if we are Nui Vanuatu, I still think and act like a Tannese. And that's something that will not easily change for many more years to come.*

Not that Europe wasn't going to try. In the 1800s in a rare attempt at cooperation, France and England declared Vanuatu a neutral territory. This meant the two countries initially did little to stop the horrendous private 'blackbirding' trade that was decimating the islands. In a fine early example of a weasel word, 'blackbirding' was coined as a more palatable term – to nineteenth-century sensibilities, anyway – than 'slavery'. At a time when the African slave trade had been abolished, up to half the adult men on many islands in Vanuatu were kidnapped and forced to work on plantations in Australia and other European Pacific colonies. French and British interests in the archipelago continued to expand, but neither power wanted to take on the responsibility of governing an ungovernable territory. And so they came up with a novel, and completely unworkable, solution. The 'Condominium'. It had nothing to do with timeshares in Miami Beach. It was derived from the Latin *com-*, meaning 'together', and *dominium* meaning 'domain'. Unfortunately for Vanuatu, it didn't result in much togetherness.

## JOHNNY KOANAPO

*I don't think it's fair to blame Captain Cook for the process of colonisation, because Captain Cook didn't come to colonise ... he came because he was exploring. Colonisation followed Cook. Then we had the French and the British. We were the only country in the Pacific that was colonised by two superpowers. We had two systems for everything. This led to the marginalisation of a lot of people because the French were focused on the French-speaking citizens, and the English focused on the English-speaking people. But we were neither French, nor were we British. If you tried to travel to the UK at that time, you would be arrested because there was no passport. We were stateless in our own land.*

The French and the English working in accord ... What on earth were they thinking? The chaos that ensued was so terrible, the locals dubbed it the 'Pandemonium'. All administrative functions – law courts, police forces, currencies, health and education systems – were duplicated. Because government bureaucracy is so much fun, why have just one when you can have two?

Things didn't improve in the twentieth century, and a push for independence led to self-governance in 1980. Thanks to European mismanagement, the newly hatched country of Vanuatu inherited no universal infrastructure to speak of. The one upside of this was that nothing much had changed over the intervening centuries since Cook's arrival, and grassroots governance remained intact. Today it forms an integral part of the government, and the locals like it that way.

## JOHNNY KOANAPO

*When we got our independence our government thought it would be good to have a common sense of identity as Nui Vanuatu, not as the French-speaking and English-speaking populations, but as a Nui Vanuatu. Now we have a council of chiefs on each of the islands, which isn't common across the Pacific. Our chiefly system is intact and informs and engages with the government.*

\*

Vanuatu's political domain proved itself to be fairly uncontrollable from a European perspective. But its unruliness doesn't stop there – it has also cornered the market in fractious natural phenomena.

## CAPTAIN JAMES COOK

*During the night the volcano, which was about four miles to the west of us, vomited up vast quantities of fire and smoke … the flames were seen to rise above the hill which lay between us and it. At every eruption it made a long rumbling noise like that of thunder, or the blowing up of large mines … the air was loaded with its ashes, which fell so thick that everything was covered with the dust. It was a kind of fine sand, or stone, ground or burnt to powder, and was exceedingly troublesome to the eyes.*

Mount Yasur is the rumbling 361-metre-high summit on Tanna that so transfixed Cook when he arrived in the archipelago. It is also an apt metaphor for the magnitude and irrepressibility of the Pacific itself.

**SAM NEILL**

*I've always been fascinated by volcanoes. They're elemental and beautiful and completely terrifying.*

Because the Pacific has the dubious honour of housing half the earth's tectonic boundaries, and tectonic boundaries equal earthquakes and volcanoes, we find in its basin the appropriately named 'Ring of Fire'.

**SAM NEILL**

*Everywhere I go in the Pacific I've seen pumice drifts from some underwater volcano in the middle of the ocean ... I've seen it in Alaska, seen it in Australia, and here I can see it on Norfolk Island. It's just a reminder of how connected the Pacific Ocean really is.*

The Pacific hosts 75 per cent of the earth's active and dormant volcanoes, and it is responsible for kicking off 90 per cent of the planet's earthquakes. It certainly makes a lie of Magellan's designation 'Pacific' (Peaceful Sea). In the past twelve thousand years, all but three of the world's twenty-five largest volcanic eruptions occurred there. And unfortunately for the residents of Japan, New Zealand and California, their countries straddle the Ring of Fire – which, as their history of destructive earthquakes proves, is at least as painful as it sounds.

The Pacific doesn't do things in half-measures. Everything about it is super-sized, including some of its most impressive permanent residents. Human beings have been zipping across its surface for three and a half thousand years or so. But we're a mere flash in the pan, relatively speaking. The gargantuan beasts that travel these waters have the strongest claim on their briny depths. While the earliest hominids were still hanging about in the African savannah, picking lice out of each other's pelts, whales ruled the seas. Today, humpbacks follow the same migratory paths in the Pacific that they have been using for countless generations.

> **JEFF LAURIE, Dive tour operator**
>
> *Anywhere between six to eight thousand kilometres each way – that's the migration path. From Tonga they head due south to the top of New Zealand – Cape Reinga – and then they travel down into Antarctic waters. Tonga and the other South Pacific countries are their breeding grounds. The cold Antarctic waters are their feeding ground.*

The 'family' of humpbacks that winter in Tonga's balmy waters have to travel there from their summer feeding grounds in Antarctica – a journey of more than six thousand kilometres that takes them up the east coast of New Zealand and along the sub-surface volcanic arch leading to Tonga.

As Cook tacked to and fro across the Pacific, he was crossing paths with these beautiful creatures.

Although he had no idea, as he travelled along Australia's east coast past K'gari – Fraser Island – on his first voyage in the *Endeavour*, Cook was following another humpback whale migration route. Many indigenous cosmological beliefs link whales to the creation and settlement of the Pacific islands, and they are worshipped across the region.

Traditional Māori beliefs assert that whales communicate messages from the gods and that the future can be divined by reading their body language. Scientific testing has shown that whale song can be heard over thousands of kilometres, and it's thought that before the cacophony of modern mechanical sounds made the Pacific noisier than a shopping centre on Christmas Eve, whale calls might well have bounced from one side of the ocean to the other in an endless loop.

If you've ever been fortunate enough to see whales in the wild, you'll appreciate their majesty and awe-inspiring presence. But to the covetous gaze of eighteenth-century Europe, whales were just another – very large and very valuable – asset to add to the ever-growing list of exploitable resources in the Pacific. Cook's charts opened the region to a tidal wave of arrivals bent on milking every last drop out of the place, with terrible consequences for the indigenous people of the Pacific and the marine mammals with whom they shared their world. Unfortunately for the locals, their vast territory was ripe for the picking. Little thought was given to the consequences of the ensuing environmental depredation.

**JEFF LAURIE**

*There's clear evidence now from the scientific community that climate change is real, that it's happening. That's going to affect everybody on this planet, in one shape or another, particularly in terms of Pacific island communities. You've seen how flat Tongatapu is – it's only a couple of metres above sea level, so the impact on an island like this is significant.*

From the European perspective, natural resources were what the Pacific was for. It was a God-given treasure house to plunder.

And, as we've seen in Australia, for the British the Pacific had another purpose that was to shape its future. It was a great place to dump people.

Which brings us to a tiny fist of volcanic rock in the South Pacific.

*

### SAM NEILL

*Cook was only here for a day, but the consequences still reverberate, and by a quirk of fate they've rattled my own family history.*

When Cook sailed to Norfolk Island on his second voyage in 1774, it was unsettled. Given the efficiency with which the Polynesians had set up shop on most of the major island groups in the Pacific, that might come as something of a surprise. But this was not an easy place to live. For one thing the main island is completely surrounded by cliffs – there is no safe harbour. And in an era when the only way to cross the waves was by boat, that was a problem. Although archaeological evidence shows that Polynesian navigators did establish a settlement on Norfolk Island sometime in the fourteenth or fifteenth centuries AD, it wasn't what you'd call a success. After a few generations, they disappeared. Whether they died out or relocated to another Pacific island, we may never know. They left behind stone tools, banana trees, the Polynesian rat and, most importantly, one of the things that would make this otherwise unremarkable place irresistible to the British government – flax. More specifically, New Zealand flax.

Cook arrived on Norfolk Island on 10 October 1774 and took a party to shore in order to explore the area now known as Duncombe Bay on the north side of the tiny island. True to form, he planted a flag and claimed it for the Crown, then gave it a name.

### CAPTAIN JAMES COOK

*I took possession of this isle as I had done of all the others we had discovered, and named it Norfolk Isle, in honour of that noble family.*

By comparison with the other Pacific territories Cook had encountered, Norfolk Island's appeal seemed limited until he spotted two things – the flax, and the towering pine trees covering the island that appeared, at first glance, to be perfect for crafting masts and spars. To draw a contemporary parallel, it was the equivalent of striking oil. With global transport and trade utterly reliant upon sailing vessels, a place that seemed to have an abundance of raw materials for ship-building and repairs was quite the find.

Chuffed as you like, Cook and his men gathered cabbages from local cabbage trees, pulled fish from the rock pools, and cooked it all up for tea. That night, they *ate fish & cabbage made into salad & were happy as possible*.

Cook knew his masters at the Admiralty would be thrilled. The flax, in particular, was invaluable as a substitute for the hemp used by the British Navy for making sails. This hemp came from Russia, and Anglo–Russian relations had begun the downward spiral that would ultimately lead to the Crimean War in the mid-nineteenth century. The navy was painfully aware of this threat, so the powers that be breathed a sigh of relief when Cook told them about the tiny island in the middle of the Pacific that looked as though it might be the answer to their prayers.

In advance of the first British settlement in Australia, the government made sure that establishing a permanent presence on Norfolk Island was a high priority for the fledgling colony.

The first governor of New South Wales, Arthur Phillip, was given instructions that he was: *'as soon as circumstances will admit of it, to send a small establishment'* to Norfolk Island to stake the Crown's claim. Lieutenant Philip Gidley King was dispatched there and given command of twenty-two men and women. Fifteen of the first arrivals were convicts tasked with felling pines, crafting them into masts and harvesting flax for canvas. Unfortunately, it didn't take long for the group to realise that neither raw material would suit their intended purpose. Although the pine could be used for many other things, it didn't cut it as a mast. And despite their best efforts, the weavers had no idea how to fashion the flax into canvas.

Norfolk Island would find its uses, though. For a start, because it was so fertile, it was the one thing that kept the early settlement in Sydney from starvation when food was scarce. But it also performed a less benign function – it became the new penal colony's offshore dumping ground. Between 1788 and 1855, Norfolk Island would be the end of the road for those convicts deemed the worst of the worst. By the mid-1830s, it was the most infamous penal outpost in the world; its reputation was such that in 1840 Charles Dickens offered to set a novel on the island in order to promote its horrors and ensure nobody wanted to risk ending up there.

One man in particular was to make quite an impression on Norfolk Island. In 1833, Captain Foster Fyans was posted there as captain of the guard. Upon arrival, he was enormously impressed by the Pacific island's natural aspects.

> **FOSTER FYANS (1790–1870), Penal Administrator, Norfolk Island, and Public Servant**
>
> *All days alike in this heavenly climate. The island is small, but luxuriantly rich, abundance of lemons, guavas, pomegranates, custard apple and other fruits indigenous to the soil. The length is not more than seven miles … the sea appeared truly grand, with a long heavy surf rolling on the island … To me for days the island appeared a fairy land, and so beautiful in comparison to New South Wales. The pine trees grow to an enormous size … the valleys are provided with numerous exotics in plants, and streams of the finest water.*

But he was less enthusiastic about the settlement and its occupants, condemning them as a disgrace to Britain. And it's here that Sam Neill's personal story crosses paths with that of the Pacific.

> **SAM NEILL**
>
> *Curiously, this is where my family and Cook and Norfolk Island intersect. The acting commandant at this gaol when prisoners rebelled and escaped was Captain Foster Fyans. His daughter married one Percival Neill, my great-grandfather. Fyans is still a family name – one I gave my son Tim. Why should this matter? Because it goes to the heart of what we call history. Foster Fyans put down the rebellion, captured the escaped convicts and administered punishment. A military man, it was his job.*

*Ice Islands with Ice Blink*, William Hodges, c.1772–75. Sailing into the Antarctic Circle in search of the Great Southern Continent, the *Resolution* and the *Adventure* met with the inevitable. In his journal, Cook wrote that the icebergs 'exhibited a view which for a few moments was pleasing to the eye; but when we reflected on the danger, the mind was filled with horror.'
*State Library of NSW, SAFE / PXD 11, FL1006760*

Sam Neill with cameraman Mark Broadbent and director Kriv Stenders at the Australian Antarctic Division base, Antarctica.
SAM NEILL: Though Cook crossed the Antarctic Circle three times, he failed to sight the continent, let alone land on it, the ice keeping him far offshore. Today it's possible to fly there and back from Hobart in less than a day. Much less effort though.
*Photo by Kriv Stenders, © 2018 Essential Media & Entertainment*

The Australian Antarctic Division's Wilkins Runway, an ice airstrip at Preston Heath, Budd Coast, Antarctica.
SAM NEILL: It took another hundred years after Cook crossed the Antarctic Circle for the first explorers to finally walk on this continent. Not hard to see why … but being here … it's immense. It's overwhelming and terrifyingly beautiful.
*Photo by Kriv Stenders, 2018 Essential Media & Entertainment*

*Dusky Bay, New Zealand*, William Hodges, 1773. Defeated by the Southern Ocean, Cook retreated to Dusky Sound, where his ships were repaired and his sailors returned to some level of health, no doubt helped by beer brewed from the local vegetation. The artist Hodges was possibly too busy to drink. This small painting on a piece of timber provided by the ship's carpenter is considered the first oil painting to be executed on site in Aotearoa/New Zealand. *The Fletcher Trust Collection*

Filming at Dusky Sound. Left to right, director of photography Jules O'Loughlin, director Sally Aitken, Sam Neill and Sam's assistant, Ziggy Golden. SAM NEILL: Nothing prepares you for waking up to dawn in Dusky Sound. It's still almost as hard to get to as it was in Cook's day, and it's almost unchanged since the *Resolution* anchored here. This place is one of New Zealand's – indeed, the world's – great treasures. *Photo by Eamon Dimmitt, © 2018 Essential Media & Entertainment*

*A View of the Monuments of Easter Island*, William Hodges, c.1776. Cook was not well enough to tour Easter Island, but his men explored the landscape and its statuary. The expedition's botanist, J.R. Forster, noted: 'The images represent men to their waist, the ears are large and they are about 18 foot high and 5 foot wide; they are ill-shaped and have a large solid bonnet on their heads.' *Bridgeman Images, PFH1172238*

Queen Elizabeth II, Queen Sālote Tupou III and the Duke of Edinburgh at the Tongan Royal Palace in 1953, inspecting Tu'i Malila, a Madagascar radiated tortoise of exceptional age, reputedly presented to the Tongan Royal family by Cook. Conditioned by the stratification of the Royal Navy and British Society, Cook felt comfortable in feudal Tonga.
*Getty Images, 105220167*

A Fakapangai ceremony at Pangai Royal Ceremonial Grounds, Tonga. This is an ancient ritual, the counting of tributes gifted to the ruler. Cook insisted on attending one and was obliged by the Tongans to go bare chested and unwigged, to the horror of his fellow officers, who felt he had let the side down.
*Photo by Johanna Gibson, © 2018 Essential Media & Entertainment*

Sam Neill attends the Free Church of Tonga. SAM NEILL: Tonga prides itself on never being colonised by the West. However, it enthusiastically adopted one of its instruments – Christianity. So much so that it is enshrined in the constitution. On Sundays it's illegal to work, shop, do chores, play sport and even swim. So what to do? Go to church.
*Photo by Johanna Gibson, © 2018 Essential Media & Entertainment*

*The landing at Erramanga [Eromanga]*, William Hodges, c.1776. Cook met with varied responses in what he dubbed the 'New Hebrides' – Vanuatu – which artist Hodges later represented in a series of paintings. The peoples of the Vanuatu Archipelago understandably viewed strangers as enemies. Cook was no exception and was repulsed on trying to land at Eromanga. His muskets killed at least four of his attackers, with only minor injuries to his crew.
*David Rumsey Map Collection, David Rumsey Map Center, Stanford Libraries*

*The Landing at Tanna*, William Hodges, c.1776. The response at Tanna was more positive; despite initial uncertainties, Cook and his men exchanged gifts with the coastal people who considered them to be spirits – and warned them against exploring the volcano, home to a cannibal tribe. The erupting Mount Yasur can be seen in the background.
*Bridgeman Images, DGA502826*

Sam Neill at Mount Yasur – the volcano Cook called 'the lighthouse of the Pacific'. Cook and his men may have been warned away from the volcano, but in the twenty-first century it's a tourist site.
*Photo by Kriv Stenders, © 2018 Essential Media & Entertainment*

TV crew and tourists at the summit of Mount Yasur.
*Photo by Johanna Gibson, © 2018 Essential Media & Entertainment*

Sam Neill at the Captain Cook Monument, Duncombe Bay, Norfolk Island. SAM NEILL: Cook was only here for a day, but the consequences still reverberate, and by a quirk of fate they've rattled my own family history.
*Photo by Kirrilly Brentnall, © 2018 Essential Media & Entertainment*

Norfolk Island Gaol. It was the tiny island's tall pine trees and abundant flax that Cook noted when claiming it for the Crown. However, on the establishment of New South Wales as a penal colony, the island was put to a less benign use – a dumping ground for the worst convicts. Sam Neill's ancestor Captain Foster Fyans, posted here as captain of the guard, put down a rebellion – earning the sobriquet 'Flogger Fyans' in Robert Hughes' *The Fatal Shore*.

SAM NEILL: For Hughes, Fyans was on the wrong side of history. Of course I disagree, and in the field of history there's often no middle ground.
*Photo by Kirrilly Brentnall, © 2018 Essential Media & Entertainment*

*Portrait of Omai*, Sir Joshua Reynolds, c.1776. Omai (or Mai) was a Ra'iatean man who boarded the *Adventure* – the companion ship on Cook's second voyage – and travelled to England. Taken under Joseph Banks' wing, he was a hit with the royal court and society, to the extent of becoming the subject of this glamorous 'celebrity' portrait by Reynolds. A goal of Cook's third Pacific voyage was to return him to his home.
*Courtesy of the Rijksmuseum*

*Bewoners van Tasmanië [Residents of Tasmania]*, Ludwig Gottlieb Portman, after Jacques Kuyper, 1803. In January 1777 Cook anchored in Adventure Bay, Bruny Island, for water, food, wood and animal feed. His interactions with the Nuenonne people were quite different from his encounters with Aboriginal people on the first voyage. Some of the men were so intrigued by the crew's cross-cut saw – cutting firewood – they ventured to operate it from one end.
*Rijksmuseum RP-P-1906-3958*

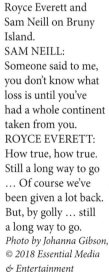

Royce Everett and Sam Neill on Bruny Island.
SAM NEILL: Someone said to me, you don't know what loss is until you've had a whole continent taken from you.
ROYCE EVERETT: How true, how true. Still a long way to go … Of course we've been given a lot back. But, by golly … still a long way to go.
*Photo by Johanna Gibson, © 2018 Essential Media & Entertainment*

*The Inside of a Hippah, in New Zealand*, John Webber, 1782. Several independent groups occupied Queen Charlotte Sound, with frequent seasonal incursions by others to harvest fish. The political fluctuations were constant and tempestuous. On Cook's visits to the various villages he had to avoid taking sides when exhorted to attack other settlements.
*SLNSW, PXD 59/Vol.01/p.F.67*

*Human Sacrifice at the Great Morai at Attahouroo*, John Webber, 1777. Cook was interested in observing religious and spiritual rituals. On Mo'orea, he witnessed a human sacrifice, writing in his journal, 'They now took the bundles of feathers and the sacrifice to the great Morai … at the foot of them the latter was placed round which the priests seated themselves and began again their prayers, while some of their attendants dug a hole at the foot of the Morai in which they buried the victim … During the ceremony we were silent but as soon as it was over … of course [we] condemned it.' Tahitians used slaves as human sacrifice, clubbing the unaware victims over the head while gardening so they were well and truly dead by the time the marae ceremony began.
*Bridgeman Images, BL3283520*

*Otoo King of O-Taheite*, John Hall after William Hodges, 1777. Tu, the high chief of Tahiti-nui (the big island), became Cook's *taio* – ceremonial friend. A vain man, jealous of Cook's friendships with other chiefs, he impressed Cook with a vast maritime display of war canoes and invited him to a ceremony with a human sacrifice. Cook formed a sentimental attachment to Tu but nevertheless refused to aid him in his ambitions to conquer the rest of the archipelago.
*David Rumsey Map Collection, David Rumsey Map Center, Stanford Libraries*

*View of Huaheine, One of the Society Islands*, attributed to John Cleveley, c.1786. Omai was returned to Huahine, rather than Ra'aitea, which was in the hands of his enemies. Before that, when the ship first arrived in Tahiti, Omai, determined to impress his countrymen, donned a suit of armour and rode a horse along the beach – only to be unceremoniously bucked off. The locals' disdain at this and his return was a portent of his unhappy future.
SLNSW DGD 27, FL 3245461

*A View of the Habitations in Nootka Sound*, John Webber, c.1782. Sailing north-east, Cook met with colder climes – and entirely different cultures – on the western coast of North America. The Mowachaht people of Nootka Sound made him welcome, at a price. Their concept of property and ownership tallied with British beliefs, and Cook paid dearly for the much-needed supplies. He ruefully commented that every patch of grass had its owner.
*SLNSW DL PXX 2/vol. 4, FL3445534*

*The Inside of a House in Nootka Sound*, John Webber, c.1782. The Mowachahts' huge houses, the largest permanent homes in the Pacific, dotted Nootka Sound. But here as elsewhere, the encroachment of traders and colonists – Spanish, Russian, British and American – had a gradual but catastrophic effect on the indigenous population. One hundred and thirty years after Cook's visit, the Mowachaht population had declined by ninety per cent.
*SLNSW DL PXX 2, FL3445535*

Sam Neill, Nootka Sound.
SAM NEILL: It always puts a shiver up my spine when I'm in the exact spot Cook was. Particularly in a place like Nootka Sound where almost nothing has changed at all … One thing that's certainly very different today is that there must have been a cacophony of noise … The place was full of people. But today, it's just me, and it's almost entirely silent.
*Photo by Kirrilly Brentnall, © 2018 Essential Media & Entertainment*

*A Man of Oonalashka*, John Webber, c.1784–86. The Unangans, who were supremely adapted to their harsh environment, had thrived for some 9,000 years before the British turned up.
*SLNSW DL PXX 2, FL3445540*

*A Woman of Oonalashka*, John Webber, c.1784–86. Cook noted that Unangan women warmed themselves by placing blubber-oil lamps between their legs and under their clothing.
*SLNSW DL PXX 2, FL3445541*

Sam Neill and Dr Rick Knecht, archaeologist, survey the remains of an Unangan Village in Nateekin Bay, Unalaska. The bulk of the houses were sensibly underground, with domed roofs above, leaving these mounds that puncture the hill top.
*Photo by Eamon Dimmitt, © 2018 Essential Media & Entertainment*

*The Resolution Beating through the Ice*, John Webber, 1792. In their search for the North-West Passage, Cook's men endured three months' worth of ice, gales, fog and sub-zero conditions – as well as Cook's insistence that they eat walrus meat, which the captain described as 'sweet as marrow'. The crew took the opposite opinion and briefly went on hunger strike until Cook restored normal rations.
*NLA, PIC Drawer 1219 #S1627*

Sam Neill with Raymond Kowelut, and his daughter Jessica Downey, Nome, Alaska.
RAYMOND KOWELUT: My people have lived on walrus for thousands of years ... You got to get used to it. When I was growing up we had to eat it at a young age because that's all we can eat sometimes – just walrus or seal. But the taste of walrus is ... well, you have to get used to the taste.
*SAM NEILL:* It tastes like rancid fish!
*Photo by Kirrilly Brentnall, © 2018 Essential Media & Entertainment*

*A View of Kealakekua Bay*, John Webber, c.1781–83. Cook chose to return to Hawai'i to wait out the winter before making another attempt on the North-West Passage. When Cook anchored in Kealakekua Bay, his welcome was a carnival. Thousands of canoes surrounded the ships, 10,000 people lined the cliffs and hundreds of men and women swarmed on board and up the rigging, almost capsizing the *Discovery*. They were unceremoniously hauled down and tossed overboard. This enthusiasm was not to last.
*SLNSW DL PXX 2/vol.6, FL5602644*

*Scarlet Hawaiian Honeycreeper*, Vestiaria coccinea, George Shaw, 1791. Red feathers were highly valued in Tahiti and Hawaii. When Cook arrived on Hawai'i, the paramount chief, Kalani'ōpu'u, presented him with his own 'ahu 'ula (feathered cloak) – estimated to contain four million feathers. It was an act of generosity that Cook and his men failed to reciprocate.
*SLNSW, ML 591/13 vol. 3*

Sam Neill with Anne LokomaikaʻI Lipscomb at the Bernice Pauahi Bishop Museum in Honolulu.
SAM NEILL: Never outstay your welcome. If there's one moral to this story, it's that, isn't it?
ANNE LOKOMAIKAʻI LIPSCOMB: That's right. Hospitality is so valued, but the flip side is that if it is not respected then there are enormous consequences.
*Photo by Kirrilly Brentnall, © 2018 Essential Media & Entertainment*

*A chief of the Sandwich Islands*, John Webber, 1787. This painting of a Hawaiian chief was created by Webber seven years after the third voyage, to show the warlike nature of the Hawaiians, with the shifty eyes of the chief's followers suggesting the imagined uncertainties and suspicions of Hawaiʻi's people towards their leaders. It was an attempt by Webber to show that the people who killed Cook were untrustworthy and violent – a notion modern Hawaiian activists have fought hard to right.
*National Library of Australia, PIC T265 NK1*

*Death of Cook*, John Webber, c.1781–83. The exact events leading to Cook's death are contested. Webber's version aligns with the noble description provided in the official edition of the journals and has Cook bravely trying to hold off the fire from his men in the boat.
*State Library of NSW, DG 26, FL3234891*

Sam Neill at Kealakekua Bay. SAM NEILL: I've been thinking about Cook's killing here and there seems a terrible inevitability about it. Cook had enjoyed such good luck throughout his three voyages around the Pacific and that luck had finally run out. That luck had led to hubris and that overconfidence had consequences.
*Photo by Kirrilly Brentnall, © 2018 Essential Media & Entertainment*

A plaque in Kealakekua Bay – here drowned by a high tide – reads, 'Near this spot, Capt. James Cook met his death February 14 1779'.
*Photo by Kirrilly Brentnall, © 2018 Essential Media & Entertainment*

Sam Neill and Gordon Kanakanui Leslie, Ho'ala Kealakekua, at the Cook memorial at Keakakekua Bay.
GORDON KANAKANUI LESLIE: I don't think our leaders back then wanted to kill him. I think they had great respect for him … they liked him. They probably didn't like some of the behaviour in the short time Cook and his men were here. But I think they revered him as a great navigator.
*Photo by Kirrilly Brentnall, © 2018 Essential Media & Entertainment*

Sam Neill, Cook memorial, Kealakekua Bay.
SAM NEILL: 'Cook discovered these islands' it says … that's just the sort of thing that 250 years later still gets poor old Cook into trouble all around the Pacific. A claim – incidentally – that he himself would never have made.
*Photo by Kirrilly Brentnall, © 2018 Essential Media & Entertainment*

The ditty box Cook's crew created for his wife, Elizabeth. Along the edge of the box is the inscription: 'Made Of *Resolution* Oak for Mrs. Cook by Crew'. Inside is a tiny painting showing his death, and a lock of his hair.
*Photos by Bonnie Fan, © 2018 Essential Media & Entertainment*

Sam Neill with Matahi Tutavae (left) and Henarii Hoffman (right) of the Tahitian Voyaging Society, at Matavai Bay, Tahiti.

MATAHI TUTAVAE: Our ancestors got it right. That's why they were one people, even though the ocean is so huge. We were able to communicate and go back and forth. We were just one people back then … Unfortunately with colonisation we went in different directions … Now we need to reconnect to our cousins of the Pacific because we have common stories, even though we're so far apart from each other.
*Photo by Kirrilly Brentnall, © 2018 Essential Media & Entertainment*

Sam Neill in Tahiti.
SAM NEILL: Mo'orea's volcanic spires are a Pacific icon, like the ocean ageless and eternal. As good a spot as any for me to contemplate the past, the future and what I've learnt from my journey travelling in the wake of James Cook.
*Photo by Owen Hughes, © 2018 Essential Media & Entertainment*

Foster Fyans had a pretty clear idea  
keep convicts under control.

**FOSTER FYAN**

*I am a great advocate for convicts an*  
*better than I with them ... I say do the*  
*but you must be strict wi*

Australian writer and commentator R  
Norfolk Island that it was a *'place of per*  
*was reckoned to be good and where the u*  
*norm'*. In Hughes' international best-se  
European settlement of Australia, *The*  
Fyans' was established as an arch-villain of  
Described as a 'sweaty' and 'dishevelled  
Fyans was a symbol of the brutal colonia  
foundations for modern Australia:

> *In a prolonged sadistic fury, Fyans and the so*  
> *set out to make the mutineers wish they had n*  
> *It took the blacksmiths nine days to make new*  
> *prisoners; they were double or triple weight, wi*  
> *the basils jagged to lacerate the flesh ... Fyans u*  
> *special cats made 'to strike terror into these hard*  
> *fellows ...' The mass floggings went on into the e*  
> *light of flambeaux, until the 'desperate and lawl*  
> *listless mob' had been battered into submission.*

Needless to say, Sam and his family have taken u  
tenor of Hughes' portrait.

**SAM NEILL**

*When the late Robert Hughes came to write his history of Australia's foundations – The Fatal Shore – he found more fault in Foster Fyans for administering punishment than the convicts who admitted they planned to cut the throats of the prison staff, rape their wives and abscond on a stolen ship. He dubbed him 'Flogger Fyans'. He transposed the convicts' notoriety to Fyans' character. For Hughes, Fyans was on the wrong side of history. Of course I disagree, and in the field of history there's often no middle ground.*

or Foster Fyans, he lived to the grand old age of eighty after a ble career in the early Australian public service. He served as first police magistrate of Geelong, in what is now Victoria, was commissioner of Crown lands in the Portland Bay toral district. The town of Fyansford on the outskirts of elong was named for the crossing Fyans built on the orabool River to access his police camp.

**SAM NEILL**

*Is this all just a matter of unintended consequences? Cook, convicts, Bligh, the mutiny on the Bounty, Pitcairn, Norfolk Island and my besmirched ancestor? I don't know but I do know this small island is a reservoir of Pacific history.*

f the story of the Pacific tells us one thing, it's that history is told by the victors. But every now and then, the marginalised have the chance to write their own narrative. That's how it was for the descendants of the mutineers from HMS *Bounty* and their

Tahitian wives who ended up on Norfolk Island in 1856 after it was abandoned by the British. Queen Victoria gifted it to the Pitcairn Islanders who had outgrown their remote island home. One hundred and ninety-three men and women took advantage of the well-constructed and attractive buildings deserted by the British and relocated, though the new residents were forced to grapple with the island's grim recent history.

**RHONDA GRIFFITHS, Pitcairn Islander Descendant**

*They thought that they would have Norfolk the same way they had Pitcairn, which is ours in entirety. But when they arrived they didn't like the island because it had ghosts. There were piles of uniforms and leg irons just left abandoned, and of course this was a great horror for the new arrivals.*

Today, half the residents of the island trace their parentage to the *Bounty* mutineers, which means surnames are in short supply and the local phone book includes nicknames to distinguish between them all. You're not going to have much trouble finding the right number with names like 'Cane Toad', 'Paw Paw', 'Diddles', 'Lettuce Leaf' and 'Goof' to choose from. These whimsical nicknames give the impression that Norfolk Islanders are pretty easygoing in general, and there's certainly no shortage of quirky facts to support that conclusion – for example, local laws give cows right of way on the island's few roads.

But the Norfolk Islanders are fiercely proud of their Pacific heritage. The local lingo is Norf'k, a blend of eighteenth-century English and Tahitian with words including *nor'gwen* (not going) and *do-mine* (never mind), and there has been major opposition to Australia's move in 2016 to abolish the Norfolk Island Legislative Assembly and establish the island as an Australian territory subject to the same Commonwealth laws as the mainland. Sixty-eight per cent of islanders reject the changes and have appealed to the United Nations to oversee a transition to self-determination.

> ### RHONDA GRIFFITHS
>
> *Yes, we could do without Australia. We've got lots of tools that you can't see, and these tools are our ability to go back to our subsistence lifestyle. We've got our land, we've got the know-how, we've got a sense of community. We always talk about our history, but I would rather see a future where we are self-governing, where Australia takes a much more adult approach to us and allows us to become part of the Pacific.*

While the Australian government now insists that the Australian national anthem is sung at official functions, it's done begrudgingly. Given a choice, the locals sing their preferred anthem: 'God Save the Queen'.

Norfolk Island is not going to be saying *do-mine* to Australian intervention anytime soon.

\*

Cook's return home via Cape Horn on 30 July 1775 was a triumph. Thanks to his rigour and a painstaking search, whose path across the Pacific resembles the marks made on a wall by a toddler with a crayon, he confidently consigned the Great Southern Continent to the scrap heap of history.

### CAPTAIN JAMES COOK

*I had now made the circuit of the Southern Ocean ... in such a manner as to leave not the least room for the possibility of there being a continent, unless near the pole and out of the reach of navigation; by twice visiting the Pacific Tropical Sea ... Thus I flatter myself that the intention of the voyage has in every respect been fully answered, the southern hemisphere sufficiently explored and a final end put to the searching after a Southern Continent, which has at times engrossed the attention of some of the maritime powers for near two centuries past and the geographers of all ages.*

For a modest man, his account reflects no small pride in this achievement.

Cook was given all the rewards the Royal Navy could grant him. He was offered an honourable discharge and a lucrative position as an officer at the Greenwich Hospital. He was acknowledged as the pre-eminent navigator of the age, was made a Fellow of the Royal Society and won the Copley Medal for contributions to scientific research. Elizabeth was waiting, and London society beckoned. For most people, it would have been more than enough. But James Cook was not most people.

The man who wrote '*I whose ambition leads me not only farther than any other man has been before me, but as far as I think it possible for any man to go*' knew that many questions were left unanswered. He had solved the southern hemisphere's greatest mystery, a puzzle that had vexed many of the world's greatest thinkers and explorers for thousands of years. But he had yet to cross into the northern Pacific, home to another great enigma that promised enduring fame and unimaginable wealth.

James Cook was not done with the Pacific, and it was not done with him.

# PART FIVE

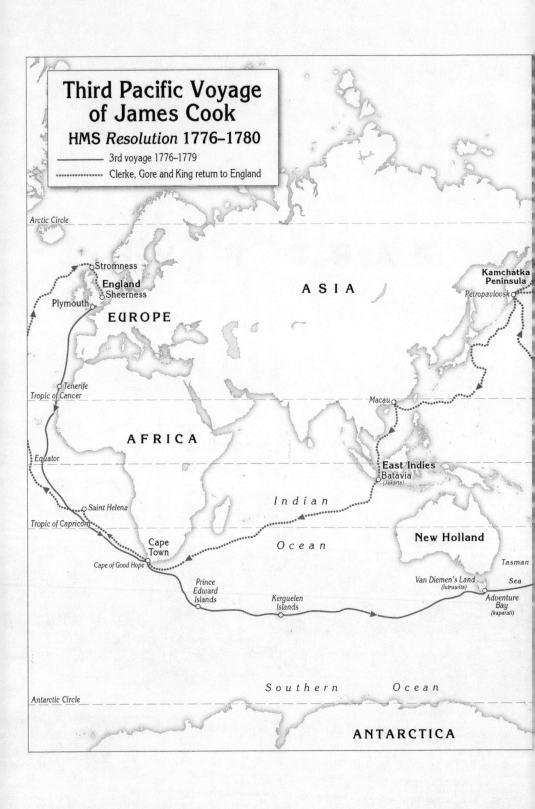

# Third Pacific Voyage of James Cook

## HMS *Resolution* 1776–1780

——————— 3rd voyage 1776–1779

·············· Clerke, Gore and King return to England

Arctic Circle

Stromness
**England**
Sheerness
Plymouth
**EUROPE**

**ASIA**

Kamchatka
Peninsula
*Petropavlovsk*

Tenerife
Tropic of Cancer

Macau

**AFRICA**

Equator

**East Indies**
Batavia
*(Jakarta)*

Saint Helena
Tropic of Capricorn

*Indian*

Cape
Town
Cape of Good Hope

*Ocean*

**New Holland**

*Tasman*

Prince
Edward
Islands

Kerguelen
Islands

Van Diemen's Land
*(lutruwita)*

*Sea*

Adventure
Bay
*(kaparati)*

Southern    Ocean

Antarctic Circle

**ANTARCTICA**

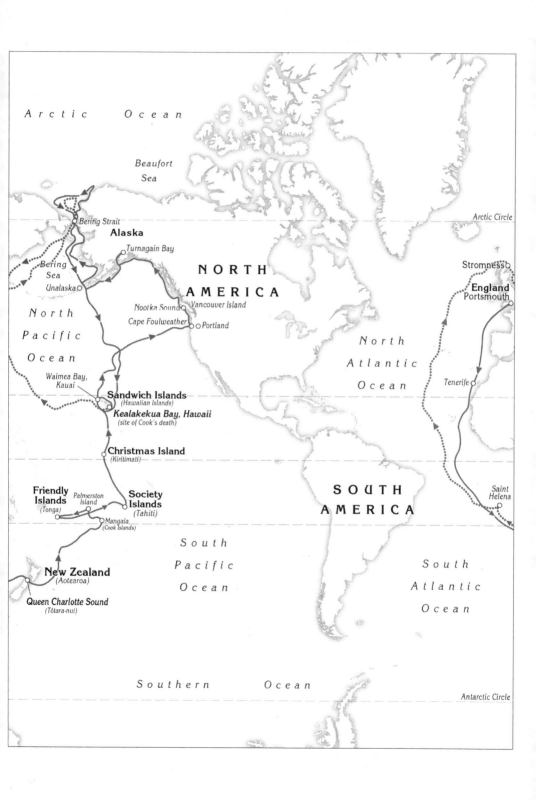

Arctic Ocean

Beaufort Sea

Arctic Circle

Bering Strait
Alaska
Turnagain Bay

Bering Sea
Unalaska

NORTH AMERICA

Nootka Sound
Cape Foulweather
Vancouver Island
Portland

North Pacific Ocean

Stromness

England
Portsmouth

North Atlantic Ocean

Tenerife

Waimea Bay, Kauai

Sandwich Islands
(Hawaiian Islands)
Kealakekua Bay, Hawaii
(site of Cook's death)

Christmas Island
(Kiritimati)

Friendly Islands
(Tonga)
Palmerston Island
Society Islands
(Tahiti)
Mangaia
(Cook Islands)

SOUTH AMERICA

Saint Helena

New Zealand
(Aotearoa)

Queen Charlotte Sound
(Tōtara-nui)

South Pacific Ocean

South Atlantic Ocean

Southern Ocean

Antarctic Circle

*THIRTEEN*

# CHASING RAINBOWS

*As soon as Cook heard of a planned voyage to find the
North-West Passage he turned his back on retirement and
domestic bliss. This was a chance to complete the Pacific
trifecta. A third voyage would encompass the northern
regions of the ocean, complete his chart, and connect the
planet's two great oceans: the Atlantic and the Pacific.
Not to mention the reward. Cook was neither a greedy
man nor was he intemperate. He had come a long way
from being a farm labourer's son. Could he go further?
Immortality beckoned as well as wealth. It would be the
biggest gamble of Cook's life.*
**SAM NEILL**

**M**en foolhardy enough to give their lives to the sea in the eighteenth century rarely made it to their three-score-and-ten. So at forty-seven years old, James Cook was well into his dotage. After his return from his second voyage, he was also famous. Cook had managed to scale the rungs of the social ladder from his humble beginnings in a tiny Yorkshire cottage to find himself a place in London's high society.

By 1775 Cook had spent most of his life at sea. No other British navigator had travelled as far as he had. After making two tremendously successful voyages of exploration to the Pacific, and garnering the recognition and acclaim of his peers, Cook could have retired. Actually, given how the next chapter of his story ended, he *should* have retired.

Instead, when the Admiralty began to scout about for someone to lead a third voyage to the Pacific, he put up his hand for the job. The admirals had been lining up Charles Clerke to fill the position and had hoped that Cook would agree to act as a consultant to the expedition. But when Cook volunteered, Clerke was quickly shunted to one side.

As the venerable mariner readied to depart in July 1776, Cook would again be leaving his wife, Elizabeth, and children – thirteen-year-old James, twelve-year-old Nathaniel and newborn Hugh. The couple had already lost three children – a daughter called Elizabeth, and two sons, Joseph and George. Having buried all three of them while Cook was at sea, Elizabeth must have farewelled her husband for a third time with a very heavy heart.

The physical and psychological pressure of commanding a ship on the high seas meant very few mariners stayed at the helm for as long as Cook. It had been barely a year since he had returned from the second voyage, so he'd had little time to recover. Yet he was determined to set sail again. Why? Was he addicted to the thrill of the chase – an extreme adventure junkie like the modern-day war correspondents who are drawn to danger like moths to a flame? Was it simply that Cook suffered from a terminal case of itchy feet and couldn't abide sitting still for long? By doing so, he was turning his back on a prestigious, not to mention safe and sedentary, appointment at the Greenwich

Hospital. Of his decision he wrote to his old employer and friend, the Quaker sea captain John Walker, that the confines of the hospital were '*far too small for an active mind like mine*'. But there certainly was something else at play. Although Cook was enjoying the advantages that came with his elevation in social standing, without the inherited wealth that kept so many of his new peers afloat, he was unable to offer his family the financial security he wanted for them. And the third great British expedition into the Pacific had the potential to be his pot of gold at the end of the rainbow.

In 1775 the Admiralty planned the third voyage in response to an Act of Parliament that offered a £20,000 prize to the person who discovered the fabled North-West Passage. Scientists had reached the conclusion that the open ocean could not ice over and so proposed that there might be a direct sea passage across the Arctic Circle. Yes, it was the Great Southern Continent all over again, but in the northern hemisphere and this time with a cash bonus – the equivalent of £3 million today, or almost AUD$5.3 million. That's a great deal of financial security.

The quest for the Passage would, over the coming century, claim many lives. To find a way across the northern latitudes would offer another way of getting to Asia other than via the perilous and protracted routes that rounded Cape Horn and the Cape of Good Hope. The projected rewards and savings in expenditure for those plying their trade between Asia and Europe were incalculable. Travel time would be dramatically reduced and there was a better chance that the valuable trade goods would make it to their intended destination in one piece. Britain was not alone in coming to this realisation, but it did intend to be the first European nation to discover and chart the Passage.

The British had another good reason to venture back into the Pacific. In August 1773, a young Ra'iatean man named Mai – or Omai – had come aboard the *Adventure*, Cook's companion ship on the second voyage, which had dropped anchor at the island of Huahine. Like Tupaia before him, Mai decided he wanted to travel to England. And also like Tupaia, he had been dispossessed of his lands by warring parties and thought that if he formed an alliance with the British they would help him defeat his enemies.

When Mai arrived in London in October 1774, Joseph Banks welcomed him with open arms. The Englishman was undoubtedly thrilled that he had an all-new South Sea Islander to squire about town after the death of Tupaia in Batavia had deprived him of the opportunity to impress his high-society friends with his 'exotic' Tahitian companion. Now the fates had delivered him a substitute, and Banks made sure Mai was the toast of the town.

*The Weekly magazine, or, Edinburgh amusement*, 1774, **volume 25**

*The Native of Otaheite, who was at court the other day, had received some instructions for his behaviour in addressing His Majesty, but so great was his embarrassment when His Majesty approached him, that he forgot everything but that of kneeling; and when his conductors endeavoured to make him speak to the King, he could only stretch out his hand, and get out the familiar phrase of How do you do? which, it seems, was the first English phrase he learnt ... His Majesty freely shook him by the hand ...*

He hobnobbed with King George and the ladies of the court, and sat for a now celebrated portrait painted by the foremost artist of the day, Sir Joshua Reynolds. If that wasn't enough, long after Mai had returned to Polynesia, he inspired a pantomime that was the hit of the season in 1785: *Omai: or, a Trip Round the World*. In it, Omai – the heir to the Tahitian throne – was bequeathed to Londina – Britannia's daughter. You don't have to look too hard to find the subtext in that plot.

After he had been swanning about London for almost two years, it was decided it was high time that he returned to Tahiti. There's no record of what he thought about the idea – not that anyone asked his opinion it seems. In the meantime, the old warhorse from the second voyage, HMS *Resolution*, and the ship intended to be its companion, the *Discovery*, were being refitted in the naval yards. Being the micromanager he was, under normal circumstances Cook would have overseen the work himself. But he was tied up preparing his account of the second voyage. So he entrusted the work to men he assumed knew what they were doing. It was a fateful decision. Before embarking on the second voyage, Cook had described the *Resolution* as 'the ship of my choice' and 'the fittest of any service of any I have seen'. With what was to come, his affection for the ship would be short-lived.

\*

On 12 July 1776, Cook set sail from England for the last time.

> **York Courant, 18 June 1776**
> *On Monday Omiah, the Otaheitean, took his leave of his Majesty, and yesterday set out for Portsmouth, where he is to embark on board Capt. Cook's Ship, in order to return*

*home. Yesterday, Capt. Cook, of his Majesty's Ship* Resolution, *who is going out for the third time on further discoveries to the South Seas, took leave of his Majesty, he being in a few days to sail in company with the* Discovery, *Capt. Clerke, now at Gravesend, on the said voyage.*

The two ships were home to a floating farmyard of livestock – a sheep, cows, goats, ducks, geese, chickens, peacocks. Not to mention the horse Mai intended to take back to Tahiti with him. The animals had been herded onto the ships as gifts from King George III to the people of the Pacific. Which was all very well and good, except he didn't have to worry about feeding them.

Cook had been instructed to round the Cape of Good Hope and then proceed directly to Tahiti. But with a shipload full of bleating, mooing, honking and gobbling animals fast running out of food, he was forced to change tack. In January 1777 he turned his ship towards Van Diemen's Land – or lutruwita, as it was known to the Aboriginal inhabitants. It's worth pausing to note here that the Aboriginal languages of lutruwita were all but lost in the attempted extermination of the Tasmanian Aboriginal peoples in the nineteenth century. In recent years, palawa kani, the language of the Tasmanian Aboriginal people, has been painstakingly revived from remnants remembered into the twentieth century and colonial documentary records. And yes, those lower-case letters are deliberate; it is the style adopted by the Tasmanian Aboriginal people of today.

In 1773, after Tobias Furneaux in the Adventure lost sight of Cook and the Resolution in the soupy fog of the Antarctic, he sought refuge on the island of lunawuni (later named Bruny Island) for five days, naming the bay he anchored in after his ship.

Of course that body of water already had a name – kaparati – but to Furneaux and the Europeans who followed in his wake, it became Adventure Bay. There was no shortage of evidence that people were living there, but Furneaux had no contact with the Aboriginal occupants. He left a selection of gifts – medals, gunflints, some nails and an old barrel with iron hoops – at a deserted campsite.

Bruny Island's Adventure Bay was the destination of choice for Cook as he sought sustenance for his ravenous menagerie.

### SAM NEILL

*Most of the early European explorers stopped in Adventure Bay: Furneaux, Cook, du Fresne – even Bligh on the Bounty. It's easy to understand why because it's the first logical stop after crossing over from the Cape of Good Hope. I like Tasmania a lot. In many ways, it's a sort of idealised version of Australia. But I'm also slightly haunted here. It almost feels like a dark place to me and that's because it had such a dark colonial history.*

The *Resolution* and *Discovery* anchored there on 27 January 1777 and took on water, food and wood. Not to mention armloads of grass to keep the animals happy.

Cook's encounter with the Aboriginal people on lunawani was quite different from his experience with the locals on Australia's east coast on the first voyage.

### ROYCE EVERETT, Ben Lomond Nation

*Well, if Cook didn't discover Australia, who would have done? It could have been the French ... the Japanese could have taken over ... who is to say we would have been any*

> *better off or worse off with anyone else, you know? It had to*
> *be discovered sometime. So I think we got the better of the*
> *worse evils.*

As the crew were busy sawing down trees, a group of Nuenonne people appeared out of the bush carrying spears.

**JOHN WEBBER (1751–1793), Artist, Cook's third voyage**

*They were quite naked & wore no ornaments except the large punctures or ridges raised on the skin ... they were of the common stature but rather slender; their skin was black and also their hair which was as woolly as any Native of Guinea, but they were not distinguished by remarkable thick lips nor flat noses, on the contrary their features were far from disagreeable; they had pretty good eyes and their teeth were tolerable even but very dirty; most of them had their hair and beards anointed with red ointment and some had their faces painted with the same composition.*

A flighty marine turned tail and fled to the boat before the Nuenonne men relinquished their weapons and showed themselves to be less interested in driving off the new arrivals than they were fascinated by the dynamics of tree-felling by saw. Cook and Mai arrived carrying some knick-knacks, along with a brace of freshly baked bread and some recently caught fish and birds. Turning their noses up at the unfamiliar smell of the freshly baked bread, the Nuenonne also refused the fish, but happily accepted the dead birds.

Cook convinced one of the men to throw his spear at a target. He missed. Mai, presumably keen to show off the military superiority of his friends' weapons, used his musket to blast the target to smithereens. The shocked Nuenonne very wisely took off into the bush. Cook was less than pleased; he assumed this would be the last he'd see of the locals. He'd struggled to make any meaningful connection with the Aboriginal inhabitants of the Australian mainland, and for a minute or two had thought he was going to do better in Tasmania.

He was wrong. As the boats from the *Resolution* and *Discovery* sailed into the cove the next morning, a group of twenty or so unarmed Nuenonne men were waiting on the beach. Cook did his usual thing and placed medals and beads strung on ribbons around their necks. The Nuenonne weren't interested in these offerings. But Cook's waistcoat? That was another thing altogether. One man was fascinated by it, so Cook handed it over. The ice was broken, and the Nuenonne broke out in what was described as the '*most immoderate fits of laughter*'. Perhaps they were delighted by the waistcoat – or perhaps they thought it the most ludicrous thing they had ever seen.

**ROYCE EVERETT:** *Now that some of our land has been handed back, the opportunities here are just colossal. When you think where it came from – this was Aboriginal land and dispossessed from the people who lived here. Now, some of it is repossessed. Which is great. I'd love to come back in fifty years' time and see all this – what has become of it. It's a great opportunity for the Aboriginal people of Tasmania.*
**SAM NEILL:** *Someone said to me, you don't know what loss is until you've had a whole continent taken from you.*

*ROYCE EVERETT: How true, how true. Still a long way to go ... of course we've been given a lot back. But, by golly ... still a long way to go.*

Bobbing about in the placid waters of karapati, the men of the *Discovery* decided they were less interested in cementing their friendship with the locals than they were determined to cut loose. Half a world away from home, they had the only fun they could – they nicked the rum rations and drank themselves silly. Being reasonably sozzled on board was par for the course, but drinking yourself into oblivion was not the done thing at all. Charles Clerke ordered the men flogged – which on top of a brutal hangover would not have been a pleasant thing – and in a fit of pique, Cook ordered the men to pack up and leave. The *Resolution* and *Discovery* departed karapati after just two days.

Yes, the irresponsibility of the harebrained drunkards got under Cook's skin. But something else was bothering him. Thanks to the shoddy fit-out of the two ships before they'd departed England, Cook had been forced to stop for repairs in Cape Town, and the *Discovery* had needed to have its leaks plugged as well. The diversion to Tasmania for stock feed had also been unplanned, and they were already well behind schedule to make it north in time for the northern summer. Cook was hoping to make it to the Arctic Circle before the ice closed in for winter. And the delays were making that less likely by the minute.

Despite the fact that an important geographic question was staring him in the face, Cook's mind was elsewhere. This is usually cited as the reason for his peculiar neglect of Tasmania.

**SAM NEILL**

*When Cook leaves the Tasmanian coast after just five days, he does something very strange. At this point in time nothing is known about what lies between here and Point Hicks, the first part of Australia that Cook spotted in 1770. Given the assiduous and curious nature of Cook the cartographer and explorer, it's strange that he didn't bother to venture north to explore. Instead he travels directly to New Zealand.*

Uncharacteristically, Cook was happy to accept Tobias Furneaux's assessment that Tasmania was joined to the mainland. It would be almost another thirty years before the body of water separating the two and now known as Bass Strait was identified and navigated by George Bass and Matthew Flinders. The Cook we know from the first and second voyages would have insisted on circumnavigating the island just to make sure. But this time round, science and geography weren't at the top of the list; for Cook and the Admiralty, this expedition was all about commerce.

\*

Before he headed for Tahiti, Cook decided to divert to Tōtaranui, which the British had dubbed Queen Charlotte Sound. The anticipation on board the *Resolution* and the *Discovery* must have been at fever pitch. Cook and his men had unfinished business in New Zealand. The grisly end of the ten sailors from the *Adventure* in Whareunga Bay – Grass Cove – was now common knowledge, and the crew expected their captain to wreak righteous vengeance upon the Māori who had killed and consumed his men.

*Portrait of a New Zealander,*
John Webber, 1774. Cook accepted
Ngāti Kuia chief Kahura's account
of the 'cannibal' incident, much to
the dismay of his men, and
angered them further by agreeing
to Kahura's request for a portrait.
SLNSW, SAFE / DL Pe 214, IE1690213

## SAM NEILL

*How on earth had this happened ... this horror? And now
the British were returning. Would he avenge the fallen
men ... would more blood be shed?*

When the Māori saw the two British ships sailing into the Sound
on 11 February 1777, they reached the same conclusion. They
expected Cook to seek revenge for what had happened. Tensions
on both sides of the beach were high. What would Cook do?

What none of them realised was that although Cook fully
intended to deal with the events in Grass Cove, he planned to do
it his way. And that involved finding out the truth about what
had happened there. None of the men involved in the skirmish
with the Māori had escaped to tell their side of the story, and so
the conclusions reached by their crewmates were based on

supposition and assumption, neither of which were things Cook placed any stock in. He was all about hard evidence. The only people alive who could testify to what happened that day were the Māori people involved in the killing.

Despite Cook's assurances that he bore the Māori no ill will, five days passed before he was able to get a local perspective on the events that had precipitated the attack on the sailors from the *Adventure*. Mai spoke with a group of Māori at Grass Cove and interpreted for Cook. A disagreement over trade terms – a British sailor had refused to hand anything over in exchange for a stone adze he had been given – had inevitably led to a tussle. Two Māori had been shot and killed, and Chief Kahura had called for reinforcements.

While the sailors were reloading their muskets, the Māori had overwhelmed them. These were not people you picked a fight with without expecting consequences and it was always going to end with death, on one side of the beach or the other. That day in Grass Cove, the Māori were the victors and they dispatched the vanquished in the customary manner.

### RAYMOND SMITH, Ngāti Kuia,
#### Rongomaiwahine Tribes, Descendant of Kahura
*Our people were giving and friendly and beautiful. But Cook's men needed to know not to cross the line, or we would defend our land. For them it was like a war, and in war there are traditions that were followed. Obviously they were killed here – our people burnt them. This was a cultural process and it was natural justice for this country ... part of our natural law.*

It seemed there was no question about why things had gone the way they had. The sailors had behaved appallingly and had been punished accordingly. Cook chose to believe the Māori account. He'd had trouble with the same sailors in Tahiti and had no reason to believe their behaviour in New Zealand would be any better.

### PETER BEECH, Eco-tour Operator

*All of Cook's men knew what had happened to their shipmates on that second voyage. And they fully expected Cook to sail over to Grass Cove, turn his ships broadside on, and blow that place to smithereens. So he did go over there and he asked Chief Kahura, 'Why did you kill my men?' Kahura told him that that the sailors had come to his bay, looking for scurvy grass. They wanted to trade but had no trade goods with them. They asked one of the Māori for a hatchet, but the sailors refused to give them anything in return. So the Māori thought he was getting stiffed and stole some bread or a coat or something, and the midshipman's mate fired on this guy and killed him. He fired a second time and killed two of the Māori. But then he had no more shots left and the other guns were back in the boat, so Kahura called out to his men to come down and overpower these guys.*

Now Cook had the facts, his men expected there to be consequences. Strangely enough, so did the Māori.

Which made what happened next all the more remarkable. Kahura, the chieftain who had led the warriors of the Ngāti Kuia and Rangitāne *iwi* in the attack on the sailors at Whareunga Bay, came on board the *Resolution* at Cook's invitation.

**CAPTAIN JAMES COOK**

*I must confess that I admired his courage and was not a little pleased at the confidence he put in me. Perhaps in this he placed his whole safety, for I had always declared to those who solicited his death that I had always been a friend to them all and would continue to be so unless they gave me a cause to act otherwise.*

When Kahura expressed a desire to have his likeness captured by the expedition's artist, John Webber, Cook agreed with delight rather than punishing him for what he had done.

Cook was oblivious to the impact of this moment. He was clear on his own motives, writing in his journal of the pride he felt about the equitable way he handled the situation. It was a most Enlightened response, as far as he was concerned.

**CAPTAIN JAMES COOK**

*It appeared to me that they were apprehensive we were come to revenge the death of Captain Furneaux's people ... they must be well assured that I was no longer a stranger to that unhappy affair, and I did all in my power to assure them of the continuance of my friendship, and that I should not disturb them on that account.*

Most tellingly, he proposed that he would continue to be a friend to the Māori *'unless they gave me a cause to act otherwise'.* Apparently the killing and devouring of ten of his crew didn't qualify as a 'cause' that would induce Cook to repeal his friendship.

Imagine how the men on board the *Resolution* and *Discovery* felt. It's difficult not to feel some sympathy for the sailors who had been on the *Adventure* when their shipmates were killed. Cook was a stern leader who tolerated no nonsense on the part of the men under his command. Yet there he was, entertaining the man responsible for killing, and eating, their comrades, in the Great Cabin. Mai, for one, was incensed. '*You tell me if a man kills another in England he is hanged for it, this man has killed ten and yet you will not kill him, though a great many of his countrymen desire it!*' he protested. The Ra'iatean, who had been on board the *Adventure* when the killings took place, was one of those who had firsthand experience of the event.

Fury bubbled over on deck. The men knew that outright mutiny was out of the question. Quiet rebellion was the only safe option. And so Cook's men concocted a most creative way to protest their captain's inaction.

### SAM NEILL

*And here followed one of the strangest events of all three voyages. Unknown to Cook, the men of the other ship, the* Discovery, *put a dog on trial for cannibalism. Now the dog had a nasty habit of biting people, but it was clearly not a cannibal. But here the poor creature is a proxy … a substitute. They find it guilty, they cook it, and they eat it.*

This was an unconscious expression of the Māori practice of *utu* (revenge) to restore *mana* (prestige). It was also a flagrant act of dissent against Cook's refusal to avenge his men's deaths.

He was never aware of it, but Cook's failure to seek revenge also undermined his standing with the Māori. As far as the locals were concerned, by not asserting *utu*, Cook was a man without *mana* – someone without any spiritual power and no better than a slave.

**PETER BEECH**

*When Cook went back to Ship Cove, everyone was very disappointed in him. The old people used to say that Grass Cove was the bay where Cook lost his* mana. *Māoris say that because* utu *was a really big part of their culture.* Utu *is like revenge – it's like an eye for an eye. If the shoe had been on the other foot they would most definitely have taken revenge. They saw his lack of action as weakness, on his part. And although I'm sure they were happy that he didn't, they kind of lost respect for him.*

There was a name for it – *taurekareka*. Cook was diminished in the eyes of the Māori and his men alike.

Better than almost all of us, Cook knew where he was geographically speaking. But even after all those years in the Pacific, he was still a man adrift in a metaphysical sense.

Just as he tracked the movement of stars in the skies and traced shorelines through his looking glass, Cook observed the people he met in the Pacific. But he could never truly understand them. Cook was a man of the Enlightenment. His was not the Old Testament God of thunderbolts and lightning, wrath and rightful vengeance. The God for Cook's age was Christ – a man of forgiveness and clemency. Turn the other cheek, do unto others and all that. But these were meaningless sentiments to the people gathered on both sides of the beach in Queen Charlotte Sound, who wanted things to play out in a far less merciful manner.

Through his inaction, Cook failed to secure *mana* for his own people. But he also failed Māori expectations by neglecting to acknowledge the importance of retribution to achieve balance.

This was a turning point, and it soured Cook's relationship both with the people of the Pacific and with his own crew.

In a sense, it was the beginning of the end.

*FOURTEEN*

# OFF THE RAILS

*The longer I'm on this journey – this exploration of the*
*Pacific – the less I'm certain about not just the present*
*but also the past because history is fluid: it's always being*
*rewritten, manipulated, reinterpreted. Bits are forgotten;*
*pieces of the jigsaw are missing. But also I'm learning that*
*history is us – we are part of history. It is within us and*
*we are part of the story. The story continues and it's never*
*anything less than fascinating.*

**SAM NEILL**

As the *Resolution* and *Discovery* packed up and readied to set sail from Queen Charlotte Sound, the relationship between the men on board and the Māori who lived there had been ruptured. Cook might have thought that his humane decision to not seek redress would inspire gratitude and fealty in the bosoms of Kahura and his *iwi*. But in this instance, Cook had grabbed firm hold of the wrong end of the stick. Any respect the Māori may have harboured for the Englishman and his comrades had evaporated. As far as they were concerned, Cook had lost his *mana*.

**DR PETER MEIHANA, Massey University, Ngāti Kuia, Ngāti Apa, Rangitāne, Ngāi Tahu Tribes, Tribal Historian**
*In terms of the way history has been written, the received version was always from the position of the outsider looking in. Now we take into account the idea of Māori agency in the events that occurred here.*

The locals gave up any pretence of attempting to establish equal trade terms when exchanging things with the visitors. They expected gifts – tribute, if you like – from men they now saw as subhuman. Lieutenant James Burney, who had been on board the *Adventure* and had the misfortune of leading the party that discovered the partially devoured remains of his shipmates, found the brazen way the Māori now flaunted their perceived superiority over the men from the British ships utterly galling.

**JAMES BURNEY (1750–1821), Crew Member, Cook's second and third voyages (later, English rear-admiral)**
*Many of them held us in great contempt and I believe chiefly on account of our not revenging the affair of Grass Cove, so contrary to the principles by which they would have been actuated in the like case ... one man did not scruple to acknowledge his being present and assisting at the killing and eating of the* Adventure's *people.*

Even after the litany of trials and tribulations endured on his first and second voyages, Cook's men had remained steadfast in their loyalty to their captain. But things were different this time round. Cook's inaction had averted further violence, but his determined moral position alienated him from the crew and caused them to question his leadership.

After leaving New Zealand, when meat was stolen from an already meagre supply, Cook cut the men's rations in an attempt to force the culprit to come forward. Nobody confessed, and instead the crew banded together and refused to eat – a gesture Cook declared 'mutinous'. It must have troubled and saddened him to see his men expressing barely veiled contempt for him.

Now at the age of forty-eight and beset by old-man-grumpiness, it certainly wouldn't have helped his state of mind. All Cook really wanted to do was head north to the Arctic Circle and do what was asked of him. But things kept getting in the way.

For one thing, Cook was paying the price of neglecting oversight of the ships' refitting back in England. The *Resolution* was no longer the reliable vessel it had been on the second voyage. Now, it was about as seaworthy as a sieve. The knowledge that he had been slipshod in his duty to ensure the ship he took to sea was in tip-top condition must have been a constant source of annoyance to him. Once they were out in the open ocean, the botched repairs to the damage that had occurred in the daunting waters of the Antarctic on the second voyage failed to hold. He was livid, accusing the shipyard's naval officers of 'barbarous neglect'.

As if the frustration caused by his tetchy crew and unseaworthy ship weren't bad enough, after Cook left New Zealand his path was blocked by adverse winds. He had hoped to head straight for Tahiti but found himself battling winds that pushed the ships to the south-east. With a demanding menagerie of two- and four-legged beasts on board, Cook couldn't spend too long between anchorages. Grass was a necessity. So he was forced to island-hop from New Zealand to Tahiti.

Of Cook's character, one of the crew observed that 'procrastination & irresolution he was a stranger to. Action was life to him & repose a kind of death.' But try as he might to avoid delay, Cook was being thwarted at every turn. It had been over a year since he'd left England and the expedition was still treading water. And it wasn't over yet. It's little wonder that Cook was feeling rather irritable. He had come to the Pacific with a new destination in his sights – yet by this stage, pretty much all he had done was go over old ground. It would have driven most people insane.

In fact, some historians have suggested that this is exactly what was happening to Cook – that he was losing his grip on reality. With irritation worming its way beneath his skin like a parasite, his behaviour became increasingly erratic. But why? What caused the rapid transformation of a man renowned for his forbearance and stoicism into a tyrant whose outbursts of temper were a constant scourge on the third voyage?

When a goat was stolen from one of the ships in the Society Islands, Cook led thirty-five armed men on a rampage across the island of Mo'orea, burning houses and canoes and plundering provisions until the cloven-footed creature was returned. As far as some of the more level-headed members of his crew were concerned, Cook had slipped a cog or two. One midshipman wrote, 'I can't well account for Capt Cook's proceedings on this occasion as they were so different from his conduct in like cases in his former voyages.' James King's assessment of the incident was scathing:

> Not being able to account for Captn Cook's precipitate
> proceeding in this business, I cannot think it justifiable;
> less destructive measures might have been adopted & the

*end gained … I doubt whether our ideas of propriety in*
*punishing so many innocent people for the crimes of a*
*few, will be ever reconcilable to any principle one can*
*form of justice.'*

The real reason for his excesses are not known. There are many opinions on the matter, but no clear answer.

**JOHN ROBSON, Map Librarian, University of Waikato**
*One of the saddest things about our knowledge of Cook is*
*that nobody who knew him wrote a biography of him.*
*We really don't have many insights about him as a*
*person.*

In her landmark book, *The Trial of the Cannibal Dog: Captain Cook in the South Seas*, Professor Dame Anne Salmond argues convincingly that Cook harboured deep resentment and a sense of betrayal after his encounter with Kahura and the Māori in Whareunga Bay, and that his irrational behaviour was attributable to a switch in attitude towards Polynesian people. Where in the past he had spoken of the Māori people in glowing terms, there's a marked shift in the way he describes them in the journal from his third voyage.

**CAPTAIN JAMES COOK**
*[Māori] kill every soul that falls in their way, not even*
*sparing the women and children, and then either feast or*
*gorge themselves on the spot or carry off as many of the*
*dead as they can and do it at home with acts of brutality*
*horrible to relate.*

Salmond also points out that there was one noteworthy difference between the first two voyages and the third. On his final voyage Cook had only one civilian with him – the astronomer William Bayly, who had also accompanied Cook on his second Pacific endeavour. But he was housed on the *Discovery*, not the *Resolution*. It is possible that the absence of independent observers on board his ship meant Cook dropped his guard, to the detriment of the men under his command.

Cook was also overseeing a second ship, and there were complications and difficulties that came with that responsibility. Although the *Resolution* had travelled with the *Adventure* on the second voyage, Furneaux's inability to keep track of his commander meant they didn't spend much time travelling in company. This time, Cook had over two hundred men making demands – for fresh food, for rest, for water. Not to mention discipline. Flogging, which had been infrequent on Cook's earlier voyages, became commonplace. Keeping things on an even keel required constant vigilance.

The question has to be asked, though: is this just wishful thinking based on a desperation to find a reasonable excuse for Cook's irrational behaviour? It shouldn't be discounted that by 1777 Cook had spent many years at sea; he was – for his chosen occupation – an old man, and his reasons for embarking this time round were pragmatic, rather than romantic. And things weren't going to plan.

Cook was also physically unwell. He was taking an opium derivative for a stomach disorder. Although opium is usually equated with euphoria and a general sense of placid wellbeing, if the pain was severe enough to require analgesia, one can only imagine that it would have left him feeling rather out of sorts.

It's likely that this would also have been affecting his judgement.

On Tahiti, a chieftain learnt of the Englishman's affliction and sent twelve women including his mother and three of his sisters, on board the *Resolution* to relieve his pain. After repeated massages, he declared himself cured and the pains 'entirely removed'.

### CAPTAIN JAMES COOK

*At first I thought that this numerous train of females came into my boat with no other view than to get a passage to Matavai. But when we arrived at the ship, they told me, they intended passing the night on board, for the express purpose of undertaking the cure of the disorder I complained of; which was a pain of the rheumatic kind ... I accepted the friendly offer ... and submitted myself to their directions ... as many of them as could get round me, began to squeeze me with both hands, from head to foot, but more particularly on the parts where the pain was lodged, till they made my bones crack, and my flesh became a perfect mummy. In short, after undergoing this discipline about a quarter of an hour, I was glad to get away from them. However, the operation gave me immediate relief.*

\*

The physical discomfort Cook had been experiencing would not have improved his state of mind. Nor would the unwelcome news that greeted him when he arrived on Tahiti that since his last visit the Spaniards had been sniffing about the islands. The Tahitians reported that two Spanish vessels from Lima in Peru had deposited two Catholic priests on the island for a ten-month sabbatical. The ships returned to collect them and left a nine-foot-high cross behind, inscribed in Spanish and asserting Spanish sovereignty over Tahiti. Furious, Cook tore down the cross and added his own inscription claiming the island for King George III.

For Cook, Tahiti and its archipelago had served up no end of irritants during the time he had spent there. The same can't be said for his men, for whom the temptations of a blissful climate and beautiful and available young women meant they saw this place as heaven on earth. On Ra'iatea, there was much gnashing of teeth and tearing of hair at the news that departure from the Society Islands was imminent. Although none of the sailors were under any illusions about the severity of the punishment that would be invited by a decision to go AWOL, some foolhardy souls attempted to flee with their lovers.

When the Ra'iateans were not forthcoming with help to corral the deserters, Cook's response was swift and high-handed. He had his mind set on his ships' next destination – the northern Pacific. The last thing he wanted to do was waste time chasing lovesick sailors around the jungle. So he gave Clerke instructions to invite the chieftain Reo's children on board under the guise of giving them some gifts, and then Cook held them hostage until the lovesick crew members were forced to return.

Reo, who was also Cook's *taio* (ceremonial friend), was livid. He hatched a plot to kill Cook and Clerke while they took their daily bath in a freshwater river – a plot that was foiled when Cook became suspicious of Reo's behaviour, and the Ra'iatean lover of a man aboard the *Discovery* warned the British about it. The absconders were returned to the ship to face their inevitable flogging on the orders of the man known in the Society Islands as 'Toote'.

**DAVID SAMWELL (1751–1791), Welsh Naval Surgeon on Cook's third voyage**

*[N]o man could be more esteemed & dreaded than Capt Cook was among them, who upon all occasions preserved his consequence with an admirable address, & the name of Toottee will be handed down to posterity as the greatest chief & a man of the greatest power that ever visited their island.*

On board his ships, Cook generally insisted on observing the strict hierarchy of naval conventions. Discipline required that the commander retain a distance from his crew, which is why Cook remained aloof from his men other than on the odd occasion when he let down his guard. Cook was expected to remain in control of the men on board his ship.

His high-handed treatment of indigenous peoples was another thing altogether. For a man who fancied himself as reasonable and fair-minded, it was a peculiar approach that inevitably engendered ill will towards him.

In Tonga on the third voyage, he and Clerke had devised a cruel way to punish thieves: they would slash crosses on the culprits' arms and shave half a head of their hair to impose on them a 'mark of infamy' that was calculated to be a grievous insult – by this time Cook and his men knew all too well the importance that Polynesian people placed upon their heads and hair.

**GEORGE GILBERT (?–1781) crew member,**
**Cook's third voyage**

*Capt Cook punished in a manner rather unbecoming of a European ... by cutting off their ears; firing at them with small shot, or ball, as they were swimming or paddling to the shore and suffering the people ... to beat them with the oars, and stick the boat hook into them ... one in particular he punished by ordering one of our people to make two cuts upon his arm to the bone one across the other close below his shoulder; which was an act that I cannot account for any other ways than to have proceeded from a momentary fit of anger.*

Remember that before travelling to Ra'iatea, Cook had just escaped a plot to kill him during his three months in Tonga. Was it any wonder, given the way he was treating the locals?

The point is, Cook didn't – and perhaps couldn't – see when he had overstayed his welcome. He kept pushing. On the third voyage, what had been a natural curiosity about unfamiliar things seemed to become an obsession. Cook may have been unflinching in his commitment to naval conventions on board a ship, but on land he was willing to overstep boundaries in order to bear witness to native rituals.

Cook returned to Tonga in July 1777. Paulaho, the Tu'i Tonga or paramount chief, had what must have seemed like a good idea at the time – and it was one that he hoped would consolidate his power over his lands and his people.

The July of 1777 was a big month in Tonga, and Paulaho was hosting the 'Inasi – a formal ceremony to lobby the higher powers for a prolific growing season.

This was the biggest event on the Tongan social calendar, attended by chiefs from across the Archipelago who came to pay homage to the paramount chief. Paulaho planned to make it even bigger this year by announcing his son as his successor. And in Polynesian society, nothing was more important at events like these than *mana* – prestige. It occurred to Paulaho that the *mana* of his 'Inasi would be enhanced if James Cook – and, by proxy, Cook's god – attended the ceremony. Needless to say, things didn't quite go according to plan.

The 'Inasi was an enormously significant occasion so completely knotted up in *tapu* (sacred protocol) it's a wonder the Tu'i Tonga took the risk. But as Paulaho was a god according to Tongan belief, he probably assumed he'd have enough authority to be able to control Cook. But Paulaho didn't figure on his guest's character. The Englishman was used to giving orders, not taking them. It was never going to end well.

Cook did begrudgingly agree to remove his hat, untie his hair and take off whatever clothes he had on his upper body – an absolute prerequisite for viewing the ceremony. What a sight he must have been; a tall, near-naked Englishman observing a passing parade of chieftains and warriors. Cook was under the supervision of some Tongan men entrusted with the impossible task of making sure he followed protocol. They tried to get him to conform by urging him to bow his head at appropriate times as the Tu'i Tonga and his son received their offerings, and to avert his eyes when sacred *tapu* rituals were underway.

**TAKAPU, Matāpule to the King of Tonga**
*Captain Cook adopted the word* tapu *from the Tongan language and took it with him to Great Britain where it*

*ended up in the English dictionaries as 'taboo'. Tapu, as we pronounce it in the common language, means some sort of prohibition, but it actually relates to the hierarchy of our system. The tapus are an obligation to keep the relationship between the hierarchy of society intact. The hierarchy contributes to the harmony of the Tongan society because it's based on blood relationships, so we are all related to one another within that system.*

For the most part Cook ignored the entreaties of the Tongan men. Eventually he left the compound where he was expected to remain, and he walked over consecrated ground. This act was the equivalent of wandering up to the altar in Westminster Cathedral during Sunday mass and helping yourself to a mouthful of Communion wine. Cook knew full well he was pushing his luck, later writing: '*I was several times desired to go away, and at last when they found I would not stir, they ... desired I would bare my shoulders.*' Yet he persisted.

Although he'd never know it, Cook had cheated death yet again. Before the 'Inasi he had been warned about the significance of the ceremony and the consequences for any breach of *tapu*.

His flagrant disregard for these sacred laws was peculiar given that by this voyage – his third – he knew Polynesian society well enough to understand the ins and outs of *tapu* and the penalties incurred by flouting the rules. He couldn't pretend he didn't know what was going on.

An early missionary who was given the Tongan perspective of Cook's behaviour at the 'Inasi marvelled at the fact that the Englishman managed to avert a sticky end that time.

**JOHN THOMAS (1797–1881), Missionary, Tonga**

*Although [Cook] was checked again and again and told it was* tapu *or unlawful for him to be present as he was with clothes, yet he persisted ... Only priests were present for a certain part of the ceremony, and being full of fear for their gods, the wonder is, that the Captain escaped being struck, or killed by some of them.*

Cook had only been given this chance to let his hair down and kick his heels up – figuratively and literally – because unfavourable conditions had delayed his ship's planned departure for Tahiti. Standing there with the wind in his hair and the sun on his bare back, he might well have been having a whale of a time. But in what was to become a common theme on the third voyage, his men were less than impressed by his performance.

**JOHN WILLIAMSON (1745?–1798), Lieutenant, Cook's third voyage**

*We ... were not a little surprised at seeing Capt Cook in the procession of the chiefs, with his hair hanging loose & his body naked down to the waist ... I do not pretend to dispute the propriety of Capt Cook's conduct, but I cannot help thinking he rather let himself down.*

It did seem to be uncharacteristically footloose and fancy-free behaviour by the otherwise sober captain. Perhaps, as has been suggested, Cook had thrown caution to the wind because he was not under the scrutiny of civilian observers. Unlike on Cook's first two voyages, where he had been attended by a clutch of scientists and civilians, the third voyage was staffed solely by military men. It's possible that Cook cared less about what they thought of him than the judgement of men he would have seen as his social and intellectual superiors. It could also be that he had taken it upon himself to cast an anthropological eye upon proceedings and record the 'Inasi from a scientific perspective in the absence of non-military observers. Ultimately, this pig-headed determination would play a part in his demise.

Cook was not a religious man. But in the name of science, he was interested in witnessing and recording cultural and spiritual rituals. As far as he was concerned, he was observing, not judging. So it is that we have from Cook a detailed account of human sacrifice he witnessed on Mo'orea during the third voyage – a ritual used to rouse the support of the gods when going into battle.

**CAPTAIN JAMES COOK**

*They now took the bundles of feathers and the sacrifice to the great* Morai *... at the foot of them the latter was placed round which the priests seated themselves and began again their prayers, while some of their attendants dug a hole at the foot of the* Morai *in which they buried the victim. As it was putting into the grave a boy squeaked out aloud, Omai said it was the* Eatua *[God] ... while two men beat at times on two drums very loud, and a boy squeaked out as before in a long shrill voice thrice, this as we were told was to call the* Eatua *to eat what they had prepared for him ... The unhappy sufferer seemed to be a middle aged man, and as we were told a* Tou tou *but I never understood he had done any crime so as to merit* *death; it is however certain that they made choice of such for these sacrifices, or else common low fellows ... During the ceremony we were silent but as soon as it was over ... of course [we] condemned it.*

\*

Although Cook was clearly keen to record details of such rituals, his main concern was to get to the Arctic Circle before the northern hemisphere winter closed in. Before he left Polynesia, though, he had to do the one thing he had ostensibly returned to the Pacific to do – return Mai to his home.

When Mai had set sail with Furneaux aboard the *Adventure*, he had hoped his newfound connections with the British would be put to use driving his enemies – the Bora Borans – from his homeland in Ra'iatea and avenging his father's death at their hands. But it was not to be. On his return Ra'iatea was still in the hands of the Bora Borans, so instead Cook acquired land for Mai on Huahine.

Whatever expectations Mai may have had about the reception he might receive fell flat. No doubt thinking he'd dazzle his countrymen with all the splendid things he'd brought back from Britain, when he first arrived in Vaitepiha Bay he donned a suit of armour and mounted a horse, intending to ride along the beach.

Unfortunately, the horse was less concerned about making a positive impression and promptly unseated poor Mai.

Even his vivid account of the splendours he'd seen in 'Pretanne', as Mai described Britain, failed to impress.

### JOHN RICKMAN (1737–1818), Lieutenant,
### Cook's third voyage

*He said, the great King of Pretanne had three hundred thousand warriors every day at his command ... and more than double that number of sailors, who traversed the globe, from the rising of the sun to his setting ... That in one city only on the banks of a river far removed from the sea, there were more people than were contained in the whole group of islands with which His Majesty was acquainted.*

Until Mai offered his countrymen red feathers from a collection he had picked up in Tonga, even his own brother-in-law treated him dismissively.

### CAPTAIN JAMES COOK

*When we first drew near the island, several canoes came off to the ships each conducted by two or three men, but as they were only common fellows Omai took no notice of them nor they of him ... At length a chief whom I had known before named Ootie and Omai's brother-in-law ... came on board, and three or four more ... yet there was nothing either tender or striking in their meeting. On the contrary there seemed to be a perfect indifference on both sides, till Omai asked his brother down into the cabin, opened the drawer where he kept his red feathers and gave him a few ... [W]ith the property he was master of he would [have] had prudence enough to make himself respected and even courted by the first persons in the island, but instead of that he rejected the advice of those who wished him well and suffered himself to be duped by every designing knave.*

As Cook described it, perhaps rather sadly: *'It was evident to everyone that it was not the man but his property they were in love with, for had he not showed them his red feathers, which is the most valuable thing that can be carried to the island, I question if they had given him a coconut.'*

On Huahine, Cook instructed his men to build Mai a wooden house, which they surrounded by a moat to fence in his horse, cows, sheep, goats, turkeys, geese, rabbits, cats and monkey. By any standards, Mai brought with him a treasure trove of British goodies – his house contained a bed, dining table, chairs, a hand organ, muskets, swords, tin soldiers, a globe of the world and crockery. And a suit of armour. But all those worldly treasures couldn't protect Mai from the hand of fate – he died just two and a half years after returning from Britain. All the splendours he'd brought with him were taken and dispersed by his family. Today, nothing of him remains in the Society Islands.

Cook's obligations fulfilled, on 8 December 1777 he departed Ra'iatea. He turned northwards, heading at last for the North American continent. The first leg of his journey had taken much longer than intended and for the first time in his life, it seemed things weren't going Cook's way. His third voyage was turning out to be a tale of thwarted ambitions.

# FIFTEEN

# GIVE AND TAKE

*For me, the strange contradiction of the wilderness – of the emptiest places of all – is that these are the places where I most readily feel the presence of the ghosts of those who have been here before ... Captain Cook and the indigenous people who lived here.*

**SAM NEILL**

Trading ... Stocks. Shares. Bank bonds. Stamps. Pokemon cards.

Everyone knows the rules of engagement. If you have something someone else wants, you trade it for something you want in exchange. If the rules of supply and demand kick in and you find yourself holding onto something scarce that someone's keen to get their hands on, you may end up pocketing more for it than you actually think it's worth. The flip side of that is if you're extremely keen to offload it, you might be prepared to hand it over for less than its perceived value. Either way, the trade should end up with both parties pretty happy about the outcome. But things can get tricky in the schoolyard Pokemon stock exchange when you have a card the neighbourhood bully wants. As he or

320

she advances towards you with 'persuasive' powers locked and loaded, it's difficult enough to keep hold of your dignity without worrying about your Pokemon, which you'll likely see torn from your sweaty little hands with nothing given in exchange except a bloody nose.

Extending this metaphor into the eighteenth-century Pacific, as James Cook hopped from island to island, he was generally observing the rules and giving objects in exchange for the necessities he required from the locals. Nails, looking glasses, axes and red feathers were exchanged for consumables. As for the men on board, they ran an enthusiastic trade in goods for many things, including the locally made cultural objects that, marketed as ethnographic curios, set collectors aquiver back in Europe.

At this point in the game things were fairly equitable between the visitors and the indigenous people he encountered. Cook was just one man seeking to boost supplies on one or two ships. In trade terms, at least, he had never shown himself inclined to behave like a schoolyard bully, but he was also in a position where he needed the supplies being offered by the people of the Pacific a great deal more than they required whatever it was he was presenting for their delectation. The indigenous people knew the value of what they had. And on the third voyage, Cook would meet a group of people on the North American coast who would prove to be the masters of the art of the deal.

But first he had to get there. And to do that, Cook knew he'd have to offer his men something more than another hunk or two of hard tack to entice them to cooperate. The delays they'd endured had depleted the ship's supplies to the extent that they wouldn't make it back to home soil without some belt tightening. Although they were able to keep the expedition going with the goods they obtained through trade with the Pacific Islanders, there wasn't enough surplus left to make it through those legs of the journey where they might expect to have trouble replenishing stores of fresh food and water. And after his experience in the Southern Ocean on the second voyage, Cook's expectations of the Arctic Circle and what it might offer from a culinary perspective were not high. So Cook put it to his men – he'd share the bonus that would come his way when, as he expected, they found the North-West Passage.

There was a catch, of course. It was a big ask, but the potential rewards were enormous.

### SAM NEILL

*To the officers' amazement, the crew agreed to the unthinkable – to give up their daily ration of rum, except on Saturdays. That way they would preserve their supplies for the chilly north. Instead, the crew took to mixing their reduced grog with coconut milk. Could this have been the first ever piña colada?*

\*

The British quest to find a faster way to Asia from Europe via the Arctic was driven by a desire to reach the lucrative and insatiable markets of China and the Far East. Britain was determined to crack it open. As Cook was making his way to the western side of the Pacific shoreline of the North American continent, unbeknownst to him the Admiralty had decided to send another expedition to approach from the east. Lieutenant Richard Pickersgill, who had accompanied Cook on his two previous voyages, was given command of the *Lyon*. But the going was tough, and his ship and callow crew not up to the task. By all reports, he was intoxicated for much of the latter part of the voyage. After he returned to London, he was found guilty of drunkenness by a court martial and dismissed from service. He drowned a short time after – not, as he might have hoped, in command of a ship on the high seas but in the muddy water of the Thames.

Putting this disappointment to one side, the Admiralty knew they had their best man on the job anyway. As Cook forged his way northwards, he was furthering British ambitions to establish itself in the North Pacific. Russian expansion into Alaska had Britain sweating, as did Spain's consolidation of power along the North and South American coastline. Spanish missions and forts were being built all along the Californian seaboard, and they had established the first European settlement on the site of San Francisco in 1776. Without a bold move or two, any hope Britain had of gaining a foothold in the region was fast disappearing. Britain was struggling to hold on to its colonies in what became the United States of America, where the locals were rebelling against the Crown in the revolution that would stretch from 1775 to 1783. Meanwhile France was attempting to assert itself, with its navigators poking around the Pacific at the same time as Cook. Having lost its Canadian territories to Britain, France was eager to find new lands upon which to impose itself.

Cook couldn't claim ignorance of these agendas – he had cut his cartographic teeth early in his career charting the coast of Newfoundland just as the British were booting the French out of Canada.

As much as all concerned liked to claim they were only focused on furthering the interests of science and exploration, that wasn't the whole story. Political and economic goals were always foremost amongst the strategies pursued by the ambitious European nations.

When news reached Spain from their colonies in Mexico that a British expedition was heading north, it caused much consternation on the Iberian Peninsula. Thanks to its settlements along the Pacific coastline and across the pond in the Spanish East Indies (now called the Philippines), Spain considered the Pacific to be its sphere of influence. It also considered much of North America its domain, and so news that the Russians had moved their fur-trading activities into Alaska must have irked them no end.

With the Viceroyalty of New Spain overseeing much of what is today the United States of America, and the viceroyalties of New Granada, Peru and Río de la Plata stretching from Central America almost to the tip of South America, Spain's territorial claims were not without good foundation from an eighteenth-century European perspective – keeping in mind that nobody in Europe had asked the people of the Pacific, who had been living there for thousands of years, what their thoughts were on the matter.

The Spanish knew that if Britain found a route into the Pacific across the Arctic Circle, this would allow the British to sneak into waters that Spain believed it had prior claim to. Word found its way back to England that any moves they planned to make towards America would be unwelcome.

The members of the Royal Society were incensed by the implication they had anything other than scientific purposes in mind. As a fellow of the Society and one-time vice-president, Daines Barrington protested, *'the English nation is actuated merely by desiring to know as much as possible with regard to the planet which we inhabit'.* The record shows he was likely protesting a little too loudly. Having authored a book in 1775 titled *Tracts on the Possibility of Reaching the North Pole*, Barrington probably had a fairly clear view of the true purpose of Cook's expedition.

*

Cook was sailing into troubled waters. Of course, that was never going to deter him. What would slow him down, though, was the constant need to restock the ships' stores.

With that in mind, Cook called halt on Christmas Eve, 1777. His two ships had reached an island that he named, unsurprisingly, Christmas Island. The enormous coral atoll – the largest in the world – was unpopulated when Cook landed, although today it's believed it was most likely used as a way station for the Polynesian voyagers crisscrossing the Pacific. Located smack-bang in the middle of the ocean, the island now known by the phonetic appellation 'Kiritimati' – say it out loud and you'll understand the connection with 'Christmas' – was first sighted by a Spaniard, Hernando de Grijalva, in 1537. Desolate and remote, it was blessed with an embarrassment of marine life. Cook and his men managed to capture two hundred green turtles during their short stay on the island.

For Cook and the early European navigators, islands like this had one use only. These were spots where the sailors could find the essentials they needed to get them to the places they really wanted to be. Which is why Cook made a habit of planting vegetables and releasing pairs of animals into the wild, in the hope they would reproduce and establish a supply of victuals ready and waiting for passing ships. With the wisdom of hindsight, we now know what an appalling idea this was – the extent of the environmental destruction caused by introduced species is beyond measure.

At the other end of the environmental catastrophe spectrum, it wouldn't take long before European powers became aware of just how rich in resources the Pacific was. Lacking the resource management skills of the Pacific First Nations, the Western approach was to take it all until there was nothing left. Which – over the centuries to come – humankind would have a very good stab at achieving.

To strip this vast maritime territory of its natural resources, the Europeans first had to control it. The skirmishes to achieve supremacy in the Pacific would be fought diplomatically, economically, and also on the battlefield.

\*

During the Second World War, one Polynesian island group and a bay named Pearl Harbor would become a tinderbox that would ignite the war in the Pacific. For our story, the archipelago would also be the place where Cook's luck would finally run out.

When the jagged peaks of Oahu appeared over the horizon on 18 January 1778, the men on board the *Resolution* and the *Discovery* became the first Europeans to lay eyes on the Hawaiian Islands, which Cook named for the First Lord of the Admiralty, Lord Sandwich.

As the British ships approached the neighbouring island of Kauai, a flotilla of canoes approached. What did the Hawaiians think of the apparition that arrived across the waves? Oral traditions record what the locals made of the peculiar vessels and their pale-skinned passengers. The masts they thought trees, the two boats an idiosyncratic double canoe. As for the men on board, the Hawaiians wondered at their 'white foreheads, sparkling eyes, wrinkled skins, and angular heads', and the way they 'breathed fire from their mouths' – presumably an impression of the sailors smoking tobacco.

When the Hawai'ians came on board, they were astounded by what they saw.

### CAPTAIN JAMES COOK

*I never saw Indians so much astonished at entering a ship before, their eyes were continually flying from object to object, the wildness of their looks and actions fully expressed their surprise and astonishment.*

Cook was also astonished by the fact the locals spoke a Polynesian dialect, which meant he could communicate with them.

The wonder of the initial contact was short-lived. As a trigger-happy third lieutenant – the brutal and generally disliked John Williamson – was attempting to land, he shot and killed a Hawai'ian.

### JAMES TREVENEN (1760–1790), Midshipman, Cook's third voyage

*A wretch, feared & hated by his inferiors, detested by his equals, & despised by his superiors; a very devil, to whom none of our midshipmen have spoke for above a year.*

But unlike with Cook's tragic first contact in New Zealand, there were no immediate repercussions.

As the lure of the Arctic called, Cook departed the Sandwich Islands after a brief visit as a god. His return visit would end on a less positive note. But, for now, the two ships tacked north-eastwards towards the American continent and a northern winter. Although they were still a long way short of the Arctic, to men who had been wallowing about in a tropical climate for an extended period, the cold was a rude shock. As Charles Clerke observed, '*We have been so long inhabitants of the torrid zone, that we are all shaking with cold here with the thermometer at 60.*' For Englishmen accustomed to European winters, fifteen degrees Celsius should have been a doddle. But they had grown soft.

The *Resolution* and *Discovery* continued to plough through the churning seas and thick fog, finally sighting the coast of Oregon on 6 March 1778. Cook leaves us in no doubt about the conditions the two ships were enduring – of the two landmarks he named, one he called Cape Foulweather. Although he struggled to make land, Cook's presence was important for Britain's colonial aspirations. When Sir Francis Drake had hauled his ship, the *Golden Hind*, ashore in 1579 at the spot now known as Drakes Bay, just north of San Francisco's Golden Gate, he claimed the continent in the name of Queen Elizabeth I from 'sea to sea' and south to Spain's territories in Mexico. Drake named it New Albion, which is the name Cook used when he wrote that he had spied '*the long looked for coast of Albion*'.

As far as Spain was concerned, Drake – who had been sent to the Pacific expressly to attack Spanish settlements and flotillas – was a blackguard and a crook. Any claims he made on the American continent were null and void, and Cook's appearance in their territory was a threat to their dominion. What they couldn't know was that Cook's greatest concern as he fought his way through the dreadful weather was simply staying afloat. The *Resolution* was far from resolute, and unless he found a safe place to repair the ship, Cook feared it would founder.

On 29 March, Cook found refuge. And not a moment too soon. On the west coast of the island that would one day be named for the man who accompanied Cook on his second and third voyages and would become a renowned navigator in his own right – George Vancouver – Cook found an anchorage that was blessed with everything he wanted and needed. Nootka Sound.

### SAM NEILL

*Cook turns in from the ocean and he's immediately surrounded by canoes with strange people he's never seen before. They start shouting at him –* ichme nutka, ichme nutka, *or something like that. What they're trying to say is 'Go in further … go round the island … there's a better place to anchor!' What he thinks they're saying is – 'We are Nootka! We are Nootka!' Big mistake, of course – but the name persists to this day.*

Of course, the area's appeal was not lost on the Mowachaht people who lived there. Beneath the shade cast by the enormous trees that Cook knew would give him the timber he needed to repair his ships, the Mowachaht lived in huge houses that were the largest permanent homes in the Pacific.

Cook described the Mowachaht lands as the richest and most abundant region he had encountered, and the locals knew the value of what they had.

When Cook dropped anchor, he did so near the tribe's summer retreat. Given its name – 'Yuquot', meaning 'wind comes from all directions' – it's little wonder the Mowachaht chose not to live there in winter.

**RAY WILLIAMS, Mowachaht Elder**

*The real name is Yuquot – where the four winds blow. This is our special place. The ancestors of the Mowachaht people are here and I choose to stay here because I want to put my heart and soul into believing this is Yuquot territory. I believe in protecting this land here.*

It wasn't the first time that the Mowachaht had seen Europeans. In August 1774, the Spanish explorer Juan Perez had stopped by on his voyage to check for troublesome British or Russian interlopers along the north Pacific coast of Spain's American territories. He didn't encounter any Europeans, but he did make contact with the locals.

The extraordinary welcome Cook received when he arrived in Perez's wake was unlike any he had experienced in the Pacific. Masked Mowachaht approached the two British ships in canoes, shaking rattles and chanting and howling in a cacophony that must have echoed around Nootka Sound. The second lieutenant, James King, appointed himself music critic and judged the fanfare '*by no means unpleasant to the ear*'. How to respond when confronted with a spontaneous serenade? '*We judged they might like our music,*' King wrote. In an age before phonographs, records, or streaming services, if you wanted to hear music, you had to play it yourself – or go to church. So most people could sing or play a tune. The crew picked up their instruments and struck up a tune. The Mowachaht people seemed impressed and responded with another ditty of their own. The finale? Cook rallied the French horn.

### SAM NEILL

*It always puts a shiver up my spine when I'm in the exact spot Cook was. Particularly in a place like Nootka Sound where almost nothing has changed at all. In Resolution Cove, the two ships were anchored – the* Resolution *and the* Discovery. *They set up an observatory on a rock you can still see today. One thing that's certainly very different today is that there must have been a cacophony of noise – people beating drums, singing, shouting at each other ... language all over the place. The place was full of people. But today, it's just me, and it's almost entirely silent.*

In addition to being musical impresarios, the Mowachaht turned out to be the canniest dealmakers in the Pacific. By this point, Cook thought he had it all worked out. He was pretty sure he knew what would tempt the locals. Metal was a sure-fire winner, for example, as were red feathers. But Cook was basing this largely upon his experiences with Polynesian people. Things would be different in Nootka Sound.

The interactions between Cook and his men and the Mowachaht were largely amicable because the locals were more than happy to engage in trade along terms the Europeans understood. There were none of the gift-giving rituals they found so confusing in Polynesia. The Mowachaht people were experienced traders in regular contact with other indigenous

American populations, and they also had a strong concept of property and ownership that tallied with British beliefs. This extended to sex, which the sailors on board pursued as vigorously here as they had elsewhere in the Pacific.

### SAM NEILL

*For Cook's men, sex in Nootka was not nearly as readily available here, as it had been elsewhere. But it was still available. The randy surgeon Samwell took advantage of that. It was transactional by nature, of course, but a rusty nail wouldn't do the job here. A pewter plate seemed to work its charms, though – it's difficult to overstate how valuable metal was to societies like this one. The sex itself must have come with its own challenges, given the proclivities of the locals who were inclined to smother themselves with a thick layer of animal fat in order to stay warm in these somewhat inclement climes. The mind boggles.*

For Cook, both pros and cons stemmed from the locals' commercial sophistication. Yes, he could get what he needed in Nootka Sound and the rate of exchange would be on terms he could understand; not to mention, the pilfering that had driven Cook to distraction in Polynesia didn't exist here. But on the flip side, the supply and demand balance sheet was tipped very heavily in favour of the Mowachaht. And they knew it.

For the first time anywhere in the Pacific, Cook was expected to pay for the grass he needed to feed his animals.

## SAM NEILL

*Here's a little family story I've always enjoyed. A great uncle of mine was having his honeymoon in Florence and he and his wife woke up early one morning to a terrible sound outside. They pulled back the shutters and outside there were a couple of Italian street urchins torturing a cat. He called the concierge and said, 'Here's some lira, give it to those kids so they let the cat go.' The cat was released, but the next morning they woke up to an even worse noise. When they opened the shutters there were about a dozen urchins torturing about a dozen cats, all looking up at the window for lira. It's all about trading when it comes down to it. And the Mowachaht were pretty canny traders, too. Cook needed grass for all the livestock on board, so he sent men to cut grass. Suddenly a bloke turns up and makes it clear that they need to pay for the grass, so he pays. And the next thing you know, there's about a dozen blokes all wanting payment and it looks like everyone owns a different blade of grass. Once Cook has spent all his money, they told him he could cut whatever he wanted.*

The locals expected far more valuable items than the knick-knacks that had served Cook so well elsewhere on his travels.

## CAPTAIN JAMES COOK

*[T]hese people got a greater middly and variety of things from us than any other people we had visited.*

The Mowachaht also took control of trade with the British vessels. Rather than the British visiting Yuquot village, as had

*Views on the West Coast of America.* Coastal profiles engraved after drawings by John Webber and William Bligh, 1785. David Rumsey Map Collection, David Rumsey Map Centre, Stanford Libraries

been the norm elsewhere in the Pacific, the locals were the ones who initiated the visits to the ships anchored in Resolution Cove.

The one person on board the British ships who willingly surrendered to the Mowachaht demands was the expedition's artist, John Webber. These days it might seem like an extravagance to include a resident artist on a maritime expedition, but it's impossible to overstate how important Webber – and the other artists who travelled with Cook on his previous voyages – were to the endeavours.

### SAM NEILL

*The importance of having a great artist on board was fully borne out on the first two voyages with Parkinson and Hodges. And so on the third voyage, Cook ensured he had someone really wonderful with him – that was the twenty-four-year-old John Webber who was, arguably, the most accomplished artist of all those who travelled with Cook.*

There's good reason for the saying that a picture tells a thousand words. In the eighteenth century, when literacy rates in Europe were extremely low, the best – and often the only – way to feed the public appetite for what they saw as exotic and unfamiliar was via the pictures Cook's artists produced to illustrate the printed accounts of his voyages. John Webber was like an Associated Press photographer and *New York Times* journalist rolled into one. And judging by Webber's prolific output in Nootka Sound, this place was deemed exceptionally newsworthy.

Webber's drawings and the engravings taken after them, along with those of the artists who accompanied Cook on his previous two voyages, became what might be described as an eighteenth- and nineteenth-century image bank. They were templates that other artists copied – unapologetically and often without acknowledgement – in countless publications across the Western world. Webber's vision of the Pacific was adopted to represent European ideas and perceptions about the region for well over a hundred years; his compositions weren't superseded until photography became commonplace at the turn of the twentieth century. Webber's vivid depictions of a pristine wilderness inhabited by people untouched by Western civilisation fed a rampant nostalgia for a pre-industrial time and a way of life that was perceived to be simple and unadulterated. At the same time, of course, the aforementioned Western 'civilisation' set in motion events and established a regime that would do its best to dismantle the traditional indigenous existence Webber had recorded.

### RAY WILLIAMS

*A lot of our people have been destroyed and many things were taken away from our way of life. The Department of Affairs ordered the authorities to take our children away from us to residential schools because they wanted to control our way of life. They tried to take our system away – our beliefs, our culture, our language – all because they wanted to control us. But we don't want that. We want to control our way of life and keep doing what we've always done – a thousand years back – just like our ancestors did. Because we're going to be here forever. Best to stay in this system here with our own way of life and our own beliefs. When I'm gone, my grandchildren got to remember those things.*

Of course, the Mowachaht were anything but 'simple'. And when Webber decided one day to draw a house, he was approached by a man who was *'seemingly displeased'*. The man blocked Webber's view of the house until the artist sliced a metal button off his coat and offered it to him. Only once his coat had been relieved of all its buttons was he permitted to draw undisturbed.

It turned out the Mowachaht had something else to offer in the exchange, beyond the day-to-day necessities Cook needed to replenish and refurbish his ships: *Enhydra lutris*. The sea otter. It is a ridiculously cute creature that chose as its home the waters of Nootka Sound. It's blessed with the thickest fur of any mammal on earth. The average human head has about 2200 hairs per square inch; the sea otter has up to one million. That's sixteen times denser than mink. Unfortunately for the otters, that made them very, very desirable to purveyors of warm – and expensive – coats.

By the nineteenth century, sea otter pelts were known as 'soft gold' – the Chinese would pay a king's ransom for them. Cook and his men had struck gold on the Pacific coast. When they arrived, it's been estimated 300,000 sea otters populated North America's west coast. Within a decade of Cook's visit, British fur traders descended on the region – including several men who had sailed on the *Resolution* and *Discovery* and wanted to make their fortunes. But as was their way, the European fur traders had no 'off' button. Eighteen thousand or so otters were slaughtered each year until the species was driven to the brink of extinction in Nootka Sound by 1830.

It wasn't just the sea otter whose fate was sealed by the arrival of Europeans who were determined to exploit the natural riches of the North Pacific.

### RAY WILLIAMS

*The people arrived in our land at the time that the government was formed, and they ordered First Nations people to live on a reservation to make room for the newcomers to live there. They came ashore and raided our*

> *smokehouses and made our men drunk and raped our*
> *women because they wanted to control our way of life and*
> *take our beliefs and our language away. They sent boxes of*
> *food – shipped it up here – and each family had the same*
> *kind of food ... They wanted us to be dependent on them.*
> *Now today it's totally different because it really messed up*
> *our system and our way here. It's not right.*

When Cook arrived at Nootka Sound, it was dotted with the long houses that were the traditional communal living spaces of the Mowachaht people. He left after a month or so, having repaired and restocked his ships. What came in his wake would disrupt Mowachaht lives forever.

> *SAM NEILL: How many people left speak Mowachaht?*
> *RAY WILLIAMS: On my hand, I can probably name*
> *seven or eight people in our nation that can speak the*
> *language.*

In 1789, the Spanish arrived in the Sound and built a fortress – Fort San Miguel – at the entrance of the place Cook called Friendly Cove. It was intended to protect the settlement of Santa Cruz de Nuca – the first Spanish settlement in British Columbia established to assert Spanish claims over the region. Predictably, the new settlers chose as their base the Mowachaht village of Yuquot, which was completely levelled to accommodate the fortress.

After altercations with British and American fur traders, a war between Spain and Britain was narrowly averted and the fortress abandoned in 1795 according to the terms of the

Nootka Convention. As the fur trade boomed and destructive government policies in centuries to come intruded on the indigenous way of life, the impact on the Mowachaht was catastrophic.

The indigenous Alaskan population endured the same seismic shift in fortunes as experienced by the Mowachaht in Nootka Sound.

**AARON LEGGETT, Dena'ina Tribe, Historian**

*The Russians arrived here in the 1790s. But probably the greatest impact that led to a change in the power dynamic came with the introduction of European diseases in the 1830s. There was a terrible smallpox epidemic from 1836 to 1839 where it's estimated about half of my people died from this illness. In about three years 2500 people of a total of 5000 disappeared. This was also the time when the Russian Orthodox Church was starting to get a foothold in this area. If you went to church, you got inoculated and when you didn't die, you attributed that to the power of Christ. Sometimes people ask why I want to speak Dena'ina. Well, this is the language that has been spoken here for over two thousand years. I say, when English has been spoken here for two thousand years, we can give up on Dena'ina. So we've only got nineteen hundred more years to go.*

A century after Cook arrived, 90 per cent of the Mowachaht population had been wiped out.

Cook's adventures in Nootka Sound drew to a close when he directed his two ships to weigh anchor in April 1778.

> *SAM NEILL: Tell me what you think about Captain Cook?*
>
> *RAY WILLIAMS: Captain Cook was good in a way and bad in another way. He was bad because after he arrived, diseases came here – syphilis, whooping cough, chicken pox, German measles.*
>
> *SAM NEILL: Were there any good things about Captain Cook?*
>
> *RAY WILLIAMS: Yes, there were good things about Captain Cook because he brought nails and hammers to our people. It made it easier for our people to build our homes – the long houses. Our people used to have to pack their lumber in canoes to carry it from location to location. But Captain Cook saw that and so his idea was to make a good relationship with our people by bringing nails and hammers and saws to make it easier for our people, instead of moving the lumber each time.*

*

From Nootka Sound, Cook's ships sailed headfirst into a week-long storm. Slowly progressing north, they hit monumentally cold conditions. As they approached Alaska, it was April – northern spring. But the world was blanketed in snow and the sea blocked with ice.

To keep his British American first lieutenant, John Gore, happy, Cook agreed to explore an opening that Gore was certain was a passage, but Cook was equally certain was an enclosed body of water. However, Cook indulged him – not without reservations – and when, as Cook had expected, they found themselves hemmed in at the end of the body of water now known as Cook Inlet, Cook named it 'Turnagain River'.

### AARON LEGGETT

*Renaming is a loss of place names and language. The English-speaking world would first know this area as Cook's River. It was eventually renamed Cook Inlet. In Anchorage we have a Campbell Creek – Campbell was a buddy of Vancouver's and the former Governor of Jamaica with no connection at all to the area. Nevertheless, these names live on. The loss of indigenous place names is a first step towards the loss of languuge and, ultimately, a loss of control.*

The commander's decision to please Gore provides a glimpse of Cook the diplomat. The window of opportunity to head north was tiny and rimmed with ice, so to pursue a red herring was a complete waste of time. Yet Cook still did it.

Although Cook was in a tearing rush, he stuck around long enough to make quite an impression on the local Dena'ina, and to draft charts of the area so accurate that they remained in use until well into the twentieth century. Although Cook didn't disembark there, some members of his crew did reach shore, where they engaged in trade with the local Dena'ina people.

### AARON LEGGETT

*At a place now called Point Possession there was a small Dena'ina settlement. Cook's men came ashore and traded a dog they were going to take back to the ship. Dena'ina oral tradition and the journals of Cook actually line up very nicely, and this is how we know it was Cook because it was handed down in the oral tradition for almost two hundred years. This story was told about the dog that was being taken back onto the boat, but after it bit somebody one of Cook's men shot the dog dead. This upset the Dena'ina – it was a good dog and we value dogs. There's also a theory that Cook's men shot the dog as an act of dominance – to show us the power of their firearms. These oral traditions and Cook's journal accounts are important because early historians were not convinced about the ethnicity of the people Cook came in contact with in this area, but thanks to the oral tradition about the dog and its confirmation in the ship's journals, we can prove it was our people who were here when Cook arrived.*

And, of course, Cook didn't miss the opportunity to raise a flag and claim the territory in the name of the King.

**SAM NEILL**

*Just before leaving the inlet – and almost as an afterthought – Cook directed James King, the second lieutenant, to land and to raise the flag and take possession of this territory in the name of King George. It's unlikely that the local Dena'ina, who watched the ceremony, understood the symbolism of what this meant.*

Cook was still determined to find the North-West Passage. It's tempting to give him the benefit of the doubt and say that he had no idea what he was doing as he probed and charted the

American coastline and opened the Pacific up to whoever would follow in his wake.

Whether or not Cook suspected what would happen after he left this place, he persisted.

By the time he began to tackle the Alaskan Peninsula in earnest, it was early June. Summer. Cook was racing against the clock to exploit a tiny window of opportunity before murderous conditions made the seas impassable. He knew he'd have to push his ships, his men and himself further than he'd ever had to push them before in pursuit of what could be an impossible dream.

**AARON LEGGETT**

*You can't help but marvel at what Cook achieved – the travel and the distances and the sheer exploration. That, to me, is rather remarkable – to travel all the way from Australia to New Zealand and Hawai'i, then up the north-west coast into Prince William Sound, into Cook Inlet, down the Alaskan Peninsula, and all the way up to the northern part of Alaska. I mean, it is quite remarkable.*

But retreat wasn't in Cook's vocabulary. He'd finish the task … or die trying.

# PART SIX

# SIXTEEN

# CONTESTED TERRITORIES

*In history we tend to celebrate those great empires ... the Romans who conquered the world and built monuments and so on. But perhaps the greatest achievements can be found here, in these societies on the edge of the world – a place where people have lived for many thousands of years and left very little imprint on the environment. They lived harmoniously with their surroundings – they lived sustainably and they knew about subsistence.*
### SAM NEILL

Planet earth has no end of picturesque and delightful places. And when those places also happen to be blessed with an abundance of natural resources and a strategic – and defensible – geographic location, it's not hard to see why humankind has been known to get quite grabby. If things were going well for the early-modern European empire builders, those regions were also easily accessed, furnished with all the things fledgling colonists required and generally pleasant to occupy once any combative indigenous people had been defeated. Throw a pleasant climate into the mix, and everything was chipper.

And then there was the far north Pacific – a remote and isolated corner of the globe that remains almost as difficult to get to today as it was during Cook's era. All right, that may be a slight exaggeration. But only slight. And there's no quibble to be had with the statement that – for visitors, at least – the region's dauntingly inhospitable climate hasn't mellowed with age.

### SAM NEILL

*Our plane to Unalaska has just arrived ... people are getting off and, well, they look very pale and worn and shaking ... some of them are actually kissing the ground. That's not a good sign, is it? One of the passengers said later that in the twenty years he's been flying to Unalaska, that was the roughest flight he'd ever had. So there's a bit of a delay and I'm a little bit anxious about it – it's already one of the most notorious flights in the world and we've had a bit of an update from a friend on the ground who tells us we have scattered snow flurries, a screaming wind out of the north, and rough seas.*

In the eighteenth century, any concerns about the feasibility of establishing a presence in a place that, as far as Europeans were concerned, was designed to discourage human settlement were put to one side amidst growing interest in the region's strategic and economic importance.

The close proximity of the two great continents of America and Asia was a major selling point for the European would-be masters of the universe. At its narrowest point, the Bering Strait is just eighty-eight kilometres wide. This geographic feature made it possible for the human migration that spread from Asia to populate the American continent. During the Pleistocene, which ended about twelve thousand years ago, expanding polar caps locked in a significant volume of water. This resulted in sea levels that were up to 110 metres lower than we're familiar with today, a phenomenon that explains why Tasmania was once connected to mainland Australia, and how a prehistoric British adventurer could have crossed a bone-dry English Channel and stormed the beaches of Normandy without getting his or her feet even slightly wet.

In the furthest reaches of the northern Pacific Ocean, this exposed a body of land known as Beringia that once joined Asia and America. The land bridge was a steppe covering over 1.6 million square kilometres and blessed with fertile grasslands. It was here that three migrations of people crossed from Asia into America. And although Native North Americans dispute their findings, scientists believe that one of those groups had the itchiest feet of all – DNA testing has shown that all Native American and Inuit populations, including the Mowachaht people, can be traced to the same small tribe of wanderers who took the leap and crossed into a new world. They migrated along the Pacific seaboard and broke off in groups to branch inland as they continued south. Eventually, they populated the entire landmass, from Alaska in the north to the icebound southern tip of Chile.

As the polar caps began to melt, sea levels rose. Eleven thousand years ago Beringia was inundated, leaving the migrants stranded. The indigenous inhabitants of the northern reaches of the American and Asian continents, and those who occupied the islands that lie between them, lived happily and largely undisturbed for thousands of years. It was only once European powers decided there was a whole, potentially profitable, slice of the globe they had been neglecting that these remote regions saw their first serious incursions.

That, of course, was why Cook voyaged there. If he could find the ever-elusive prize – the North-West Passage – he could trump them all by gifting the Mother Country ready access to the lucrative commercial markets of Asia.

*

Cook was in a hurry when he made his first visit to the islands that are scattered like a string of pearls in a gentle arc that begins at the long finger extending westwards from Alaska across the northern reaches of the Pacific. Most of the Aleutian Islands are technically part of Alaska, but they stretch so far to the west that most maps of the United States don't include them. They are sometimes lucky enough to be added in a little breakout box, just like the other remote American possession that features in the final chapter of James Cook's story: Hawai'i.

The Aleutian Arc, as it's known, comprises fourteen large islands and fifty-five smaller ones that stretch 1900 kilometres across the Pacific. Because we're talking the Pacific, with its much-celebrated Ring of Fire, the Aleutian Islands are also volcanic.

### SAM NEILL

*I think everybody's got somewhere they really want to go to once in their lifetime and that place for me has always been the Aleutian Islands ... I love volcanoes.*

One of the most active of these pyroclastic giants – the Makushin Volcano – is found on the island of Unalaska, which is today home to the largest city in the archipelago. Its population is just 4400, and amongst those residents live people descended from the adventurous souls who first crossed from Asia to America – the Unangan, often referred to by non-indigenous people as the Aleut.

Cook's first encounter with Unalaska was fleeting. With supplies on board the two ships running low, he needed to restock before they headed further north. He approached Unalaska with a view to refreshing water, anti-scurvy greens and fish. A thick fog descended, and he heard the ominous crash of breaking waves – not a particularly reassuring sound when you're trying to find your way to safety and can't actually see where you're going. But even sailing blind as he was, Cook still managed to navigate a way to safe harbour. It was only when the fog cleared that he realised how close they had come to disaster.

### CAPTAIN JAMES COOK

*We could not help being struck with horror at the sight of the dangers we had escaped, having three or four patches of rocks above water about a third of a mile from one another and the land half a mile distance on the other ... a more providential escape from instant destruction being scarce to meet with.*

Not only had Cook managed to find his way between two razor-sharp lines of rocks, he'd avoided beaching the two ships on a shoreline that was perilously close. To top it off, he'd happened upon one of the most sheltered anchorages on the island.

*Canoes of Oonalashka*, John Webber, c.1773–84. Cook, in his journal, wrote: 'they paddle in most excellent time, the foremost man every 3d or 4th stroke making flourishes with his paddle'. The top canoe from Prince William Sound is broad, with a solid platform for inland waters. The bottom kayak from Unalakska is bespoke, built for survival in the more tempestuous seas of the island chain. SLNSW, SAFE / DL PXX 2, 455685

Even today, English Bay – or Samagunda – is considered one of the safest harbours in waters that are unremittingly awful.

**CAPTAIN DAVE MAGONE, Marine Surveyor**

*There are lots of places around the island where you can hide. In English Bay, you can hide from the weather no matter which direction it's coming from. You've got the Pacific Ocean on one side and the Bering Sea on the other. The tides run back and forth through that area and it can give you some really bad sea conditions. The flood tide will*

> *come this way then it will go up to nine knots as the tide turns round and comes back this way – you've seen a white-water rafting trip? It gets like that in here. It's like a washing machine. But English Bay is always as smooth as a lake.*

After their near miss, Cook named the island 'Providence', though he amended that after a brief visit by the locals, who paddled out to the ship on their kayaks and told him their home was named 'Oonalaschka', meaning 'near the peninsula'.

\*

Cook must have been tempted to track down the Russians he was certain were in the area. When they had been on the Alaskan coast – at a place Cook gave the rather unimaginative name, of 'Foggy Cape' – the two British ships had been approached by kayaks whose occupants bowed and passed over a piece of paper marked with Russian writing.

Although none of Cook's men could read Cyrillic – they later learnt it was a receipt for taxes that Russian fur traders imposed on the locals – this was undeniable evidence of a strong Slavic presence in the area.

But now was not the time to go chasing after Russian will-o'-the-wisps. It was July already, and each day of summer that passed was another day wasted. There was a nice breeze, and the north was calling.

Besides which, in the *Resolution*'s Great Cabin, Russia was causing Cook a monumental headache. He had the utmost respect for fellow navigators and took their maps at face value, so when he headed north, he did so with copies of Russian charts drafted by two Germans working in the Russian Crown's employ – Gerhard Friedrich Müller, the founder of the Russian Imperial Academy of Sciences, and Jacob von Staelin-Storcksburg.

Müller, who's widely credited with being the progenitor of the science of ethnography, participated in the first expedition that Peter the Great sent to Siberia under the Danish captain, Vitus Bering – the same Bering who gave his name to the strait. So Müller's maps carried some weight, as did those revised by Staehlin. The fundamental problem was that until late in the eighteenth century, Russian mapmakers produced what they called *chertezhi* – manuscript maps lacking coordinates and drafted using river systems as reference rather than the astronomical observations Cook and his peers used when drawing up a nautical chart. Distances were often expressed in the rather imprecise measurement of days of travel, and details were recorded based on second-hand accounts relayed by fur traders and other travellers.

Cook had sailed into the great unknown with these charts, assuming they weren't leading him up the proverbial garden path. That was a mistake – it has been suggested that Staehlin's map, in particular, may have been deliberately crafted to be misleading to the English, Spanish and French ambassadors in St Petersburg. Whatever the reason for their errors, the charts compounded Cook's difficulties in this already daunting region. As he followed the Alaskan Peninsula south, the Russian charts showed him heading north. Staehlin's map plonked an island – Alaschka – in the middle of Bering Strait.

Confused by errors in the maps, by August 1778 Cook was on the edge of the Arctic Circle but found himself blown off course to the Asian continent without really knowing where he was. For a man who prided himself on keeping track of such things, it was infuriating – a sentiment captured unambiguously in his journal entries.

## CAPTAIN JAMES COOK

*A map that the most illiterate of illiterate seafaring men would have been ashamed to put his name to.*

\*

When the *Resolution* and the *Discovery* arrived in Siberia, it was 10 August – St Lawrence's feast day, according to the Church of England's calendar – so Cook named the bay in Chukotka 'St Lawrence Bay'. The settlement on the same site is today called 'Lavrentiya'. According to Staehlin's fantastical map, they were on the island of Alaschka. But as Cook observed a group of people on shore heading away from the coast, he had other ideas about their location.

Approaching shore with three boats manned by well-armed marines, Cook – as always – led from the front. Forty or so locals approached with arrows drawn and spears brandished. In his journal, Cook described the men as quite different from the people he had encountered in North America, both in terms of their physique and their attire. Impressed by the intricate ornamentation of their weapons and the practicality of their clothes, houses and canoes, he concluded that the people who fiercely opposed his landing were the same people described by Vitus Bering in 1728 – the Tchutschians. This told Cook that he and his men were not, as indicated by Staehlin's map, on an island, but were actually in Asia.

The Chukchi – as they're now known – are of Mongolian descent. But it's also recently been discovered that they carry the same DNA as the first wave of people that populated the continent on the opposite side of the Pacific. This shows there were Eskimo-Aleut speakers who travelled back to Asia after the initial migration – not an easy journey by any measure, and proving beyond doubt the Chukchi maritime credentials.

**SAM NEILL**

*For millennia, like the Polynesians, the Chukchi had been master mariners. They traded all around the Bering Sea and went to places like Nome – they'd travel over the ice in the winter, and in summer by boat.*

The Chukchi reputation as mariners par excellence had made an impression in the court of Tsar Peter the Great. Rumours of the great land they had visited across the strait played a part in convincing the Tsar to sponsor an expedition to North America. But on Vitus Bering's second expedition from Kamchatka, the navigator met his end after his ship was wrecked on Bering Island in the Aleutian archipelago. Survivors from his crew salvaged timber from the ruined vessel and cobbled together a ship that carried them to safety. The pelts they brought with them back to Russia were of such high quality, they inspired a rush eastward – it was the first wave of Alaska's 'soft gold' rush. The Russian traders who subsequently set up shop in the Aleutian Islands would make quite the impression later in Cook's Arctic adventure.

The Chukchi people Cook encountered in St Lawrence Bay were less than enthusiastic about Slavic incursions into their territory, and that had an adverse effect upon his reception – it's thought that the aggressive response to the British ships was largely thanks to a case of mistaken identity. The Russians had acquired most of their knowledge of the region at the easternmost extreme of their empire from attempts to subjugate or avoid the Chukchi, who classified the Russians as their traditional enemies. Being master mariners, the Chukchi understood that there would be no Russian maritime exploration or expansion if they did not have seagoing vessels, and so the indigenous people embarked upon a concerted – and very successful – campaign to destroy any Russian ships that appeared off the coast. This made it impossible for Russian expeditions to winter in the relatively hospitable surrounds of Lavrentiya and restricted their navigational season. So when the Chukchi saw Cook and his men, it seems they assumed they were more Russians. Cook, with his customary apparent fearlessness, persisted.

Although he didn't manage to persuade the Chukchi to trade with him and his men – or even to lower their weapons – for the three hours the ships were there, Cook did encourage some exchanges of trinkets for artefacts. Word of Cook's visit would eventually find its way back to the ear of Catherine the Great, who assumed the interlopers were American. Furious, and determined to assert her claim over the area, she demanded that her coat of arms be nailed to tree trunks along the coast ... being unaware that there are no trees in the region.

Today, the Chukchi remain fiercely independent. The Chukotka Autonomous Region is populated by 55,000 people spread out over more than 700,000 square kilometres, which is traversed by only 600 kilometres or so in roads and has no other overland means of transport. As recently as the 1970s, it was reported that the Chukchi still refused to speak Russian.

For Cook's men, the Chukchi greeting didn't alter the fact that, having endured horrendous conditions in the Bering Sea, the brief change of scenery was appreciated.

**CHARLES CLERKE (1743–1779), Naval Officer, crew member on Cook's first, second and third voyages**
*[F]ine cheery day ... gave even this wretched, barren country a more pleasing appearance; we all feel this morning as though we were risen in a new world.*

If there is any doubt about just how terrible their experience in that body of water must have been, consider how it was that two shiploads of men who had recently spent months wallowing in the tropical climate of Polynesia could wax lyrical about Siberia – a place that is, by any measure, bleak, barren and rather uninviting to the uninitiated.

It would have been with considerable dismay, then, that the crew heard the order to head out to sea again.

\*

Having found no indication yet that a passage through the sea ice existed, Cook was determined to continue his search. But it was August and summer was on the wane. And as winter approached, so did the ice sheet. Despite the danger, Cook forged his way through terrifying seas as he pushed north.

**CAPTAIN PHIL PRYZMONT, Arctic Fisherman**
*Sledge Island is about twenty miles east of us right now, and after Cook clears that, he's going to turn north and go*

*around the end of the Bering Strait. Out there it gets bumpy.*
*You've got a prevailing northerly wind with a prevailing*
*south to north current, so you get some pretty steep waves.*

Approaching the ice sheet on 17 August 1778, Cook recognised an atmospheric phenomenon he knew from his time in Antarctica: ice blink – a peculiar glow in the sky near the horizon that's caused by the reflection of the sun off an icefield.

### CAPTAIN PHIL PRYZMONT

*When you get close to the ice, even within about twenty miles, you can see the sky above it is white. It's reflecting the sunlight off it, so you have a pretty good advance notice that it's coming. When you get to the ice you're going to get to the pancake ice where pieces of them are banging into each other in the swells. It's round enough and the edges are usually pretty thin. But then as you get further into the ice pack, you lose the swell first and start noticing that the water gets calmer and calmer. Then the pancake ice pieces get bigger and bigger and pretty soon you start to meet up with the icebergs.*

Cook knew what that meant, and it wasn't good news. Large chunks of frozen water slamming and grinding together did not bode well for two timber ships whose seaworthiness had been giving Cook headaches ever since they had departed England.

It was the Great Barrier Reef all over again, but in sub-zero conditions and with terminally dangerous chunks of ice that moved. At least coral stays in the one spot.

Still Cook pressed on. On 18 August 1778, he reached as far

north as Icy Cape. He was just beyond seventy degrees in latitude and at a point so far north that it was as far from Icy Cape to Unalaska as Unalaska was from Hawai'i. It was almost exactly the same latitude Cook had reached in the southern hemisphere when he crossed the Antarctic Circle. But as the seasons turned and the ice sheet began its inexorable march south at a rate of up to a mile an hour, the ice pressed in on him – 'as compact as a wall and seemed to be ten or twelve feet high', as Cook put it – at times threatening to crush the two ships.

For a time, Cook tacked back and forth along the wall, probing to find any gaps that might hint at a passage beyond. The chart that shows Cook's zigzagging about the Bering Sea and the northern Asian and American shorelines bears witness to his determination to probe every corner of the northern Pacific until he found evidence of – or disproved – the existence of a passage through the ice. But conditions worsened, and he realised he could push his men no further.

### CHARLES CLERKE

*A thick fog and a foul wind are rather disagreeable intruders to people engaged in surveying and tracing a coast … We have now a very staggering gale. This seems upon the whole a damned unhappy part of the world.*

### JOHN RICKMAN (1737–1818), Lieutenant, Cook's third voyage

*Ice was seen hanging at our hair, our noses and even at the men's finger ends. Hot victuals froze while we were at table.*

Cook knew it was the end of the line.

360

**CAPTAIN JAMES COOK**

*The season was so far advanced ... I didn't think it consistent with prudence to make any further attempts to find a passage this year in any direction so little was the chance of succeeding.*

On 29 August, he decided to retreat from the frozen north.

It surely came at no small cost to Cook's pride for him to turn back without resolving the question he had travelled so far, and endured so much, to answer.

**JAMES TREVENEN (1760–1790), Midshipman, Cook's third voyage**

*Indefatigability was a leading feature of his character. If he failed in, or could no longer pursue, his first great object, he immediately began to consider how he might be most useful in prosecuting some inferior one.*

Did Cook consider the voyage a failure? There's no doubt he would have preferred to find a way through the ice to the other side on his first attempt. But he had every intention of returning the following summer – the next time travelling with fresh eyes and his own charts after having been led on a wild goose chase in 1778 by the substandard Russian maps.

**CAPTAIN JAMES COOK**

*It was with me a matter of some consequence to clear up this point this season, that I might have but one object in view the next.*

He certainly didn't plan to give up – though as he sailed south, he had begun to question the plausibility of there being a North-West Passage, writing that he had observed 'the polar part is far from being an open sea'.

Cook's scepticism was based on observations he had made while journeying around the Antarctic on his second voyage. Along with the naturalist Johann Forster, Cook had questioned the prevailing wisdom as put forward by the leading lights of the Royal Society that ice was a freshwater phenomenon and that seawater did not freeze. The explanation they had for sea ice was that it was formed in rivers before entering the ocean. All of which was complete bunkum, of course.

It would take nearly two hundred and fifty years and the helping hand of global warming for the North-West Passage to become a reality – and only then in summer with the assistance of icebreakers.

*

Cook's decision to abandon the search must have come as a relief to the men on board the ships. Not that the return to Unalaska was without its challenges. As they retreated south, they had to fight through heavy snow flurries and bitterly cold temperatures. To top it all off, on 25 September the *Resolution* again defied its name and sprang a new leak.

Visibility was appalling, which meant that Cook was often sailing blind. He found a surprising – and unwitting – ally when navigating the icefloes through sea fog. The mournful bellow of walruses lolling about on the ice warned Cook when he was getting too close for comfort.

Before turning south again, the other thing Cook had thought walruses might be useful for was as a source of protein. Given they looked for all the world like legless marine cows – or 'sea horses' as the men on the British boats called them – it wasn't an unreasonable assumption to make. For the people who inhabited these desolate outer reaches of the globe, walruses were a crucial natural resource.

### RAYMOND KOWELUT, Inupiat/Eskimo

*My people have lived on walrus for thousands of years. When I was sixteen years old, I went walrus hunting and they wanted me to harpoon without using the rifle, but we couldn't find a walrus. I'm glad we didn't because if I had gotten it with just a harpoon at sixteen, it would have been my time to get married – it was tradition back then. When you're hunting, your adrenalin is really high – some people get nervous because a walrus is a big animal. Once you harpoon it, it's like catching a big fish. If you're going too fast it can almost rip your arm off – the bearded seal can get to about maybe eight hundred pounds, and a walrus can be half a tonne maybe. Sometimes the young bulls will come up to your boat and try to flip it over. I like hunting – you get that natural high.*

It's unlikely Cook's crewmen experienced the raw thrill of the hunt as described by traditional hunters.

Judging by the illustration that the ship's artist, Webber, made of the 'sea horse' hunt, where sailors in a low-keeled rowboat unload shot into walruses with tusks the length of a man's arm, it must have got their hearts racing nonetheless. They brought down nine walruses – some as large as nine feet in length.

Cook sampled the walrus meat and deemed it quite delicious, declaring its fat as *'sweet as marrow'*.

### CAPTAIN JAMES COOK

*The fat at first is sweet as marrow but in a few days it grows rancid unless it is salted, then it will keep good much longer, the lean is course, black and rather a strong taste, the heart is nearly as well tasted as that of a bullock. The fat when melted yields a good deal of oil which burns very well in lamps, and their hides, which are very thick, were very useful about our rigging.*

The crew disagreed. To their taste, the fat resembled *'train oil instead of marrow'*, and was *'disgustful'* and *'too rank both in smell and taste as to make use of except with plenty of pepper and salt'*.

### SAM NEILL

*It kind of has a blubbery look about it. So if I'm careful, I can avoid the blubber, and just go for the meat … Urgh … it's got a slight gag reflex thing about it … That's decidedly one of the worst things I've ever eaten in my life … it's kind of rancid – fishy tasting – really an instant stomach churn. Having said that, if I was cold and hungry, and I was nearing the Arctic Circle, I'm not entirely sure if I'd go on hunger strike … No, come to think of it, I probably would.*

Cook, they decided, may have been a commander and navigator without peer, but a gourmand he was not.

### JAMES TREVENEN

*Captain Cook here speaks entirely from his own taste which was, surely, the coarsest that ever mortal was endured with.*

'Disgustful' or not, Cook wasn't about to give in. He halved regular rations and left them with one choice. Eat the walrus, or starve. Many amongst the crew voted with their spoons – it was an Alaskan stand-off as the men refused to eat. Many of those who did eat the walrus were violently ill.

### RAYMOND KOWELUT

*You got to get used to it. When I was growing up we had to eat it at a young age because that's all we can eat sometimes – just walrus or seal. But the taste of walrus is ... well, you have to get used to the taste.*

Within days, Cook's malnourished men were ready to collapse and next to useless. He had no other choice but to give in and reinstate salt beef in the rations, though he did so begrudgingly, describing his men as *'[d]amned mutinous scoundrels'*.

There's no doubt this incident caused another rift between Cook and his crew. In a sense, it was a point of critical mass – the culmination of all the ill will that had been building up during the voyage.

In the past, Cook's men had the highest regard for their captain.

**ALEXANDER HOME, (c.1739–1823), crew member,
Cook's third voyage**

*In the midst of the greatest jeopardy, [Cook] could judge
and reflect calmly and always had the skill and good
fortune to extricate himself and his people ... By degrees a
habit grew upon us of placing such confidence in him, that
although surrounded by dangers in shallow seas, fogs and
storms we could go calmly to rest placing our safety in the
skill and fortune of our leader.*

But although there had been glimpses on this third journey of
the composed leader they knew from previous voyages, Cook's
reputation as a commander who was fair-minded and even-
handed had suffered a mortal blow.

**JAMES TREVENEN**

*[Cook] would sometimes relax from his almost constant
severity of disposition and condescended now and then to
converse familiarly with us. But it was only for a time; as
soon as on board the ship he became again the despot.*

Although many factors contributed to his end, this rupture
between Cook and his crew would play an important part in the
tragic events that led to his death.

\*

Other than their very brief sojourn in St Lawrence Bay, by the
time they arrived in the (relatively) safe harbour in Unalaska at
the beginning of October, the men on board the *Resolution* and

the *Discovery* had endured three months worth of ice, gales, fog and sub-zero conditions.

On 2 October, the *Resolution* and *Discovery* dropped anchor in Unalaska, and Cook ordered the men to set about refitting, repairing and replenishing the ships, and recaulking their leaking timbers.

They would spend almost one month in Unalaska, during which Cook allowed his men to take shore leave while he indulged in long walks in the hills ringing English Bay, cataloguing the many berries that grew on the exposed hillsides. While he directed some of the crew to harvest the berries with a view to fending off scurvy in months to come, Cook also instructed the blacksmith to rework a damaged anchor from the *Discovery* into knives and adze blades to use as trade goods when they returned to Hawai'i. If he'd known what was to come, Cook might have chosen to do something else with the waste metal.

While on shore, Cook also found time to cast an anthropological eye over the Unangan people who lived in what were to him surprisingly heavily populated settlements, given the apparent paucity of natural resources on the island.

*DR RICK KNECHT, Archaeologist, University of Aberdeen: There would have been five or six hundred people in these settlements. That contrasts to the Eastern Arctic, where you could have had no more than five hundred people in total on the entire Ellesmere Island. Because they had so many marine resources here, they were able to have a fairly complex and sophisticated culture even though they were non-agrarian because you*

*had all that food out there in the ocean in big packages ...*
*all you had to do was harvest it and process it. So rather*
*than put in all the labour cultivating, planting ...*
*SAM NEILL: ... and weeding.*
*RICK KNECHT: Yeah ... weeding.*
*SAM NEILL: No weeding. This is a dream.*

Cook marvelled at their ingenuity and ability to thrive in what he knew from firsthand experience was a harsh and forbidding environment. The Unangan wasted nothing. Take a sea lion, for example: yes, it yielded the obvious – food and blubber oil – but it went a whole lot further than that. Its bones were used to craft tools, teeth became fishhooks, and sinews were dried and used as fishing lines. Flippers were shoe soles and, most extraordinarily, intestines and gut lining were used to make water-resistant parkas and skylights for the subterranean houses the Unangan carved into the earth.

### SAM NEILL

*In Unalaska, Cook encountered people who had adapted*
*brilliantly to their harsh environment. And the Unangans*
*had thrived for some nine and a half thousand years when*
*the English ships showed up. They lived in homes built*
*about a metre underground – where a wooden post was*
*both a ladder and structural support for the building. Cook*
*was impressed by Unangan genius in surviving in these*
*adverse conditions. And, frankly, so am I. There's a parka*
*in the Museum of the Aleutians which is made of seal gut.*
*It's not only an exquisite piece of clothing, it's also*
*completely practical. Before the invention of Gore-Tex, it*

*was the most waterproof and breathable thing you could*
*wear on the planet.*

Cook made note of the rye grass baskets carefully crafted by the Unangan women, and he recorded how they warmed themselves using blubber-oil lamps by placing them between their legs and under their clothing.

As has occurred with depressing regularity across the Pacific, in Unalaska the accounts written by Cook and the other men on board would ultimately prove to be valuable resources for present-day Unangans seeking to re-establish ancient cultural traditions that had previously been transmitted from generation to generation through oral means.

Their houses were also quite remarkable and perfectly suited for the environment. For thousands of years, the Unangan occupied subterranean huts accessible via a ladder that popped out of a hole in the hut's roof.

**DR RICK KNECHT**

*We get a tremendous amount of ethnographic information from Cook's written diaries and records, and also the drawings. Because of the conditions, many things don't survive, archaeologically-speaking, so we really rely on the historical records for that detail. We known the Unangan people lived in semi-subterranean houses. There are some we've found that are probably two thousand years old. Some of the largest house pits in Alaska are in the Aleutians. By the time Cook arrived, multiple families lived in long houses that could be up to one hundred metres long. But it's a long way from the Arctic tree line so they*

> *were dependent on driftwood for wood supplies. One of the prime reasons for locating a village was to access driftwood. This timber was reused and recycled – probably for centuries. Some of those timbers used in these long houses were probably heirlooms.*

It was down one of these hatches that David Samwell descended, along with a brace of other sailors, determined to sample the local women – whether they were interested or not. What followed was rape.

**DAVID SAMWELL (1751–1798), Welsh Naval Surgeon on Cook's third voyage**

*[We] immediately made love to the handsomest woman in the company, who in order to make us welcome refused us no favour she could grant though her husband or father stood by.*

The Russian fur traders had already forced the Unangan people into servitude. Cook's men were more than happy to take advantage of the fact the women would have been too terrified to say no to any demands made of them. The crew also very quickly worked out that the Unangan were gripped by the scourge of tobacco addiction, which proved to be most convenient for anyone looking for sex with one of the locals.

**CAPTAIN JAMES COOK**

*There are few if any that do not both smoke and chew tobacco, a luxury that bids fair to keep them always poor.*

### CHARLES CLERKE

*The compliment usually paid for a beauty's favours was a hand of tobacco: for one of inferior charms, a few leaves of this valuable weed.*

Cook concluded that the Unangan were *'the most peaceable and inoffensive people I ever met with'*. He couldn't help but notice how they had incorporated Western conveniences into their daily lives – things like kettles and European fabrics. But he also suspected that this came at a heavy cost. Let's consider, for a moment, why that might have been the case. The Russian occupation of the Aleutian Islands was not a state project. It was initiated by trading companies, and there were up to eighty of those operating in the region. As is the way with such enterprises, their only concerns were with commercial imperatives, and they had a short-term view of the exploitation and rapid depletion of resources no matter the cost to the local population. The Unangan were 'peaceable and inoffensive' because they had no choice.

*

In 1759 when the first Russian fur-trading company arrived under Stepan Glotov, Unalaska and Amaknak islands were home to twenty-four settlements and more than one thousand Aleut inhabitants. The locals had no intention of cooperating with the new arrivals, and between 1763 and 1766 the Aleuts destroyed four Russian ships and killed 175 hunters and fur traders. Predictably, the Russians retaliated. Brutally. After an attack that killed many hundreds of Aleut, the local women and children were held hostage until the men agreed to hunt furs for the Russians. The final blow came when Aleut men were stripped of their arms and their chieftains forced to pay tribute in the form of furs. Young men were taken from their families and raised as Russians, children were forced to work in the Russian fur-processing plants, and the great majority of Aleut at the very least paid lip service to being Russian Orthodox converts.

When Cook arrived, the Aleut were living as serfs under Russian overlords.

### SAM NEILL

*On Unalaska, Cook witnessed something he'd never seen before in his decade of voyaging – a traumatised people struggling to survive the first impacts of contact with Europeans. Russian fur traders had been at work for decades. He sensed it hadn't gone well – but he didn't know the half of it. The Russians called themselves traders but that was misleading. They were here to pillage – to take as many animal pelts as they possibly could, whatever it took. By the time Cook arrived half the population had been annihilated. It left Cook conflicted – it was a portent of things to come. The Unangan people were enslaved, raped, massacred, traumatised and ravaged by disease. Within a few years of Cook's departure, 90 per cent would be gone.*

Cook noted that the indigenous people had been disarmed and observed 'the great subjection the natives are under'. Although he came from a society that was characterised by an extremely rigid hierarchy, serfdom as a form of quasi-slavery was – by the late eighteenth century in Britain – very much on the out. We can't know for certain what Cook would have thought about the conditions the Unangan were living under. But it seems unlikely it would have sat at all well with him.

**JOHN ROBSON, Map Librarian, University of Waikato**
*We would need to go get Doctor Who and go back a couple of hundred years to ask the Europeans why they did it. I think they had this attitude of superiority that led to the slave trade. It was very similar to what happened in the Pacific – this whole idea that the peoples of other countries were inferior to Europeans, and were there to work for them. So by acquiring land and peoples they were perpetuating that. There was a body of people at the time who were anti-slavery and amongst the most ardent anti-slavers were the Quakers. Cook had been strongly influenced by his time with a Quaker sea captain when he was growing up, and the Quaker influence was probably very strong with him. Most likely, he himself would have been anti-slavery. But, really, we just don't know.*

\*

One person from Cook's crew who had the opportunity to witness the relationship between the Russians and Unangans in person was the American marine John Ledyard. The encounter began in a most peculiar way. The British ships had been at anchor for a couple of days when a delegation of locals arrived bearing a surprising gift – a salmon pie.

## CAPTAIN JAMES COOK

*A very singular present considering the place – a rye loaf or rather a pie made in the form of a loaf, for some salmon highly seasoned.*

Cook rightly concluded it was an offering sent by the Russians – a fair assumption given it was highly unlikely the locals had independently mastered the art of European pastry-making.

> *SAM NEILL: So a kayak turns up. Remarkably, one of the crew members hands over a pie – it's a gift from the Russians. It was a gesture of hospitality. Why a salmon pie?*
>
> *DENIS ROBINSON, Unangan Tribe, Chief: Because that is probably the freshest protein they have on the island, unless they wanted to eat seal or sea lion. And in October, when he landed, it was right towards the end of a major salmon run. It was probably the freshest protein they could present – the Unangan people had been eating it for thousands of years, but the pie is a very Russian thing.*

Curious to find out how long the Russians had been in residence, Cook tasked Ledyard with accompanying the Aleut guides back to the Russian settlement in Dutch Harbor to reconnoitre, arming him with bottles of wine and rum as a reciprocal gift. A full day's trek across the island proved to be hard on Ledyard's feet, though that was to be expected after such a long time at sea. On the second day, his Aleut companions stuffed him headfirst into the prow of a skin kayak to make the sea crossing to Dutch Harbor where he was greeted by the Russians and treated to a hearty meal of boiled whale as the Slavs tucked into the alcoholic beverages he'd carted along with him.

That evening, he joined the Russians and Unangans in an Orthodox prayer service.

> **JOHN LEDYARD (1751–1789), British American Explorer, crew member, Cook's third voyage**
> *The Russians assembled the Indians in a very silent manner, and said prayers after the manner of the Greek Church.*

This was followed by a somewhat less wholesome exchange. A plug of tobacco bought Ledyard some time with one of the local women. After what must have been a welcome night's sleep, he was introduced to the wonders of a Slavic steam bath where he promptly passed out, only to be revived by a good slosh of brandy and a plate of whale meat, bear and walrus – '*A composition of smells very offensive at nine or ten in the morning*', as he put it. This was a memorable experience, and one that made a mark on the Connecticut-born Ledyard, who got a taste for adventure and would go on to become one of the greatest solo explorers of the eighteenth century.

Ledyard escorted the three Russians who had entertained him at Dutch Harbor back to English Bay. Once on board the *Resolution*, they proceeded to drain the boat's supplies of hard liquor and entertain the men with their first European contact outside the ship's company in years.

**JAMES KING (1750–1784), Officer, Royal Navy, crew
member, Cook's third voyage**

*To see people in so strange a part of the world who had
other ties than that of common humanity was such a
novelty and pleasure and gave such a turn to our ideas and
feelings as may easily be imagined.*

A change is as good as a holiday, right? One of the guests was of particular interest to Cook – Gerasim Gregoriev Izmailov, a student navigator. Ismailov gave Cook a letter of introduction to the Russian Governor of Kamchatka and Petropavlovsk, a letter that would be of no use to Cook but would prove extremely useful to the two men who would lead the expedition after his death, Charles Clerke and John Gore.

Cook also took advantage of the Russian presence to write a letter to the Admiralty, which would be his first contact with home since he had departed the Cape of Good Hope two years previously. The letter, in which he outlined his intention to return to the Arctic Circle in order to continue his search the following summer, would end up being a voice from beyond the grave – it arrived in London via St Petersburg in January 1780 after news of Cook's death had already reached home.

The spirit of camaraderie embodied in this exchange did not persist in centuries to come as the dominant world powers came to blows over the region. In August 1788, the Spanish came into contact with the Russians on Unalaska for the first time. Esteban José Martínez and Gonzalo López de Haro weren't to be discouraged after meeting Potap Zaikof, who was then commander of Russian Unalaska. The Spaniards brazenly claimed the island for their Crown and renamed it Puerto de

Dona Maria Luisa Teresa. After returning to America and reporting to Manuel Antonio Flores – the Viceroy of New Spain – that the Russians intended to occupy Nootka Sound, Martinez and de Haro were dispatched again to protect Spanish interests in the region, so initiating the Nootka Crisis that brought Britain and Spain to the brink of war.

In the meantime, the inevitable wave of missionaries arrived – in this instance of the Russian Orthodox variety. Orthodox monks and priests turned up at the Aleutian fur-trading camps some fifteen years after Cook's visit, and it's fair to assume their appearance was greeted with some ambivalence by the Russians who – until that time – had been running the islands as personal fiefdoms without any answerability to a higher power.

For the Unangans who'd been subjugated by the traders, the arrival of the Church had two relatively positive outcomes.

**LARESA SYRESON, Unangan Descendant**
*Like my grandma always told me, there was some slavery happening at the same time as the fur trade. But there were also some very good things that came out of Russian contact ... like our language being documented and our alphabet being created. So that was very helpful for my generation and others who would like to learn the language. But there was also a lot of bloodshed and maltreatment due to the fur trade.*

As long as the locals converted, they were inoculated against smallpox, a disease that was laying waste to the Alaskan and Native American populations in the early 1800s. Forget the inconvenient truth that the Orthodox new arrivals had transmitted the disease to the indigenous communities in the first place. Between 1836 and 1840, epidemics of nasty imported bugs almost wiped out the population; by the end of the decade, only two to four hundred Aleuts remained in Unalaska.

What was the other upside of the Church's arrival? In 1825, the Russian Orthodox Church of the Holy Ascension was established in Unalaska by its founding priest, Ivan Veniaminov, who was later canonised and became St Innocent of Alaska. St Innocent created the first Aleut writing system and translated scripture into Aleut.

Unfortunately, that positive development came with its caveats. As the Church schools were established, Aleut customs and forms of cultural expression were discouraged in preference to a Russian way of life. For a preliterate society that relied on oral storytelling in order to preserve its culture, that meant many links to the past were lost forever.

### DENIS ROBINSON

*There were two different waves of Russian arrivals – first were the fur traders. They were ruthless and killed a lot of people and enslaved the Unangan people. Next came the missionaries. They built schools and started trying to structure the life of the Unangan people. But Unangan culture is not a written history. It was passed along by word of mouth. So a lot of Unangan history and culture was lost.*

If this sounds familiar, it's because this is also the tale of the Pacific after Cook.

## DR RICK KNECHT

*It's estimated only one in ten Unangans survived after European contact. But that may be conservative. They had very limited experience with the diseases from the old world – they had no immunity. In a preliterate culture, this mortality rate was like your library burning down … your entire repository of hard-won knowledge, lost. In one generation. Those who survived were younger and relatively unskilled, so you see evidence of a decrease in skill levels and knowledge in the very early ethnographic collections. Things are beautifully crafted and made but as time goes on that knowledge is lost.*

But that wasn't the end of the story for the Aleutian Islands. Scooped up in the United States' 1867 Alaska Purchase when a cash-strapped Russian Empire sold its North American territories for USD$7.2 million – amounting to about AUD$130 million today – the archipelago became strategically important when the United States entered the Second World War after the Japanese attack at Pearl Harbor. Dutch Harbor was attacked by Japanese forces in June 1942, and the indigenous residents were relocated and interned in ill-equipped camps in south-east Alaska for the duration of the war, ostensibly for their own protection.

## DENIS ROBINSON

*Prior to World War II, we had a really good economy here. All of our people worked in the salted herring industry. Hundreds and hundreds of barrels of salted fish were exported every year. Then in 1942 the Japanese bombed us. The US government decided they were gonna take all of the Unangan people out of the area. But nobody would tell them where they were going. So they were dropped off in south-east Alaska in abandoned fish-canning factories with no roofs, no windows, no doors. My mum remembers lying under the one blanket they gave her and looking up through the cracks of the roof to see the stars. And there were trees! Out here, we don't have trees. Most of the Aleut people will tell you that trees block the view. I was talking to a lovely old lady who said she gets anxiety when she's among trees. So when it was over the military had filled in the lagoon on Unalaska where the herring spawned ... so that killed the herring industry.*

Only several hundred made it back to their islands after the war. The Aleut on the islands occupied by the Japanese were taken to internment camps in Japan. Only twenty-five of those people survived.

The legacy of all these events, from first contact with the Russians and through the Second World War, endures today.

*SAM NEILL: So that first contact means that 90 per cent of the people were dead. How do you recover from that?*
*DENIS ROBINSON: We didn't – we haven't. If we were wolves, we'd be on the endangered species list. In 1974, when the Alaska Native Land Claims Settlement Act was enacted, there were only about three thousand Unangan people registered as a quarter blood or more. So we really are pretty much an extinct people.*

Although there is a strong will among the Aleut to revive the traditions of the past, so much has been lost – particularly when considered in light of the number of them who died – that it seems to be a Sisyphean task. Not that it will stop them trying.

**LARESA SYRESON**

*I got interested in tattooing because I saw one woman when I was very young – she was beautiful and she was very old. She must've been from up north. Just seeing her, it made me start asking my grandma about our traditions. The chin tattoos had to do with your status within the community. But it could also have been the status of your family within the community – maybe your husband was a well-established hunter for your village and that would be communicated in your tattoos.*

Across the reaches of the far northern Pacific, indigenous people continue to find expression through traditional means and are fighting to keep their culture alive, even as it seems the world is doing its best to shut them down.

\*

This future was already mapped out as Cook made his farewells and departed English Bay on 24 October 1778. He had been given an insight into the cultural disruption that would occur in the wake of his visits to previously isolated communities across the Pacific. His charts were exposing these worlds to foreigners and, in effect, mapping their demise.

## SAM NEILL

*Throughout his decade of voyaging, Cook had met Pacific peoples who'd experienced brief European contact. Unalaska was the first place where he saw the upheavals brought to indigenous culture after sustained contact with the Russians. For Cook, it must have been an unsettling preview of what potentially lay ahead for the societies he himself had opened up to the West.*

Although Cook's observations about the subjugation of the Unangan people reflect an unease about what he saw, it's impossible to know whether that translated to a broader concern. All we can be certain of as he left the Aleutian Islands were his intentions for the rest of his voyage and the mission he had been sent to complete.

## DR RICK KNECHT

*The big prize, of course, was the North-West Passage. He must've been terribly disappointed when he didn't get through the ice. When he went down to Hawai'i and made a few bad decisions and things ended so badly for him, I wonder whether that disappointment kind of caught up to him. I wonder if it contributed to the uncharacteristic moves on his part.*

Cook might have been a little disappointed he'd been unable to crack open the North-West Passage. But his achievements were significant. After leaving Nootka Sound, Cook had charted most of the north-west American coastline for the first time. He determined the extent of Alaska and mapped all the way to the

Bering Strait. Ensuring no other mariner would ever suffer as he did from the inaccuracies in the Russian maps, he corrected their errors, while also filling in the gaps in the Spanish and Russian charts of the northern Pacific.

The Admiralty had been unequivocal in their instructions. If Cook failed to find the North-West Passage, he was to winter in Petropavlovsk in Kamchatka and try again the following summer. But the Russians on Unalaska had told him provisions in Kamchatka were thin on the ground and would cost him an arm and a leg. With that in mind, he cast his mind back to the fertile and inviting islands he'd named the 'Sandwich Islands' as he'd travelled north from the equator … Hawai'i.

Ignoring the instructions he'd been given, Cook turned south.

It was a fateful decision, and one that would cost him dearly.

# SEVENTEEN

# BEYOND THE MORTAL
# REALM

*I've been thinking about Cook's killing here and, there
seems a terrible inevitability about it. For right or wrong,
he was the man at the front, taking action. Taking the
lead. Cook had enjoyed such good luck throughout his
three voyages around the Pacific and that luck had finally
run out. That luck had led to hubris and that
overconfidence had consequences. I see shades of Joseph
Conrad's* Heart of Darkness *here ... Captain Cook as
Mr Kurtz ... weariness, anger, illness, arrogance –
possibly even madness – and then death.*

**SAM NEILL**

Hands up who's been to Hawai'i? OK – hands up who'd *like*
to go to Hawai'i?

American popular culture has done a great job at promoting
Hawai'i as everyone's ideal tropical island getaway. From Elvis
Presley's hip-swaying endorsement in *Blue Hawaii* to *Hawaii
Five-O*, the marketing of the exotic American possession in the
centre of the Pacific has worked like a charm.

Not that its reputation is unwarranted. Like Tahiti, Hawai'i is blessed with soft sandy beaches; towering mountains clad in lush green forests; crystal clear water; rolling surf and more coconut palms than you can shake a stick at. So imagine how badly the men on board the *Resolution* and the *Discovery* wanted to get there once Cook made the announcement they were heading south to the balmy climes of the Sandwich Islands to escape the Arctic winter. They had been in the inhospitable northern Pacific region for nearly twelve months and stuck with the same group of men for two and a half years. They were about due a change of scenery.

> *SAM NEILL: Cook when he's up here, it's been years at sea with the same crew. Can you imagine what that's like?*
> **CAPTAIN PHIL PRYZMONT, Arctic Fisherman:** *My guys would have strangled each other.*
> *SAM NEILL: ... And then strangled you?*
> **PHIL PRYZMONT:** *No ... strangled each other.*
> *SAM NEILL: You've just been to sea for two months with the same guys. Did anyone strangle each other?*
> **PHIL PRYZMONT:** *Yes.*
> *SAM NEILL: They strangled each other?*
> **PHIL PRYZMONT:** *Close enough. They beat the hell out of each other.*

For four days, Cook's ships were battered by the worst gales of all his three voyages. And considering the brutal weather he'd endured at sea, that was saying something. Once they had survived that, imagine the itchy feet on board when the island of Maui loomed over the horizon on 26 November 1778, a month after they had departed Unalaska. But it wasn't only the men's feet that were itchy – Cook knew they were riddled with venereal disease and didn't want them spreading the love on shore.

### SAM NEILL

*Cook forbade his poxy crew from having sexual contact with the women … Well that was never going to work. But he feared the spread of venereal disease through the islands, though of course he was already too late because they'd already dropped anchor here a year ago and deposited nasty diseases that were by then running rampant through the Hawai'ian Islands.*

To the sailors' distress and frustration, Cook stayed offshore, navigating around the islands for eight weeks.

When he approached the largest island in the archipelago – Hawai'i – he struggled to find a suitable harbour. The men on board could see white banners flying on shore. They couldn't have known, but it was a warning that the island was under sacred restrictions for the festival of Makahiki, a celebration that heralded the return of the ancestor god Lono-i-ka-Makahiki, also known as Lono. Canoes paddled out to the ships carrying gifts of pigs, breadfruit, taro and sugar cane. But Cook wouldn't relent – he had no intention of allowing his men to infect the people living on these islands. It was only when the Hawaiians on the canoes showed him their pox-riddled genitals and asked what might be done to cure them that Cook realised the sexually transmitted horse had already bolted after their first visit.

Beyond his men's tainted X-rated bits, there was another reason that Cook wanted to delay their visit to shore – he was determined to control the going rate for metal goods by limiting supply. As long as the men weren't allowed on shore to exchange nails for sexual favours, demand for what Cook had to offer would remain high. But once the iron-for-sex trade was in full swing, the value of his goods would drop, and it would cost him a lot more to get the provisions he needed. So he intended to keep the crew on board as long as he could.

The sailors were beyond antsy. The straw that broke the camel's back was when Cook reduced the daily grog ration and ordered sugarcane beer brewed to supplement the diminishing supply of spirits. A letter of objection was penned by the men, and Cook responded by punishing his crew and cutting their grog allowance altogether.

> **JOHN LEDYARD (1751–1789), British American Explorer, crew member, Cook's third voyage**
>
> *This conduct of the commander in chief was highly reprobated and at last remonstrated against by the people on board both ships ... he was evidently sacrificing not only the ships, but the health and happiness of the brave men, who were weaving the laurel that was hereafter to adorn his brows.*

It was the walrus meat affair, all over again.

As Cook struggled to maintain order on board, from shore the Hawaiians watched the progress of the new arrivals around the island with mounting excitement. Their anticipation had nothing to do with the prospect of boatloads of randy sailors disembarking on the beach, or the metal they might bring with them. It was a whole lot more momentous than that. Arriving as he did aboard two peculiar vessels at a time that coincided with the festival that celebrated the imminent return of the ancestor god Lono, the Hawai'ians' first thought was that perhaps, at last, this was their sacred high chief and god of peace and fertility returning to them as prophesied.

According to tradition, Lono had departed the islands and portended his *'return later on an island bearing coconut-trees, and pigs, and dogs'*. With Cook's floating islands sprouting trees and accompanied by both pigs and dogs, the Hawaiians reached a logical conclusion. Cook was Lono.

**TRACY TAM SING, State Archaeologist**

*Makahiki is the season of agriculture, and it's a time when the Hawaiians worship the god Lono. Many gifts were given to Lono – feather cloaks, copper, and food such as sweet potato. These were paid in the form of taxes, and the procession to gather the taxes would go clockwise around the island with the priests of Lono carrying an image of the god. When Cook came here it was perfect timing. One of the reasons the Hawaiians received him as Lono was that the god was thought to have gone away into the ocean. The legend tells that he would one day return to Hawai'i. So here we have Cook – a foreigner – arriving at the islands. More than that, he's going around the island in a clockwise motion, which is the same way that the image of Lono would be carried around the island by the priests. Also, Lono was represented as a long staff with a crossbeam and along its sides hung white sheets of* tapa *cloth – it closely resembled the mast and the sails of Cook's ships.*

*An offering before Captain Cook in the Sandwich Islands*, engraving after John Webber, 1784. Arriving in the Season of Fertility, Cook is feted by the Hawaiians with the generous gift of a pig. The artist doesn't suggest what – if anything – Cook might have given in return. David Rumsey Map Collection, David Rumsey Map Centre, Stanford Libraries

Cook was – as yet – unaware of all this. All he was concerned about was finding a place to drop anchor, which was proving to be no small feat given the ubiquity of cliffs, shallow reefs and Hawai'i's famed towering surf. Having at last found a bay that looked as if it had potential, he directed the *Resolution* and *Discovery* into Kealakekua Bay – meaning 'the pathway of the gods'. The bay was beautiful and heavily populated. From the deck, Cook saw cliff-top gardens and arable land crisscrossed with stone walls and hedges that delineated lush breadfruit forests and fields. But what struck the men on board more than anything was the boisterous welcome that awaited them.

Ten thousand or so Hawaiians were in and around the bay. Cook estimated there to be over one and a half thousand canoes in the water, supplemented by other people who swam out to meet the new arrivals.

### JOHN LEDYARD

*The crowds on shore were still more numerous. The beach, the surrounding rocks, the tops of houses, the branches of trees and the adjacent hills were all covered, and the shouts of joy, and admiration ... formed one of the most tumultuous and the most curious prospects that can be imagined.*

On Cook's exploration of Tahiti with Joseph Banks during the first voyage, the two men had been treated to the sight of locals taking to the waves atop wooden boards – the first European record of *he'e 'ana*. Surfing. They would see more of it in Hawai'i, and confirm that the cabalistic etiquette and hierarchy that prevails in today's surfing culture has a long history. In Hawai'i, where surfing had more to do with a ritual practice than recreation, the chieftains had first claim on the best breaks and were given boards made of the best wood.

\*

When Cook dropped anchor, the Hawaiians had more important things on their minds than surfing. Heading out on their boards and canoes, the rapturous Hawaiians swamped the two ships. So many people clambered onto the *Discovery* that it keeled over onto its side. Narrowly averting disaster, the men on board were forced to push many of the men and women in the welcoming party off the boat's side – an indignity they bore with surprisingly good humour.

**DAVID SAMWELL (1751–1791) Welsh Naval Surgeon on Cook's third voyage**

*[T]he decks both above and below were entirely covered with them, so that ... we could not come at the ropes without first driving the greatest part of them overboard; which they bore with the utmost cheerfulness and good nature.*

A new visitor approached the *Resolution*. Koaʻa, Lono's high priest, came on board and quickly identified the man who was the commander of the crew of pale-skinned sailors. To the Hawaiians, who were master navigators and knew all about nautical hierarchy and the ritual regalia that went with it, there was no mistaking it. Cook was their man.

**ASSOCIATE PROFESSOR MARK D. MCCOY, Southern Methodist University**

*There's probably a sense of being kindred spirits – these are clearly ships that were doing long-distance navigation, and that's something that's extraordinarily familiar to Polynesians. The Polynesians would also have recognised the hierarchy of the ship, down to the uniforms and the hats and the regalia. You can't just be in charge – you have to look like you were in charge, and Cook certainly did that.*

Koaʻa began chanting and wrapped Cook in red cloth, offering him gifts of pigs and coconuts. Although Cook had enjoyed an enthusiastic welcome or two from indigenous people, this was one out of the box.

But that wasn't the end of the story.

It was 17 January 1779. Koaʻa escorted Cook to shore where a company of Hawaiians carried the Englishman on their shoulders to the beach. Heralds walked before the two men crying 'the great Lono is coming!' as all the people on the beach – other than the god's own priests – prostrated themselves before Cook. Leading him up to a stone shrine, or *heiau*, known as Hikiau, the priests made a series of rituals and offerings to Cook.

**TRACY TAM SING**

*The Hikiau* heiau *is a religious structure built by the Hawaiians. It was probably built around 1400 to 1500AD and was used for human sacrifices to please the god Kū. It was also used to serve the god Lono during the Makahiki season.*

As far as the men on board the British ships were concerned, their commander was being venerated as a living god.

**DAVID SAMWELL (1751–1791)**

*[T]housands of people prostrated themselves as they passed along and put their hands before their faces as if it was deemed violation or sacrilege to look at them ... a ceremony was performed by the priests in which he was invested by them with the title and dignity of Orono, which is the highest rank among these Indians and is a character that is looked upon by them as partaking something of divinity.*

This wasn't a ridiculous assumption to make considering the pomp and ceremony that accompanied Cook's arrival, although amongst indigenous Hawaiians today, there's no consensus about whether or not the locals were worshipping him as a god incarnate, or just being hospitable to a new – and important – visitor to their shores.

### TRACY TAM SING

*Cook was met by the chief, Kalaniʻōpuʻu. He actually brought Captain Cook here to the shoreline and brought him up to the temple – the* heiau *– where they conducted religious ceremonies in front of Cook, offering him pig and wrapping him in red* tapa *cloth. That's where they declared him the human manifestation of the god Lono.*

### GORDON KANAKANUI LESLIE, Hoʻala Kealakekua

*In some accounts they talk about all the women going out to visit the ships when they pulled into their bays and the women spending all night below deck with the sailors. Now Lono is very sacred. And fornication is not one of those things you exercise during that period. So I doubt that the ruling chiefs would have allowed that to happen if they did think Cook was Lono.*

Whether or not the locals regarded him as a deity, this was but a taste of the veneration Cook would enjoy for much of his stay in Hawaiʻi. Whenever he went ashore, he was accompanied by a priest who announced that Lono had landed, and the people he encountered would prostrate themselves before him.

Cook's standing on the island was consolidated by another important visitor to the *Resolution* – Hawaiʻi's high chief, Kalaniʻōpuʻu. As the chieftain of the largest island in the archipelago, Kalaniʻōpuʻu was the most important man around. When he came on board, he presented Cook with a gift of three small pigs and fresh fruit and – most significantly – his black-and yellow-feathered helmet, or *mahiole*, and his exquisite *'ahu 'ula*, or feathered cloak, both of which were ceremonial regalia worn only by chieftains.

**ANNE LOKOMAIKA'I LIPSCOMB, Senior Culture Educator**

*When Captain Cook arrives on the Island of Hawai'i, Kalani'ōpu'u is the paramount Chief of that island. So he is in a position to not only welcome anyone who comes to the island, but also to bestow upon them all sorts of riches and to feed them. I think that's an important thing to keep in mind … It's a part of our culture to greet one another with generosity – with an open and welcoming spirit. So Kalani'ōpu'u was coming from a place of generous relationship building. He gifts Captain Cook many things, among them his own* 'ahu 'ula *and* mahiole. *The* mana *of the wearer is enhanced and reflected by these materials in that they themselves are filled with* mana. *It's estimated that the* 'ahu 'ula *given to Cook includes four million feathers in total taken from about twenty thousand birds. These feathered pieces were worn into battle so that they carry with them the* mana *of those birds and also the* mana *of the hands that made that beautiful object so they would be supported and protected in their efforts. Kalani'ōpu'u places them upon Cook's body, which is a tremendously significant gesture. He is giving up himself because his own* mana *from the many, many times he's worn it – the many adventures and achievements – all those years of living are imbued in these treasures when he transfers them to Cook.*

Cook and Kalaniʻōpuʻu exchanged names – a ritual Cook knew well from his time in Polynesia – and Cook reciprocated his ritual friend's gift by presenting him with his own naval sword.

**ASSOCIATE PROFESSOR MARK D. MCCOY**

*I think it went in stages. It probably depended on a lot of things – so from the perspective of the priests, they had to look at the signs around them and say, 'Yes, this is Lono.' But ultimately the person who was in charge of religion in Hawaiʻi was the King. So when the King finally received Cook here and acknowledged him as Lono, then he officially became Lono.*

There's no doubt the crew – and, presumably, Cook – believed the Hawaiians were exalting him as the manifestation of their god. As a man who shied away from overt expressions of religious belief and seemed to maintain a fairly sceptical outlook when it came to questions of faith, what did Cook make of all this? He had failed in his first attempt to achieve the sole purpose of the voyage, while coming to the brink of mutiny with his men on more than one occasion. It's safe to assume that when he landed in Hawaiʻi he had been feeling rather dejected.

Cook's career had been a rollcall of lucky escapes, and his heavy-handed management of relationships with crew and indigenous people alike on the third voyage suggests he now considered himself above recrimination. Perhaps his long absence from the world he'd grown up in, where social conventions would have kept him in check, not to mention his many near misses, had cultivated a sense of immortality in him – a sense that the normal rules no longer applied to him.

In Hawai'i, his fearlessness and determination to lead from the front had crossed the line and entered the realm of recklessness. If he believed the Hawaiians recognised him as a deity, that would hardly have helped him keep a lid on his sense of mortality and human frailty.

### SAM NEILL

*Cook got the first taste of the extraordinary adulation that persisted wherever he went in the next few weeks … What's equally interesting, I think, is what Cook was thinking. Could he be forgiven for imagining himself as something more than human? We'll never know because the journals from that part of the journey no longer exist.*

Uncharacteristically for a man who had always shown a determination to keep a record of his adventures, it seems Cook gave up on diarising just before his life's last leg. Or perhaps all his journal entries from this time have been lost. Or some question whether the Admiralty or Charles Clerke, who assumed command after Cook's death, might have decided to do a little judicious editing because Cook's account reflected a mental fissure in his last days that didn't measure up to the grand myth being constructed posthumously around his name.

\*

Possible delusions of grandeur aside, Cook's stay in Hawai'i was generally delightful thanks to the Hawai'ians' eagerness to make things as comfortable as possible for him and his men. Two chieftains, Kanina and Palea, voluntarily posted themselves as sentries on board the two ships to police their compatriots – any thieves were severely punished, and female visitation was restricted to the hours after dark. While on board, the two Hawaiian men impressed the officers with their insights and sophisticated questions about the British way of life.

### JAMES KING (1750–1784) Officer, Royal Navy, crew member, Cook's third voyage

*[They] asked after our King; the nature of our government; our numbers; the method of building our ships; our houses; the produce of our country; whether we had wars; with whom ... and many other questions of the same nature, which indicated an understanding of great comprehension.*

The men on board the ship had many opportunities of their own to observe the Hawaiians going about their everyday lives. One thing that baffled them was the prevalence of homosexuality. The Hawaiian king, Kalaniʻōpuʻu, was attended by a number of *aikāne*, or male lovers, who tended to his needs – amongst them Palea, the chieftain who was acting as mediator on the British ships.

### DAVID SAMWELL (1751–1798)

*Their business is to commit the Sin of Onan upon the old King ... it is an office that is esteemed honourable among them & they have frequently asked us on seeing a handsome young fellow if he was not an* aikāne *to some of us.*

As a side note, the term 'Sin of Onan' is a delicate way to describe the spilling of seed, or masturbation, and named for the Old

Testament figure, Onan, who defied his father's orders to impregnate his deceased brother's wife by withdrawing before the deed was done.

For almost three weeks, Cook enjoyed the hospitality of the Hawai'ian people. It came at no small cost to the locals – finding enough food to support two hundred men who had arrived with scant supplies of their own meant Kalani'ōpu'u had to call on villagers from across the island to satisfy the constant demands being made on the people of Kealakekua Bay.

### GORDON KANAKANUI LESLIE

*Now keep in mind even though the people greeted him like a royal guest when he arrived here, Cook and his men were somewhat disrespectful in a sense that you know when you have that one guest who spends a little too long in your house. Provisions for Cook's men – there's almost two hundred of them – for twenty days, well, it takes a lot of food. So their resources were being tapped to the point where they had to go to a nearby district which is about sixty miles [one hundred kilometres] from here to ask them to bring food to help take care of their guests in here. And Cook and his men were rather disrespectful in that when they needed firewood for their stoves they removed all the fence posts from around the temple and when that wasn't enough, they took the tikis and cut them up for firewood as well. But because the Hawaiians respected him, they allowed him to do it. But it left them with a really bad taste in their mouth.*

When Cook's men struggled to find firewood in the interior of the island, he was granted permission to dismantle the fence around the Hikiau *heiau* – the temple where he had been honoured when he first arrived – to burn as firewood. Although the Hawaiians begrudgingly agreed to let him do it, they were less than pleased. Cook had outstayed his welcome, god incarnate or not.

> *ANNE LOKOMAIKA'I LIPSCOMB: ... Everything was made available to you and sometimes that gift comes with great expectation. But, perhaps you take that generosity for granted and go too far. Then those actions have repercussions that again change everything.*
> *SAM NEILL: Never outstay your welcome. If there's one moral to this story, it's that, isn't it?*
> *ANNE LOKOMAIKA'I LIPSCOMB: That's right. Hospitality is so valued, but the flip side is that if it is not respected. then there are enormous consequences.*

Kalani'ōpu'u and the other chieftains approached Cook and asked when he planned to leave. He told them it would be soon, and their relief was evident. Second Lieutenant James King, who would end up captaining the *Discovery*, had made a strong connection with the Hawaiians, and Kalani'ōpu'u, thinking he was Cook's son, asked if King might be permitted to stay on the island. Cook, of course, declined the generous offer. If King had known he was to die of tuberculosis just four years after the *Resolution* and *Discovery* returned to England, he might have chosen to live out his remaining years in Hawai'i.

\*

With much fanfare, the two ships departed Kealakekua Bay on 4 February 1779. Cook's plan was to visit Maui and explore the rest of the Hawaiian Islands. For Kalaniʻōpuʻu and his subjects, this was perfect synergy. It was the day Lono's departure was predicted to occur. The prophecy as proclaimed by the King and the priests of Lono had been fulfilled.

But it didn't go quite as planned. Sometimes the smallest things can be your undoing. During the voyage, there must have been many occasions when Cook looked at the irresolute *Resolution* with its shoddy caulking and rotting timbers and thought that it would be the death of him. Unfortunately, he was right.

A foremast that had been replaced in Nootka gave way, rotten and weakened by the constant battering it had endured in the Arctic. Just three days after the British ships left Kealakekua Bay, the mast snapped in a storm and – to add insult to injury – the *Resolution* sprang another serious leak. What to do but to return for repairs to the bay where Cook had enjoyed the most hospitable welcome of all his voyages?

If the men on board had been expecting a ticker-tape parade and bunting when they reappeared in Kealakekua Bay, they would have been sorely disappointed. Unlike their previous arrival, there was nobody around to greet them. Those locals they encountered were sullen and less than happy to see them.

Again, Cook had revealed his inability to truly understand local traditions and belief systems, despite having spent so many years amongst Polynesian people.

Kalaniʻōpuʻu came on board and was clearly irritated to see Cook again. For one thing, he suspected the British were back because they were planning to stay and establish themselves on the island. But what caused him the greatest displeasure was that it violated the King's will. By returning to the island, Cook had undermined his and the priests' authority by defying expectations about how Lono was meant to behave.

### ASSOCIATE PROFESSOR MARK D. MCCOY

*So Cook had broken generations of rules about how Lono is expected to act. He left from the place where Lono was ritually put in a canoe and sent off but by returning he had flown in the face of the priests and the King who had received him as Lono by not doing the things that Lono would do. This was seen as a bad omen and so their reception was very chilly when he returned.*

Tensions mounted, with neither party really wanting the ships to be there – including the men on board, who were eager to move on.

### JOHN LEDYARD

*Our return to this bay was as disagreeable to us as it was to the inhabitants, because we were reciprocally tired of each other. They had been oppressed and were wary of our prostituted alliance, and we were aggrieved by the consideration of wanting the provisions and refreshments of the country.*

As the crew attempted to repair the ship, canoes ferried supplies out to them. But unlike during the previous visit, the Hawaiians indulged in rampant thievery and were flogged when captured red-handed. On shore, where once the sailors had been welcomed they were now mocked and attacked. George Vancouver and the

*Discovery*'s master, Thomas Edgar, set off to retrieve a purloined pinnace and ended up in a dispute that resulted in Palea – Kalani'ōpu'u's lover and the chieftain who had kept order on board the *Discovery* – being beaten about the head. This was a dreadful breach of *kapu* (sacred power). As was the case elsewhere in Polynesia, in Hawai'i the hair and head of a chieftain was revered. Palea was gracious and stopped his warriors from seeking retribution. But things were going off the rails fast. And it was about to get a whole lot worse.

On 14 February 1779, a cutter was stolen from the *Discovery*. Furious, Cook commanded Charles Clerke to go ashore and take Kalani'ōpu'u hostage. Clerke, a veteran of all three of Cook's voyages, had contracted tuberculosis between journeys when he agreed to serve time in prison for a debt incurred by his brother. The disease plagued him on the third voyage, and he was severely ill when Cook called on him to retrieve the stolen boat.

Cook decided to take matters into his own hands. His high-handed method of punishing behaviour he deemed unacceptable on the part of indigenous populations – hostage taking – had proven to be effective in the past. But it had also been the cause of numerous near misses, with Cook barely escaping violent retribution and doing untold damage to his relationship with the indigenous people of the Pacific. Kalani'ōpu'u was Cook's ritual friend – they had exchanged names and the King had given Cook extremely significant gifts steeped in *mana*. In the Polynesian belief system, the two men were now fused, in a way. Kalani'ōpu'u was Cook, and Cook was Kalani'ōpu'u. So for Cook to consider taking the King hostage was absurd. But because hostage taking had worked for Cook before, he assumed it would work again. So he went ashore with ten armed marines intent on the course of action and oblivious to the dangers inherent in the undertaking.

Cook did not for a moment think Kalani'ōpu'u was responsible for – or even aware of – the theft, but he believed this was the only way to resolve the issue. He was led to Kalani'ōpu'u's side by the King's two sons.

Kalani'ōpu'u was sleeping but was roused to receive his visitor. Cook invited the King to visit the *Resolution* and escorted him down to the beach. On the way, a shocking piece of news reached the village. A party from the *Discovery* had shot and killed another chieftain, Kalimu. On hearing this, and fearing the worst, Kalani'ōpu'u's senior wife begged the King not to accompany Cook. Kalani'ōpu'u responded with a form of peaceful protest. He embraced Cook, explained he could go no further with him, and sat down.

There are differing opinions about what happened next.

### SAM NEILL

*There is much conjecture about the day that Cook was killed. But what is generally understood is the Hawaiians made a series of small thefts but when one of Cook's important boats was stolen, Cook flew into a rage and went ashore with a plan that had served him well in the past – to take the chief hostage in order to get it back. But as to the details – well, everyone has a different take.*

Contemporary accounts of Cook's death are contradictory, perhaps because those on board were concerned about protecting their own reputations when, as they expected, recriminations would be sought for the death of their commander in circumstances that should have been avoidable. But certain details are generally accepted as being accurate.

Kalaniʻōpuʻu was surrounded by a crowd of two to three thousand people, all urging him to resist Cook's entreaties. The marines were lined up on shore facing the crowd, their guns raised.

Determined to get Kalaniʻōpuʻu to cooperate, Cook attempted to lift him to his feet. But laying your hands on the King was an appalling breach of protocol. A warrior stepped in to attack Cook, who pulled the trigger on his pistol and peppered his attacker with small shot – to no effect.

### ASSOCIATE PROFESSOR MARK D. MCCOY

*Cook made a number of missteps that really set things off. It's also important to remember he was killed in a very chaotic moment. I doubt in the ten minutes prior to the event that the King could have predicted that Cook was going to be killed. Certainly, Cook had no idea or else he would have gotten out of there faster. What we know from the written accounts is that Cook arrived here and sought out King Kalaniʻōpuʻu. This was not unusual – he had talked to the King and the King had been on board his ship before. So Cook was trying to entice the King to come with him, but the King's family and his retainers saw it for what it was and knew things were going badly. So Cook's plan starts to unravel when the King just sits down on the beach. And you can't move a king – Cook should have known this. Imagine if one of Kalaniʻōpuʻu's warriors went to the court of King George and tried to grab King George by the collar and take him out to his Polynesian canoe! That wouldn't have gone down well either.*

The marines opened fire and Cook loaded his gun, shooting and killing another Hawaiian. From the boats offshore, the sailors who had brought Cook to the beach also opened fire. Turning to the boats, Cook waved at the men to put their guns down and implored them to come to shore. Because Cook couldn't swim, he needed his men to carry him and the marines to safety. He had no way of retreating from the menacing crowd on the beach without a boat. He was stranded.

As Cook appealed for help, one warrior struck him on the back of the head with a club. Another stabbed him in the neck with a knife – one of the blades that had been fashioned from the *Discovery*'s anchor in Unalaska.

With a single cry – 'My God!' – Cook fell into the water between two rocks and was beaten to death.

### GORDON KANAKANUI LESLIE

*Some people tell me that the Hawaiians knew about Cook taking hostages in Tahiti so when Cook approached Kalani'ōpu'u, who was just getting up – he was hungover from kava – thousands of people followed them, trying to discourage the chief from going with Cook. When his wife begged him not to go, Kalani'ōpu'u sat on the ground. Cook put his hand out to pull the chief to his feet. But commoners and foreigners are not allowed to touch this man, so when he did that, the women and children in the crowd retreated. But at that moment, they heard cannons and gunshots going off. When Cook had left the ship he had given his officers instructions not to let any canoe leave the bay. So another famous chief was shot by the men on the ship and that's when the warriors started mustering up their weapons.*

*Captain Cook sees all this and he ordered the marines to the water's edge to face the crowd. When they fired into the air, the natives went nuts. Cook runs down to the water's edge to get away from the crowd. But then he gets stabbed, he gets clubbed, and then pushed under the water to die.*

### ALEXANDER HOME (1739–1823), crew member, Cook's third voyage

*Captain Cook stood on the edge of the rock waiting for the boat for [he] could not swim and when he stood in that position one of the chiefs came behind him and stabbed in the back with an iron dagger ... which had been forged on board the ships ... Captain Cook being thus mortally wounded tumbled down the rock into the sea and his head fell into a gully betwixt two narrow rocks. He attempted to get up, could not and I believe was suffocated in the water.*

And, just like that, Cook was gone.

Four marines and many Hawaiians were killed in the chaos that followed. The Hawaiians, for the most part, fled the shore and left Cook's body and the bodies of the fallen marines lying on the beach. This would have been an opportunity for the generally disliked lieutenant, John Williamson, to retrieve his comrades' remains. But feebly citing concerns about the viability of weapons that may have been exposed to water and deciding his men didn't have enough ammunition to fend off an attack, Williamson gave the order to return to the ships, so forsaking the lifeless body of his commander.

\*

Cook's death was fast and it was brutal. Yet it had also been a long time coming.

### ASSOCIATE PROFESSOR MARK D. MCCOY

*Cook's luck ran out right here. Rather than ask why Cook was killed, a better question is to ask why it took so long. How did he last as long as he did? How did he survive Aotearoa, Tonga and Tahiti and finally meet his end here in Hawai'i? It's puzzling how this person managed to impose himself on his hosts all over the Pacific – it speaks to the wonderful spirit of these people who honoured their obligation as hosts that he survived as long as he did.*

In years to come, a man who claimed to have struck the fatal blow gave his version of events. His account seems to confirm that chaos and confusion played a part in Cook's death.

### PIHERE, Hawaiian warrior

*I arrived just as the disturbance began and heard my countrymen crying out that the white men were going to kill the King ... I have a* Parhoavah *in my hand – all was confusion and in a short time I think Capt. Cook fired, but as nobody was hurt we thought it was only harmless thunders, shortly after a number of men fired & killed several of my countrymen. We then rushed on & I being near the Lono his back turned towards me struck him quite through with the dagger and he fell.*

But there were so many other factors. When Cook returned to Hawai'i, it was the wrong time of the Makahiki cycle. The god

Lono was on the wane and the god of war, Kū, was in the ascendency – if Cook had elected to continue to Maui rather than return to Hawai'i, things might have ended differently. If the marines had stood fast ... If Williamson had ordered the men in the boats to come to Cook's aid ... If Williamson – who had a chequered history with Cook – hadn't been in charge that day ... If the mast hadn't broken in the first place ... If Cook had paid more attention to the *Resolution*'s outfitting in England ... If Clerke hadn't been ill ... If Cook had restrained himself and accepted the loss of the cutter ... If his men had forged the *Discovery*'s anchor into spoons rather than knives ... If he'd just been content with retirement in Greenwich ...

At his death, Cook was fifty years of age.

### ASSOCIATE PROFESSOR MARK D. MCCOY

*Cook had good days and he had bad days ... I think by opening up the Pacific to the European maps, he started an exchange that was unlike any other in world history, at least in this part of the world, and that ultimately is something that he'll always be remembered for.*

Cook had been at sea for over thirty years. He had taken no time for rest and recuperation between his three voyages, and he had endured the crushing stress of command under conditions that would have shattered many men.

### HEINRICH ZIMMERMANN (1741–1805), crew member, Cook's third voyage

*He would often sit at the table with his officers without saying a word, and was always very reserved. In small matters he was stricter with the crew than the officers, but at times was very affable. He was born to deal with savages and he was never happier than in association with them. He loved them and understood the languages of the different islanders and had the art of captivating them with his engaging manner. This was probably the reason that they honoured him and at times even worshipped him, and also further reason that when they ceased to honour him, or sometimes even ridicule him, he burned with rage.*

Cook had failed in his first attempt to find the North-West Passage – the prize that he'd been so desperate to find to ensure financial security for his family – and his behaviour on his third voyage showed a man whose defining characteristics of humanity, resolve and fairness had devolved into cruelty, pettiness and volatility.

Because Cook – the faithful journal keeper – was silent for the last month of his life, what was going on in his mind is, and will most likely always remain, a mystery to us. Perhaps one day a missing journal will reappear. But even then, Cook's words would be unlikely to shed any light on why it was that this man who had cheated death for so many years met his end on this beach, on that day. The conclusion reached by the pre-eminent Cook scholar Professor Dame Anne Salmond, in her book *The Trial of the Cannibal Dog* is that Cook's long engagement with Polynesia and the cultural contradictions he encountered and could never quite penetrate culminated in a tragic event that was as inevitable as it was avoidable:

*[T]here is no good morality play, colonial or post-colonial, to be made of Cook's killing. Over a decade in Polynesia, he was caught in intractable contradictions. As the trial of the cannibal dog at Tōtara-nui showed, when he acted with calm restraint, he invited humiliation – his sailors and the islanders alike considered him to be weak ... When he acted in anger and sought* mana *by force, he invited retaliation. His men became mutinous, and the islanders sought to kill him ... At Hawai'i it happened, but there was no one cause. It was a cross-cultural combination of forces that killed him.*

Cook had given much of his life to the Pacific. His arrival in its waters would alter it and the lives of the indigenous people he had encountered irrevocably. No matter the cause, it seems only fitting that it was there that he met his end.

**SAM NEILL**
*Cook devoted his life to charting the Pacific, and that is where he rests, in this great ocean.*

*EIGHTEEN*

# APOTHEOSIS

*Of the many monuments I've seen to Cook, the one in*
*Kealakekua Bay is probably for me the most poignant*
*because it was erected about a hundred years after his*
*death – just a few feet away from where he was actually*
*killed. A curiosity about it was that the land itself was*
*actually gifted to Britain. It's just a shame about the*
*words inscribed on it ... 'Cook discovered these islands', it*
*says ... that's just the sort of thing that 250 years later*
*still gets poor old Cook into trouble all around the*
*Pacific. A claim – incidentally – that he himself would*
*never have made.*

## SAM NEILL

One year is not made up of 365 days – not exactly. When, in 46BC, Julius Caesar decreed a reform of the Roman calendar that didn't accommodate the slight anomaly embodied in the solar year, Europe began to gain a day every 128 years. By the mid-eighteenth century, this meant the Julian system was eleven days out of whack, which meant the whole seasonal calendar was shifting. To amend this, in 1750 Great Britain adopted the Gregorian calendar now used in the West, which incorporates a leap year to keep things in check.

What does this have to do with the story of James Cook? It means that – like so many other things about him – Cook's date of birth is a contentious point. According to the Gregorian model, he was born in 1728 on 7 November. That's what Wikipedia tells us, so it must be right, right? Not necessarily – proving that judicious use of online resources behoves us all. Because if – as was customary at the time – we follow the Julian dates that prevailed at his birth, Cook was actually born on 27 October.

One thing that's beyond doubt is that he died at the age of fifty on Valentine's Day, 1779, in Kealakekua Bay, Hawai'i.

The earth did not shake. The sky did not rain fire and brimstone. To the best of our knowledge, the heavenly host did not weep. Cook was, after all, just a man.

Would Cook have considered his life's work a triumph? Would he have deemed his death a tragedy and seen himself as a man gone before his time? Or would he have assumed it was the high price he was obliged to pay for cheating death so many times? It was almost as if all the transgressions Cook made, time and time again, in his encounters with the indigenous people of the Pacific had been accumulating in a simmering pot that finally bubbled over in Hawai'i.

**ASSOCIATE PROFESSOR MARK D. MCCOY,**
**Southern Methodist University**

*Cook could map a coastline but he couldn't see the very subtle boundaries and borders that existed here. He came here and, according to Native Hawaiian measures, he*

*behaved badly, just as they were trying to civilise him. The*
*Hawaiians were trying to show him by example … 'Look,*
*we're giving you these gifts, this is what civilised people do!'*
*So they gave the gifts and tried to explain that it would be*
*good to respond in kind. But Cook was only really looking*
*at it as a rest stop on his way. He wasn't interested in*
*setting up an embassy or establishing a long-term*
*relationship between King George and our King*
*Kalani'ōpu'u. So I think that short-sightedness and his*
*missing the social cues were the things that got him into*
*trouble.*

Not that the people of Kealakekua Bay were aware of all the
details of Cook's long history in Polynesia. They could only
measure his behaviour by what they had witnessed themselves.
And overall, other than the incident that ended his life, the
Hawaiians do appear to have held Cook in reasonably good
regard.

*SAM NEILL: On the anniversary of Cook's death this year,*
*there were people all over the Pacific saying to me things*
*like – 'Godspeed to the great people of Hawai'i who did the*
*thing that should have been done … they killed Captain*
*Cook.' What do you think of that?*
*GORDON KANAKANUI LESLIE, Ho'ala Kealakekua:*
*I don't think our leaders back then wanted to kill him.*
*I think they had great respect for him … they liked him.*
*They probably didn't like some of the behaviour in the*
*short time Cook and his men were here. But I think they*
*revered him as a great navigator.*

*The Apotheosis of Captain Cook*, Francesco Bartolozzi (engraver), after Philippe-Jacques de Loutherbourg from a drawing by John Webber, 1794. Cook's death met with an outpouring of grief in Britain, and he was memorialised in all media of the day. Here Cook is carried from Kealakekua Bay towards Heaven, in the arms of Britannia and Fame – though there are still Hawaiians today who would rather he had been consigned to hell.

National Library of Australia, PIC Drawer 82 #S1089

For one Hawaiian man, Cook's death triggered an existential and spiritual crisis. Kalaniʻōpuʻu was mortified that Cook, with whom he had formed the bond of ritual friendship, had been killed. He retreated to a cave cut into the rocks above the bay where his friend had died. It was accessible only by rope, and during the King's period of self-imposed exile, supplies had to be lowered down to him. Because Kalaniʻōpuʻu and Cook had exchanged names, according to the Hawaiian belief system, when Cook was killed the King's life force was also struck a blow. By all reports, the ritual connection between the two men didn't diminish after Cook's death.

That's not the end of the story of the Hawaiian King and James Cook. It's a tale that captures the shifting currents in today's Pacific, as the indigenous people of Polynesia find ways of reconciling the past with the present. Having passed through many hands over the centuries since Cook's death, the ʻahu ʻula and *mahiole* gifted to Cook by Kalaniʻōpuʻu when they exchanged names found their way to New Zealand's Te Papa Museum. In 2016, in a significant and moving gesture of restitution and Polynesian kinship, Te Papa returned the feathered cloak and helmet to Hawaiʻi's Bishop Museum.

The Pacific Ocean and the people who called it home would be transformed forever in the wake of James Cook's arrival. At points during his three voyages, there are hints in his journal that he was aware of how his work might fuel European ambitions, with earth-shattering repercussions for the region and its original inhabitants. But he could never have imagined that, at his end, he would become one with the Polynesian cosmos – literally and figuratively.

\*

As Kalaniʻōpuʻu confronted his loss, the Englishman's body was taken up by the Hawaiʻians. It was then dealt with in a way that would inspire a cross-cultural misunderstanding, indicative of the cultural chasm that existed between the people of the Pacific and the Western ethos. The Hawaiians handled Cook's remains with veneration, following the rituals they would have observed if he were a fallen chieftain. In the Hawaiian burial tradition, the most important parts of the deceased were the bones. To extricate them, the body was dismembered and interred in an earth oven until the flesh fell away. There's disagreement today about whether or not part of that process also involved the priests and chieftains ingesting some of Cook's flesh.

**TRACY TAM SING, State Archaeologist**

*They took Cook's body up to the cliffs to another smaller heiau. When a chief would die, they would strip all the flesh off the bones by putting the body in an underground oven. Part of the ritual after a chief had passed away was that the next chief, who was to take his place, would partake of a little bit of the flesh of the chief that passed to absorb his mana. Because Cook was seen as a personification of Lono, the chiefs and the priest would probably have partaken in parts of his flesh. But it was a ritual. They were honouring him. He was treated with the utmost respect by the Hawaiians – in the same way they would treat one of their own chiefs.*

**LANAKILA MANGAUIL, Activist**

*People said they ate Cook ... but that's not our practice in Hawai'i. Where the confusion comes from is that the burial tradition of Hawai'i involves putting the body into an underground oven, which is also how we cook our food.*

Given what Cook's men knew of Māori traditions when it came to the treatment of a fallen enemy's body, when they saw smoke billowing from fires inland, they assumed their commander's body and those of the marines who had died with him were being prepared for consumption.

The men of the *Resolution* and the *Discovery* were reeling with shock at the death of their commander.

**DAVID SAMWELL (1751–1791) Welsh Naval Surgeon on Cook's third voyage**

*The men it must be said were most sincerely affected on this occasion ... when they came alongside they cried out with tears in their eyes that they had lost their father ... [I]n every situation, he stood unrivalled ... he was our leading-star which at his setting, left us involved in darkness and despair ... He was beloved by his people who looked up to him as to a father, and obeyed his commands with alacrity.*

At that moment, the entire expedition was rudderless.

**GEORGE GILBERT (? – 1781) crew member,**
**Cook's third voyage**

*A general silence ensued throughout the ship, for the space of near half an hour – it appearing to us somewhat like a dream ... Grief was visible in every countenance; some expressing it by tears and others by a kind of gloomy dejection ... all our hopes centred on him, our loss became irreparable.*

The seemingly indestructible man who had driven them through moments of inconceivable hardship with the force of his cast-iron will and unshakeable determination was gone.

For Cook's shipmates, it was unthinkable that his remains were going to be subjected to what they saw as the ultimate desecration, on an island so far from home. As their shock gave way to anger, the one thing on the men's minds was revenge.

\*

From his sickbed, Charles Clerke – the man originally tapped on the shoulder to lead the third voyage before Cook decided he wanted to head out to sea again – took over the captaincy of the *Resolution*. Replacing him as captain of the *Discovery* was John Gore, the American-born naval officer who in 1767 had been a crew member accompanying Samuel Wallis to Tahiti on board the *Dolphin*.

Gore and Clerke now faced a daunting task. Both had accompanied Cook on all three of his voyages, and so they must have been struggling to keep their own emotions in check. But they had to safely refit the crippled *Resolution* and set sail to waters that were less hostile to them. To do that, they needed to secure a new mast. And that required keeping the men – who were determined to avenge their captain's death – under control.

On shore, the Hawaiians had their own, very well-founded, reasons for fighting back. They had lost many warriors in the firestorm that followed Cook's death.

James King, who had formed a good relationship with the priests in Kealakekua Bay, mediated a truce with a party of Hawaiians who came alongside the British ships. But on shore, a group of warriors taunted the sailors, parading along the beach wearing Cook's jacket and trousers and brandishing weapons taken from Cook and the marines who had died alongside him. It was too much for the sailors on board, and ignoring their commander's orders, when a water party went to shore some days later, they inflicted brutal reprisals on the Hawaiian villagers.

### SAM NEILL

*The crew were overwhelmed by grief and a thirst for vengeance, and they were further enraged by the taunts of the Hawaiians. It was never going to end well. Clerke, who was now in command, advised restraint. But a couple of days later, a water party at the beach ran amok ... they burnt a village, they destroyed canoes, they slaughtered villagers and they paraded their heads on poles. It was a brutal and gruesome response.*

Kalaniʻōpuʻu interceded. He expressed deep regret that Cook had been killed and declared himself willing to renew his friendship with the visitors.

James King had learnt that Cook's bones had been distributed amongst the chieftains so that they could all share in his *mana*, but Clerke wanted to retrieve his remains so he could bury him according to Christian traditions.

The next morning, peace held long enough for the *Resolution* to be fitted with a new foremast.

That evening, two Hawaiians paddled out to the ships carrying a parcel wrapped in cloth. It contained flesh from Cook's thigh. When King asked them whether they had eaten the Englishman, the Hawaiians were horrified, assuring him they were not cannibals. They were clearly terrified, asking whether Lono would one day return and seek revenge for his murder.

Some time later, another bundle arrived on the boat draped in a black feather cloak. In it the sailors found both of Cook's arms disarticulated from his hands, one of which bore the distinctive scar from an injury caused by an exploding powder-horn early in his naval career in Newfoundland.

### LILIKALĀ KAMEʻELEIHIWA PhD,
#### Professor of Hawaiian Ancestral Knowledge

*They kept the bones – that's what they did with Cook ... except for the hands and his buttocks. The Lono priests took those down to the boat and said, 'Oh you want your share of Cook? Here he is.'*

Clerke also retrieved Cook's skull and scalp with one ear attached, and sometime later, his lower jaw and feet were returned to the newly minted commander.

James Cook's scant remains were placed into a coffin and

buried at sea in Kealakekua Bay with full military honours and ceremony befitting his status.

After the two British ships pulled up anchor, they blasted their cannon at the cliffs beside the bay to create a landslide blocking access to the pathways that led to other villages on the island. This grim tradition was commemorated by Australian and Canadian naval vessels each year until 1960, permanently scarring the landscape.

\*

Cook's memory was kept alive on Hawai'i after the departure of his men. European visitors in the late eighteenth century reported that he was venerated on the island as 'Lono-nui', and that two new volcanoes that had exploded to life after his death were attributed to a posthumous expression of his rage. *Heiaus* (temples) were erected in his memory and sacrifices made in the hope that Lono-nui would one day return to forgive those who had murdered him.

Visitors to the island were shown bones they were told belonged to Cook, the legend being that they had been passed on to the man who inherited Kalani'ōpu'u's throne, Kamehameha. And when George Vancouver – a midshipman on Cook's final voyage – returned to the island in 1793 in command of his own voyage, one of his crew reported that Cook's bones were revered and kept with Kalani'ōpu'u's own remains at the Hikiau *heiau*.

The stories brought back to Europe were embellished further still; it was said that during the annual tribute to Lono, Cook's bones were kept in a wickerwork basket covered in red feathers and carried around the island.

News of Cook's death reached Tonga in the earliest years of the nineteenth century. The English sailor William Mariner, who had been spared by the Tongan chieftain, Finau, in his attack on the British privateer *Port au Prince* was told that the Hawaiians were shocked they had been able to kill Cook as they believed him to be superhuman.

**WILLIAM MARINER (1791–1853), English Sailor**
*His bones ... they devoutly hold sacred. They are deposited in a house consecrated to a god, and are annually carried in procession to many other sacred houses, before each of which they are laid on the ground, and the priest returns thanks to the gods for having sent them so great a man.*

So were these stories about Cook's posthumous veneration on the island of Hawai'i fact or fiction? We'll likely never know, but they must be considered in light of the fact that they coincide with the rise of Cook's legend across the Pacific. And legends have a funny way of perpetuating themselves.

The veneration in which Cook was held in Hawai'i was undermined and then completely demolished by the American Calvinist missionaries who arrived in the 1820s. As far as they were concerned, Cook's death was inevitable because any man who had allowed himself to be worshipped as a heathen god would incur divine wrath. The missionaries were also less than keen about the extramarital fornication that had spread venereal diseases amongst the locals. Not to mention, in the wake of the American War of Independence, preaching the American gospel meant shunting aside any lingering attachment the locals might have had to England. Cook was an enduring symbol of Britain and her Empire and all the things the Revolutionaries had fought to drive away from the United States. Cook's shade could not reside unchallenged on the Hawaiian Islands.

**HIRAM BINGHAM (1789–1869), American Protestant Missionary, Hawai'i**

*How vain, rebellious, and at the same time contemptible, for a work to presume to receive homage and sacrifices from the stupid and polluted worshippers of demons and of the vilest visible objects of creation.*

Given what happened to the Hawaiians soon after Cook's death, it's little wonder that today they feel a great deal less positive about his influence on their lives than their ancestors may have.

**LANAKILA MANGAUIL**

*In Hawai'i he's known as Captain Crook! We have quite a lot of bitterness towards him in Hawai'i. There are many stories of how he knew the sicknesses of his crew, yet he allowed them amongst our people. In the fifty years after Cook arrived in the late 1700s, we lost 90 per cent of our population due to the diseases his men introduced.*

The European diseases brought to the islands decimated the population, making it next to impossible for the Hawaiians to defend themselves against the colonial incursions that came later.

# THE PACIFIC

## LILIKALĀ KAMEʻELEIHIWA

*There are many bad feelings about Cook in Hawaiʻi. Some people say that he didn't know his men were going to give the natives venereal disease and tuberculosis so that wasn't really his fault. But he did know what was going to happen when he allowed them to go ashore and stay overnight. When those sailors got on shore they weren't just looking for water. He knew the diseases were going to be passed on to us. So by the time we get to 1893 when the American military invaded, there were only forty thousand Native Hawaiians left. The collapse of the population caused us to lose our sovereignty. Easy pickings, right? Now, we've been under American military occupation for over a hundred years.*

It was the same story across the Pacific. Was it Cook's fault? He has certainly become a symbol for a much bigger narrative of dispossession and loss in the region. But some indigenous people of the Pacific have a different way of looking at things.

## NAINOA THOMPSON, Master Navigator Hōkūleʻa

*As a sailor, as a captain and as a scientist, Cook was amazing. His record matters to us because Banks and the others on board were good observers, and they left us important records. So one part of me is grateful for that. I do think that unlike many of the other explorers, Cook did try to be more respectful than the others. The brutality of some of the other European explorers is just absolutely unbelievable. There's no way that we can forgive that. But Cook was a different breed.*

# APOTHEOSIS

## TRACY TAM SING

*Personally, I have no bad feelings against Cook. If it wasn't Cook, eventually someone else would have come here, so, I have nothing bad against the man. The only thing that bothers me is that people say he discovered Hawai'i, but it's hard to discover a place when there are people there already.*

What's certain is that Cook's observations led him to reach conclusions about the Polynesian people that wouldn't be acknowledged by European scientists for many years to come. By accommodating ideas that were inconceivable to many of his peers – that the Polynesians were accomplished navigators who were deliberately and effectively finding their way from island to island around the Pacific – Cook knew instinctively what the indigenous people of Polynesia never questioned. They were one people.

## ASSOCIATE PROFESSOR MARK D. MCCOY

*As an anthropologist I can't divorce thinking about Cook from thinking about his impact on what otherwise was a rather insular society. It was like dropping a rock into a pond of still water. I find the Hawaiian reaction to him much more interesting than I do Cook himself. But he certainly was unparalleled in terms of his exploration of the Pacific and his keen observations. Cook looked at all these places in Polynesia, and he described them as a nation. It's taken a long time for archaeology, cultural anthropology, historical linguistics and biology to put those puzzle pieces together and deduce where Polynesians came from. But, to his credit, Cook saw that right away.*

*

The treasure house of knowledge that Cook encountered in the Pacific is today being resurrected and celebrated across a broad and ever-growing segment of the population, beyond the domain of the indigenous people who were custodians of their culture during periods of brutal repression.

**SAM NEILL**

*The centuries that followed Cook, I think it's fair to say, were at best dismal for the Polynesian people. But everywhere I've been in the Pacific there's been evidence of a vigorous revival of Polynesian culture.*

A powerful symbol for the cultural renaissance that's taking place within indigenous communities in Polynesia is the great voyaging canoe, the *Hōkūle'a*.

**NAINOA THOMPSON**

*The genesis of Hōkūle'a began in the late 1950s. Academics and researchers here in Hawai'i worked together to draw up a design of the canoe using all the historic information we had – it was launched on 8 March 1975 and it changed my life. It was the first voyaging canoe to be in Hawaiian waters for many hundreds of years. But there were no Native Hawaiian master navigators … or anywhere in Polynesia. So they set off in 1976 on the first voyage in six hundred years along the old road that's paved on the ocean, and thirty-one days later they arrived in Papeete. Seventeen thousand met them on the beach – over half the population of the country.*

Scuppering the theory of 'accidental drift' forever, the *Hōkūleʻa* was navigated from Hawaiʻi to Tahiti using traditional techniques learnt from a master navigator from Micronesia. This voyage spawned the rebirth of Polynesian navigation and Nainoa Thompson would become the first Native Hawaiian to master traditional navigation in the modern era and sail from Hawaiʻi to Tahiti and back.

### SAM NEILL

*I think the first time I saw the Hōkūleʻa was on set one day for Paul Cox's* Molokai: The Story of Father Damien, *when I was wearing a Victorian costume and I wasn't needed so I walked down to the beach. There was no one else around … just cliffs, and no sign of any human habitation at all. then this beautiful craft with two red sails appeared, and I thought, 'Have I slipped in time somehow, or am I having some kind of fantastical mental event?' It was the most surreal thing that's ever happened to me. And I just watched as the ship disappeared over the horizon towards Oahu.*

It's impossible to overstate how momentous this was for the indigenous people of Polynesia. As the *Hōkūleʻa* crisscrossed the Pacific, it brought together kin from all corners of the Polynesian triangle and celebrated their shared heritage.

### MATAHI TUTAVAE, Tahitian Voyaging Society

*Our ancestors got it right. That's why they were one people, even though the ocean is so huge. We were able to communicate and go back and forth. Now, we need to reconnect to our cousins of the Pacific because we have common stories, even though we're so far apart from each other. We were just one people back then. But unfortunately with colonisation we went in different directions. But thanks to the canoes and the voyaging societies and the Polynesian cultural renaissance, we're coming together again.*

The voyaging canoe is a tangible – and impressive – embodiment of Polynesian navigational superiority and cultural continuity.

### NAINOA THOMPSON

*Hōkūleʻa restored Native Hawaiian dignity and pride. We were on the edge of everything being lost. That's extinction. We know what it feels like; we know what it smells like. The healing needs to come from us. This was an ocean country. The ocean is not what divides us – it connects us. Hōkūleʻa has helped us heal ourselves and helped us believe in ourselves. You see indications that we're going to teach our children differently – that our culture does matter. All of a sudden there's this new idea, which is also an ancient idea – we were the greatest voyagers and the greatest explorers of our time. This has changed everything. Today, there's twenty-seven voyager canoes and 2500 active sailors in Polynesia. The restoration of Hawaiian culture is not just about honouring the past – it's about shaping a better world for our children in the future. I owe almost everything to Hōkūleʻa.*

# APOTHEOSIS

> **LILIKALĀ KAMEʻELEIHIWA PhD**
>
> *I'm optimistic that my students are not here because their parents tell them they have to be here, in fact most parents will say, 'What are you going to do with a degree in Hawaiian studies?' Well, our students go on to become professors, they go on to become lawyers and doctors and leaders of the nation. I feel like we've such wonderful young people, the ancestors are walking the earth again.*

The *Hōkūleʻa* and a new generation of master navigators are dismantling and dismembering Cook's legacy and unpicking the lines he drew across the map of the Pacific.

\*

Beyond the story of the repression and resurrection of Polynesian culture is the Pacific Ocean itself.

> **SAM NEILL**
>
> *One of the things we've been talking about is the Pacific as an idea – as a place, yes, but also the importance of protecting that place because it continues to sustain us just as it's sustained the people who were here for thousands of years, and the way it sustained Cook and his crew as they travelled around.*

On voyages across the Pacific, the sailors on board the *Hōkūleʻa* are unwilling witnesses to the environmental damage being inflicted upon this great body of water by human activity.

**NAINOA THOMPSON**

*This planet is an island and the ocean drives life. It drives our climate, our chemistry, our wildlife, our biology. It is a microcosm of what humanity is supposed to become. Our focus now is on the health of the oceans, because the oceans are a mirror of what happens to us on land, and what happens on land is a mirror of what happens in the ocean. This is a blue planet – it's 70 per cent water, and it gives us life. If we change it too much, I think we're in trouble.*

In the far northern reaches of the ocean, the ice wall that hampered Cook's efforts to find the North-West Passage is retreating, and with it the native flora and fauna that allowed indigenous populations to maintain a connection to a traditional lifestyle. As the region becomes more accessible, a tussle is underway in the Arctic – and, in the southernmost reaches of the Pacific, in the Antarctic – over control of the resources that can now be exploited.

The Great Barrier Reef, off Australia's north-eastern coast – which had the honour of being the one natural hazard that came close to ending Cook's career – is on its last legs. Rising water temperatures are responsible for bleaching thousands of kilometres of the reef, transforming the vivid colours of one of the great natural wonders of the world into a barren, bone-white graveyard of dead and dying coral.

Plastic pollution in the Pacific has reached catastrophic levels. Caught at the centre of the ocean's vast circuit of rotating currents between Hawai'i and California is a garbage patch of inconceivable scale. Its heart is estimated to measure one million square kilometres, with its outer edges covering a further three and a half

APOTHEOSIS

million square kilometres. That's a sodden rubbish dump that's almost half as big in area as Australia. Add to this grim tally the nuclear material that has been leaching into the Pacific from Japan's ruined Fukushima nuclear plant, and the environmental vandalism caused by the massive factory ships that scoop everything that moves out of the ocean to feed the world's appetite for fresh fish, and it's impossible to ignore the fact that the Pacific Ocean has entered a new, and perilous, stage of its evolution.

### SAM NEILL

*What I do know is we live in precarious times, and unless we start looking after this planet better – the only one that we have – this beautiful body of water will surely rise up and drown us all. So let us ensure for our grandchildren's sake, and for their grandchildren, that this never happens.*

Amongst the most vocal of all the activists fighting to save the Pacific are the Polynesian people who have called this ocean their home for many thousands of years. As they unite in this common cause, bonds of kinship are strengthened, and the idea of a Polynesian coalition of First Nations now seems possible.

### LILIKALĀ KAMEʻELEIHIWA PhD

*In the 1870s, our King wanted to make an alliance between Tahiti and Samoa and Hawaiʻi so we could keep foreigners from taking over our countries. There were too many European and American interests in the Pacific that wanted to make sure they had control over those places ... so they thought he was an uppity king. But it was a great idea and it's still a good idea.*

431

As the Cook scholar Nicholas Thomas has pointed out, the encounter between Cook and the people of the Pacific was a two-way exchange. As Cook was engaging with people and places that were unknown to Europeans, he was also introducing Europe and its ways to the people of the Pacific – for better or worse. The Enlightenment doctrine that prevailed in Cook's day saw nature as subservient to humankind. Science provided a means for bringing the ocean and its custodians to heel to exploit the Pacific's bountiful resources. This principle has done untold damage to the region. Hints in Cook's journals suggest he had a sense of some of the dangers that were looming, though there was little he could have done about them. And as is so often observed, others were on the way regardless – the Pacific's days of isolation from Western influence were at an end; Cook was just symptomatic of a bigger reality. But the fact remains that so many things Cook and his crew marvelled over disappeared in the years following his arrival in the Pacific.

Whether or not you hold Cook personally responsible for the social, cultural and environmental desecration that followed in his wake, there's no denying the fact he has proved useful as a symbol of colonisation and subjugation for the movement that's seeking to redress these wrongs.

### ASSOCIATE PROFESSOR MARK D. MCCOY

*Is it fair to hate Cook? He's got a lot to answer for if we want to judge him by modern standards. But when we're looking at historical questions – do you use the morality of his own society or the societies that he's visiting? I think that's a very difficult question to answer.*

Undermining Cook's legacy is a way for the original inhabitants of the Pacific to overturn the status quo and reassert their own, ancient, claims over their lands while recalibrating relationships with the non-indigenous people who settled there.

If history teaches us one thing, it's that revolutionaries need a common enemy.

*

Cook has been widely acclaimed as the greatest European maritime explorer of all time. There's no doubt he was at his most potent when he was on board one of his ships, and his many years at sea seemed to leave him floundering on dry land. He became addicted to the shifting landscapes, extreme climates and near-death experiences he encountered on a daily basis in the Pacific. For Cook, to stand still was to die – not for him a cushy and well-renumerated retirement amongst other old sailors, sitting by the fire exchanging salty tales from a lifetime of adventures. It seems only fitting that his life ended in the place that came to define him.

Steeling themselves after the death of their commander, the men on board the *Resolution* and the *Discovery* headed north from Hawai'i, determined to complete Cook's mission and discover whether or not the North-West Passage existed.

Here, the amicable exchange they'd had with the Russian navigator on Unalaska, Gerasim Izmailov, paid off. The letters of introduction Izmailov had given Cook proved to be of vital importance. The two ships dropped anchor in Petropavlovsk, Kamchatka, where they remained from April to June 1779. The governor, Magnus von Behm, generously agreed to provision

Clerke to the tune of 2256 rubles without expectation of payment. As a gesture of gratitude, Clerke gifted Behm a collection of cultural artefacts from Oceania and north-west America, and a map showing Cook's new cartographic observations. This important ethnographic collection ultimately found its way from Kamchatka to St Petersburg; today it's housed in the Museum of Anthropology and Ethnography.

Fighting the symptoms of consumption, Charles Clerke forged north and tackled the Arctic Circle again in June and July. The search was fruitless, and when the ships returned to Petropavlovsk, Clerke succumbed to the disease that had bedevilled him for the entire voyage. He was thirty-eight years of age. A stone memorial erected by the Admiralty marks the spot where Clerke was buried on a high hill overlooking the town.

After Clerke's death, the expedition fell under the leadership of Lieutenant John Gore, who assumed command of the *Resolution* and appointed James King as captain of the *Discovery*.

Cook's legacy would live on in many of the men who survived the voyage. William Bligh, George Vancouver, James King, John Ledyard and John Gore would all make names for themselves in the world of exploration and British naval history. As it happened, Gore's son was one of the first free settlers to arrive in Australia, and Gore's grandson, Graham, died during John Franklin's doomed search for the same thing that had drawn John Gore to the bleak northern Pacific: the North-West Passage.

*

As is so often the case with these tales of adventure on the high seas, little thought has been given to the people left behind. When

Elizabeth Cook received news of her husband's death, she was stitching a waistcoat made of the *tapa* cloth James had brought back for her from his second voyage.

Her lot in life was not easy. Nine months after Elizabeth and James were married, she had given birth to their first child, a son, while her husband was at sea. Cook was at home for the birth of only two of their six children, and only three of them survived infancy. Joseph, George and the couple's only daughter, Elizabeth, all died and were buried while Cook was away. All three of the Cooks' children who made it to adulthood died young, and had no children of their own. Nathaniel was lost at sea at the age of sixteen when the ship he was serving on in the West Indies went down with all hands on deck during a hurricane. Hugh contracted scarlet fever and died at the age of seventeen while a student at Cambridge. And the eldest son, also named James, followed in his father's footsteps and became a commander in the British Navy. He drowned at sea at the age of thirty-one. James and Elizabeth Cook left no direct line of descent.

Still, Elizabeth whiled away what spare time she had on an object that embodies hope. On the piece of mulberry-bark fabric brought back to England by her husband from a Pacific island half a world away, Elizabeth began to embroider delicate tendrils of foliage and flower buds to trim the garment she imagined he would one day wear at court – perhaps when receiving his knighthood.

The life of a naval wife in the eighteenth century was a precarious existence. With her husband gone for years on end and in the absence of any means of regular communication, a sense of uncertainty must have been a constant feature of Elizabeth's life as she waited for her husband to return. Perhaps, in a way, it was a relief when she learnt of his death – the bad news she had been dreading for so many years had finally come. Or maybe, after he had managed to return home safely so many times after so many near misses, she believed him to be indestructible.

Given an Admiralty pension amounting to two hundred pounds per annum – the equivalent of roughly AUD$60,000 today – Elizabeth Cook kept her husband's portrait with her until her death in 1835 at the age of ninety-three. Living in her home as her companion was her cousin, Isaac Smith, who had accompanied James Cook on his first voyage and was the first European to step ashore at Botany Bay. Perhaps anticipating the obsessive public fascination with her husband that would develop as the years passed, before she died it's believed Elizabeth Cook burnt all of her husband's personal correspondence with her. She seems to have judged the private moments captured between husband and wife too personal to share.

Elizabeth had no cause to complete her husband's *tapa* cloth waistcoat. It now lies in the collection of the State Library of New South Wales. Alongside it is another poignant object that captures Cook's intimate and tumultuous relationship with the Pacific. When the *Resolution* and the *Discovery* dropped anchor in Yarmouth in September 1780, the men on board carried with them a gift they had hand-crafted for their commander's widow. Using timber from the troublesome *Resolution*, the men carved a tiny, coffin-shaped box, measuring just nine by seven centimetres. Along the edge of the box is an inscription: 'Made of Resolution Oak for Mrs. Cook by Crew'. Inlaid with mother-of-pearl, the box has three silver plaques affixed to it. One is inscribed 'Captain James Cook Slain at Owhyhee 14 February 1779'. The other two record places of note from Cook's career: 'Quebec, Newfoundland, Greenwich and Australis', and, significantly, 'Lono and the Seaman's Idol'. Inside the coffin they placed a lock of Cook's hair – presumably retrieved from the scalp returned to Clerke in Kealakekua Bay. It rests on a miniature watercolour depicting the moment of Cook's death.

### SAM NEILL

*This extraordinary little ditty-box is carved of wood from the* Resolution, *and it was a gift from the crew to Cook's widow. I suppose to a modern eye, it's slightly macabre because it's carved in the shape of a coffin, and inside is a lock of what is presumed to be Cook's hair and an amazing little painting of his death. But it's a beautiful little thing because, somehow, it contains so much emotion.*

It is a tiny thing, yet it inspires great pathos – not just because it is a deeply personal memento that captures a tragic moment, but also because it reflects the respect and love his crew held for James Cook. Despite the moments of resentment the men on board the *Resolution* felt towards him on occasion during the third voyage, at the end, he was Lono, and they worshipped him: 'the Seaman's Idol'. There could be no finer memorial for Cook as a leader of men.

Professor Dame Anne Salmond has proposed that, at his end, Cook became a prince of the Pacific. A revealing exchange occurred on Ra'iatea during the first voyage, when Cook was approached by a chieftain who asked him the name of his *marae*. Cook took that to mean the place he would be buried, which he thought was a peculiar question to ask a seaman, given they were usually buried at sea. But to Polynesians, a *marae* was the hub of a man's identity. What Cook was being asked was to identify the place that was his spiritual hub – where his soul resided.

When Cook's remains were buried at sea in Kealakekua Bay, the ocean itself became his *marae*. That was where his memory would persist. For better or worse, his identity – his soul – would be tied to the Pacific and its people forever.

It was in the Pacific Ocean that James Cook found immortality.

### SAM NEILL

*After my journey, I don't know whether I now feel more or less connected to the Pacific. I've got a much clearer idea of how I came to be here. That's to say, my forebears came here 150 years ago, and I just thought that was what happens. But every act of possession is an act of dispossession. There's no denying that. So I'm grateful for the time I've spent in the Pacific, my home. I know we live in precarious times, but this great ocean will surely outlast humanity. The Pacific will endure, its timelessness and immensity a reservoir of stories for whoever, or whatever, follows us all.*

# ACKNOWLEDGEMENTS

Books like this only exist as a consequence of the relentless enthusiasm and commitment of a very large group of people. Without the contribution of the many brilliant individuals who were involved in the production of both the TV series and this book, it would be a very flimsy tome. So, I owe sincere thanks to many people.

Firstly, to Sam Neill. Thank you for your willingness to challenge your understanding of the world in which you live and to confront some daunting realities about a place and people you know and love. Your tenacity and acuity brought this project to life, and gave me the opportunity to be involved with this remarkable story. For that, I'll always be grateful.

I also owe producer Owen Hughes, who co-wrote the series and nurtured it from its early days, an enormous debt of gratitude for his passionate advocacy for this story, and for reading my manuscript and keeping an eye on its historical accuracy. Sincere thanks, also, to Paul Brunton for his unerring attention to detail in his capacity as historical consultant for the book.

The TV series captured extraordinary moments and exchanges between Sam and the people he met across the Pacific, all of which inspired the book and came about thanks to the key production staff: directors Kriv Stenders and Sally Aitken, who also co-wrote the series and served as a valued collaborator as we wrestled the storylines into shape; supervising producer, Aline Jacques; and executive producers, Chris Hilton and David Alrich. I'm deeply thankful to all at Essential Media and Entertainment for entrusting me with this project, in particular David for not throttling me when I was making demands on his time while he was attempting to put the TV series to bed. Most of all, to the researchers on the project – led ably by Kirrilly Brentnall and Johanna Gibson – who managed to wade through inconceivable amounts of material to find the gems we used to bring the series and this book to life. Joh's additional assistance with research for the manuscript was also invaluable.

At its heart, this is a book about the experiences of the indigenous people of the Pacific. I'm eternally grateful for the insights and stories I've been privileged to hear, and am indebted to those people who've guided me on this journey. Enormous thanks go to Professor Larissa Behrendt and Annabelle Lee who served as indigenous consultants for the production. The TV series – and, by association, the book – also benefitted from the generous contributions of Robin Inglis and Professor Dame Anne Salmond. With thanks to the Tasmanian Aboriginal Centre for use of *palawa kani* place names. *palawa kani* is the language of the Tasmanian Aboriginal people.

There's a long list of people whose involvement in the TV series also provided the book with its spine. In no particular order, sincere thanks to: Marguerite Lai, Josiane Teamotuaitau, Moana'ura Walker, Richard Tuheiava, Moetai Brotherson and Matahiarii Tutavae in Tahiti; Nick Tupara, James (Pop) Milner,

ACKNOWLEDGEMENTS

Annie Macguire, Kihi Howe-Ririnui, Gordon Toi, Tim Finn, Emeritus Professor Ngahuia Te Awekotuku, Peter and Takutai Beech, Tina Ngata, Kiley Nepia, Dr Peter Meihana, and Raymond Smith in New Zealand. In Australia Bruce Pascoe, Dr Shayne Williams, Rodney Mason, Warwick Thornton, Dr Brett Summerell, Professor Darren Crayn, Jody H Orcher, Gemma Cronin, David Pryce, Alberta Hornsby and Ernie Dingo. In Antarctica and the Southern Ocean: Dr Nick Gales and Tim Jarvis. We were honoured to include Princess 'Ofeina-'e-he-Langi and Princess Marcella Kalaniuvali-Lady Fotofili from Tonga in the production, and also Jeff Laurie and Sepuloni Kitekeiaho; Jocelyn Usua, Joseph Jimmy, Johnny Koanapo, and Chief Sam Usua Eskar in Vanuatu; Ray Williams in Canada; Aaron Leggett, Raymond Koweluk and Captain Phil Pryzmont in Alaska; Dr Rick Knecht, Captain Dave Magone, Laresa Syreson and Denis Robinson in Unalaska; and Nainoa Thompson, Associate Professor Mark D. McCoy, Anne Lokomaikli Lipscomb, Lanakila Mangauil, Lilikalā Kameʻeleihiwa, Gordon Kanakanui Leslie, and Tracy Tam Sing in Hawaiʻi. And finally, a dedication to the memory of the late Kingi Taurua, who was a passionate advocate for Ngāpuhi and its people, Māori self-sovereignty and *Te Reo*.

Of course, without a publisher, there is no book. And the staff at HarperCollins managed to maintain their aplomb and good humour with a complicated project that sometimes seemed to combine the worst aspects of marathon running and speed dating. Sincere thanks go to my wonderful publisher, Catherine Milne, who nurtured this book from the beginning and to my patient and generous editor, Nicola Robinson, who could never have predicted she might, one day, become an expert in Polynesian punctuation. Thanks are also due to the book designer, Hazel Lam, and typesetter, Graeme Jones, who did an extraordinary job under (very, very) challenging conditions.

On a personal level, I'd like to thank my agent, Clare Forster, for her wise counsel and advocacy. Thanks also to Spencer Scott Sandilands, a mentor and friend who – many years ago – introduced me to the wonders of cartography and inspired in me a fascination with early European exploration, and to Alan Erson who brought me aboard *Uncharted* when it was little more than a log raft in a wide ocean. To Loretta, Victoria, Phoebe, AB, Adrian, and little Stella, thank you for contributing so much to the delightful whirlwind that is my life. And to Willie, for your obsession with George Bass.

As always, and in all ways – to my soul mate and best friend, Andrew, and our just about perfect children, Roman and Cleopatra. Thank you for your love, encouragement and general lunacy. You keep me sane (yes, I know that's a contradiction in terms). And, this book owes you an Easter.

Thanks are due also to Captain James Cook, who I believe would be horrified by many of the things that occurred in his wake and mortified by what has been perpetrated in his name.

And thank you for joining us on this journey. If there's one thing I hope this book achieves, it's that one or two of you out there may be inspired to think a little differently about the 'history' so many of us are taught to believe.

*Meaghan Wilson Anastasios*

# FURTHER READING

Peter Adds [et al.]; introduction by Marilyn Head, *The Transit of Venus: How a Rare Astronomical Alignment Changed the World*, Awa Press, 2007

James K. Barnett and David L. Nicandri, preface by Robin Inglis, *Arctic Ambitions: Captain Cook and the Northwest Passage*, Heritage House, 2015

J.C. Beaglehole (ed.), *The Endeavour Journal of Joseph Banks: 1769–1771 (Second Edition)*, Trustees of the Public Library of NSW in association with Angus and Robertson, 1963

J.C. Beaglehole, *The Exploration of the Pacific (Third Edition)*, A. and C. Black, 1966

J.C. Beaglehole, *The Life of Captain James Cook*, A. and C. Black, 1974

Joel Bonnemaison; translated and adapted by Josee Penot-Demetry, *The Tree and the Canoe: History and Ethnography of Tanna*, University of Hawai'i Press, 1994

Daniel J. Boorstin, *The Discoverers*, Random House, 1983

Ian C. Campbell, *Island Kingdom: Tonga Ancient and Modern (Third Edition)*, Canterbury University Press, 2015

Paul Carter, *The Road to Botany Bay: An Essay in Spatial History*, Faber and Faber, 1987

Inga Clendinnen, *Dancing with Strangers: Europeans and Australians at First Contact*, Cambridge University Press, 2005

Vanessa Collingridge, *Captain Cook: Obsession and Betrayal in the New World*, Ebury Press, 2002

Wade Davis, *The Wayfinders: Why Ancient Wisdom Matters in the Modern World*, Anansi, 2009

Joan Druett, *Tupaia: The Remarkable Story of Captain Cook's Polynesian Navigator*, Random House New Zealand, 2011

Martin Dugard, *Farther Than Any Man: The Rise and Fall of Captain James Cook*, Washington Square Press, 2002

Philip Edwards (ed.), *James Cook: The Journals*, Penguin Books, 2003

Robin Fisher and Hugh Johnson (eds), *Captain James Cook and His Times*, University of Washington Press, 1979

Georg Forster, *A Voyage Round the World, Vol 1 & 2*, University of Hawai'i Press, 1999

John Gascoigne, *Encountering the Pacific in the Age of Enlightenment*, Cambridge University Press, 2014

Michelle Hetherington (curator) in association with Iain McCalman and Alexander Cook, *Cook & Omai: The Cult of the South Seas*, National Library of Australia, 2001

Tony Horwitz, *Into the Blue: Boldly Going Where Captain Cook Has Gone Before*, Bloomsbury, 2003

K.R. Howe (ed.), *Vaka Moana: Voyages of the Ancestors: The Discovery and Settlement of the Pacific*, David Bateman, 2006

Robert Hughes, *The Fatal Shore*, Alfred A. Knopf, 1987

Geoffrey Irwin, *The Prehistoric Exploration and Colonisation of the Pacific*, Cambridge University Press, 1992

Murray Johnson and Ian McFarlane, *Van Diemen's Land : An Aboriginal History*, NewSouth Publishing, 2015

Alison Jones and Kuni Jenkins, *Words Between Us: He Korero*, Huia Publishers, 2011

Rüdiger Joppien and Bernard Smith, *The Art of Captain Cook's Voyages*, Oxford University Press in association with the Australian Academy of the Humanities, 1985

John McAleer and Nigel Rigby, *Captain Cook and the Pacific: Art, Exploration, and Empire*, Yale University Press, 2017

Frank McLynn, *Captain Cook: Master of the Seas*, Yale University Press, 2011

Granville Allen Mawer, *Ahab's Trade: The Saga of South Seas Whaling*, Allen & Unwin, 1999

Alan Moorehead, *The Fatal Impact: The Invasion of the South Pacific, 1767–1840*, Penguin Books, 1968

Eileen Norbert (ed.), *Menadelook: An Inupiat Teacher's Photographs of Alaska Village Life, 1907–1932*, University of Washington Press, 2016

Maria Nugent, *Captain Cook Was Here*, Cambridge University Press, 2009

Patrick O'Brian, *Joseph Banks: A Life*, Collins Harvill, 1987

Gananath Obeyesekere, *The Apotheosis of Captain Cook: European Mythmaking in the Pacific*, Princeton University Press, 1997

Ray Parkin, *H.M. Bark Endeavour: Her Place in Australian History: With an Account of her Construction, Crew and Equipment and a Narrative of Her Voyage on the East Coast of New Holland in the Year 1770: With Plans, Charts, and Illustrations by the Author (Second Edition)*, The Miegunyah Press, 2003

Sydney Parkinson, *A Journal of a Voyage to the South Seas*, Caliban Press, 1984

John Robson, *Captain Cook's World: Maps of the Life and Voyages of James Cook R.N.*, Random House New Zealand, 2000

John Robson, *The Captain Cook Encyclopaedia*, Random House New Zealand, 2004

Anne Salmond, *Between Worlds: Early Exchanges Between Māori and Europeans, 1773–1815*, Viking, 1997

Anne Salmond, *The Trial of the Cannibal Dog: Captain Cook in the South Seas*, Yale University Press, 2003

Anne Salmond, *Aphrodite's Island: The European Discovery of Tahiti*, Viking, 2010

THE PACIFIC

Anne Salmond, *Two Worlds: First Meetings Between Māori and Europeans, 1642–1772*, Penguin, 2018

Laurence Simmons, *Tuhituhi: William Hodges, Cook's Painter in the South Pacific*, Otago University Press, 2011

Bernard Smith, *European Vision and the South Pacific*, Harper & Row, 1985

Ngahuia Te Awekotuku; with Linda Waimarie Nikora, Mohi Rua and Rolinda Karapu; new photography by Becky Nunes, *Mau Moko: The World of Māori Tattoo*, Penguin, 2007

Alice Te Punga Somerville, *Once Were Pacific: Māori Connections to Oceania*, University of Minnesota Press, 2012

Nicholas Thomas, *Cook: The Extraordinary Voyages of Captain James Cook*, Walker Publishing Company, 2003

Nicholas Thomas, *Discoveries: The Voyages of Captain Cook*, Penguin Books, 2004

Nicholas Thomas (ed.), *The Voyages of Captain James Cook: The Illustrated Accounts of Three Epic Voyages, From the writings of James Cook, John Hawkesworth, Georg Forster, and James King*, Voyageur Press, 2016

Glyndwr Williams, *Captain Cook: Explorations and Reassessments*, Boydell Press, 2004

Glyn Williams, *The Death of Captain Cook: A Hero Made and Unmade*, Profile, 2008

Glyn Williams, *Arctic Labyrinth: The Quest for the Northwest Passage*, Penguin, 2010